The Dragon of Destiny

And the Saga of Shanghai Pooley

AUTHOR'S AUTOGRAPH

Hello Bill,

Thank you for all your support over the years.

Jim Phillips

Publisher.

14 Feb. 2014

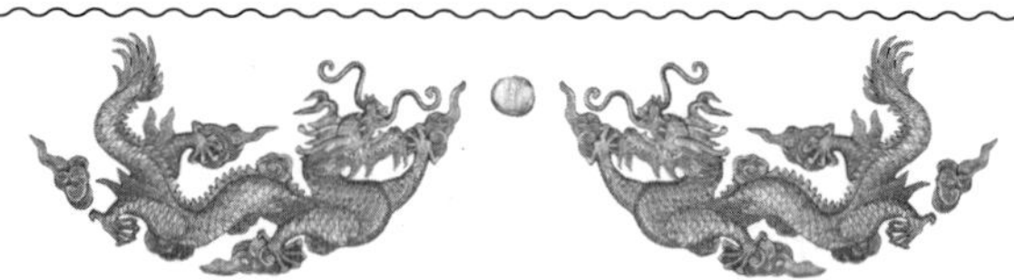

THE DRAGON OF DESTINY

And the Saga of Shanghai Pooley

Major Rick Spooner, *USMC, Ret.*

Also by the author:

The Spirit of Semper Fedelis
Phillips Publications, 2004

A Marine Anthology
Phillips Publications, 2010

Published by:
Phillips Publications
P.O. Box 168
Williamstown, NJ 08094

Tel. (609) 567-0695 ♦ Fax (609) 561-4967
email: greenberet1@verizon.net

ISBN: 978-0-9849605-2-1

10 9 8 7 6 5 4 3 2 1 14 15 16 17 18

First Edition: January, 2014
Printed in China

Dedicated

To the Corps

the Old Corps, the New Corps, the Marine Corps

and to those who proudly serve.

As Gunnery Sergeant Paul Pooley once
said to Lieutenant (jg) Max Shapiro,

". . . the Marine Corps is my life,

it's not just a job or a career,

it's my life."

Marine mascot "Jiggs 1" on board for his flight.

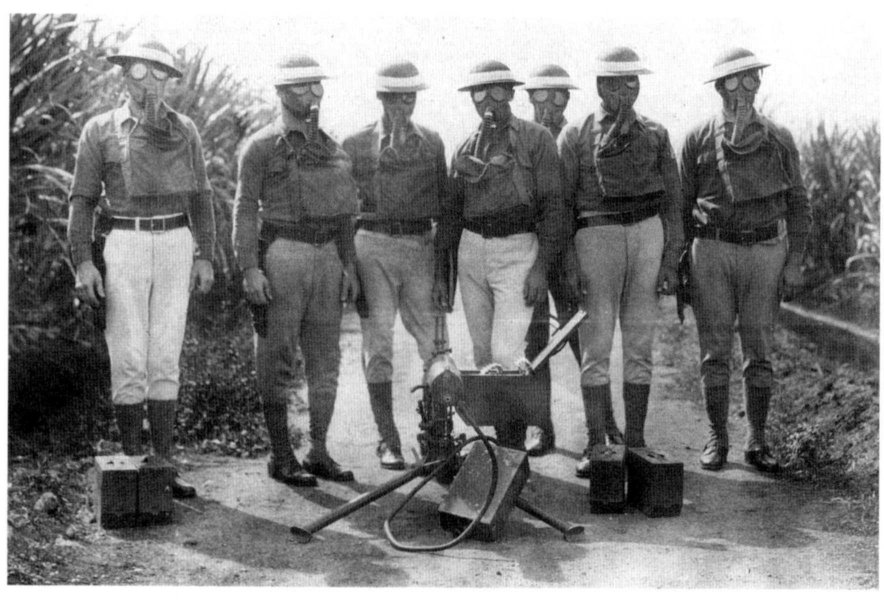

Marines train in Hawaii.

Table of Contents

Infantry weapons school instructors, 1930.

King Neptune and his court await new Marines.

Introduction

Duty on "The Old Asiatic Station" was much sought after by Marines of the 1920's and '30's. Many tales abound concerning duty with the American Legation Guard at Peking and Tientsin or the 4th Marine Regiment in Shanghai. The monetary exchange rate favored the Americans and a dollar went much further in China than it did at home in the United States.

For young adventurers new to the Corps a tour on the old Asiatic station could mean cheap liberty, plentiful liquor, beautiful Asian and Eurasian women, excitement around every corner and a succession of good times with good buddies.

For the "Old China Hands" A return to Shanghai meant a return to the place where the cultures of the east and west co-existed in one colorful and exciting place. It was a time of intrigue, adventure, special friendships and a marked degree of professionalism among military men in general and Marines in particular.

There was a certain mystique about duty in China that lent special status to Marines who had served there. Marines entitled to the Yangtze Patrol Medal or the China Service Medal were ever after referred to as "China Marines."

In addition to "showing the flag" and the multitude of routine military and security duties performed by the China Marines there was in their midst a handful of professional Navy and Marine personnel who had an additional mission, they were vitally concerned with gathering, evaluating and

disseminating intelligence information from this hotbed of intrigue, mystery, corruption, violence and every type of criminal activity imaginable.

This is a work of fiction though it is based on some factual incidents. Some names may be recognized as those of real people while others are contrived. The dialog is a product of the author's imagination.

MEMORIES OF A MARINE

I met Sweet Marie in gay Paree,
And Fifi in Port au Prince,
And Nan Osan in old Japan,
Tho I haven't seen her since.
There was Molly Brown in far Cape Town,
And Marabelle in Peru,
A Norway maid who wore a braid,
And an Edinburgh lass named Sue.

Cute Kate O'Rorke I met in Cork,
And Alma, the Danish kid,
Some Turkish belles near the Dardanelles,
And Isabel in Madrid.
I met girls galore in Singapore,
And Rita who lived in Rome,
But I winked my eye and said good-bye
When the cruiser sailed for home.

I knew some queens in the Philippines,
And some in the South Sea Isles;
I met a peach on Waikiki Beach
And basked in her sunny smiles.
I'll flirt no more, as in days of yore,
For my sea-bag is stowed away,
And I'm tied for life to a little wife
I met in the U.S.A.

Memories of a Marine Poem.

Prologue

It was to be their last full day on Saipan and they especially wanted to visit the museum and the American Memorial Park with its Flag Circle and Court of Honor. The old man was glad to have returned to Saipan after an absence of 68 years. It was to be a pilgrimage to honor his many friends and buddies who had died here so many years ago and an opportunity to see and visit with his US Park Ranger friends Brian Piercy and Nancy Kerschner here at the westernmost outpost of the US Park Service. The island had changed; it was nothing like the bloodstained battlefield he remembered. Gone were the many grisly reminders of death and destruction that he had witnessed on his first trip.

Ranger Nancy said, "Come over to the museum, we've arranged for you to do a book signing from 12:30 until 2:30 this afternoon." The old man answered, "What, two hours! Nancy, No one on this island wants to buy a book about a bunch of Marines fighting in a war that occurred almost seventy years ago." Nancy commented, "Perhaps not but its what we've planned so you just come along and cooperate." Then she added, "You'll see." When they arrived Brian was there to greet them. Nancy said, "Let's have some cake and coffee."

A large cake was wheeled out. It was decorated to resemble his last book and was beautifully executed and except for its size it was an exact replica of the book's cover.

Prologue

Looking up he saw people queuing up and waiting; books in hand. He was told that some had even flown in from the outlying islands.

After two hours had passed, he was still signing books. When he had finished Alexi Sotamajor approached and stated that she was from the Saipan Tribune and was here to interview him along with Gemma Casas a reporter from the Beach Road Magazine and a third reporter who had flown in from one of the other islands and was also waiting. He happily granted the three interviews.

Later Brian commented that he knew the old man would want to take a few moments to go over to the Flag Circle and visit the Court of Honor and say hello to some of his old friends. The names of all the Marines and other service members killed on Saipan and Tinian were inscribed in the Court of Honor. When they arrived, Brian said, "They are alphabetically listed by division, starting right there on your left. You can just read your way around the Court and you'll wind up right back here." The old man said, "Okay Brian, I would like to look for a few of my buddies names but I won't take long, I should be back to you in less than ten minutes." The Chief Park Ranger had a knowing smile on his face as he said, "Okay Major, I'll be right here waiting for you."

As the old man looked at one name, several others seemed to be calling out to him. What an eerie experience. They were the names of men he had known intimately and thought he could never forget, but he had.

As he recognized the long forgotten names, faces, personalities and memories came flooding back. They were all young Marines when they died. He could see them as he remembered marching beside them on parade, standing next to them at inspection, going on liberty, training, living in crowded troop transports, fighting their way ashore on a hostile beach, sharing a fighting hole and he remembered some of them in their last moments as they died beside him. How cruel life can be. They have all been dead for sixty-eight years and he was still alive and well. How could he have forgotten any of them? His old squad leader had always said, "No one is really dead until he's forgotten." The old man felt considerable remorse; he should not have forgotten a single one.

Prologue

Much time had elapsed when the misty-eyed old man finally arrived where Chief Park Ranger Brian Piercy had been patiently waiting. They started walking back to the museum when the ranger said, "One thing has bothered me for a long time, I know most of your characters were actual people or were composites of guys you knew during the war. The one character in your books that has intrigued me the most is the one you called Shanghai Pooley. Who was Shanghai in real life?"

The old man said, "I was just up there talking to him." He turned around and said, "Come on Brian, let's go back up, I want to show you something." They walked together back up the steps to the Court of Honor. The old man stopped and pointed to one of the thousands of names etched on the memorial as he said, "Look Brian, there it is. Now you know. Shanghai was no composite, he was a real Marine and one of the best." The ranger said, "I'd really like to know more about him; what can you tell me?" The old man replied, "Well, you and Nancy are joining us for dinner tonight at the Pacific Islands Club. Perhaps after dinner we'll have some time to sit out on the patio. I'll be glad to tell you all I can about him."

The Pacific Islands Club was a beautiful four-star resort and hotel that was located very close to the beach where the old man had landed sixty-eight years before. At the conclusion of a delicious dinner they walked out to the patio beside the pool. The colorful lighting turned the dark night into a glorious rainbow of colors making the pool and the spacious patio resemble what he thought a Hollywood movie set might look like.

They were seated at a large round table. The old man thought of the many blessings in his life. He could think of no place he would rather be at this moment than right here sitting next to his son and such good friends as Andy Traynor and Pam Flynn along with John Hoy, Ron Keene, Shayne Jarosz and Bob and Justin Palmer and of course, the rangers. The rest of the party, all good friends, had drifted off to other interests. The old man and his son lit their cigars and sitting back and relaxing he finally looked at Brian and said, "You asked me about Shanghai Pooley so I'll tell you what I can.

"It was to the southeast of where we are sitting right now and was less than a half-mile from here. The island of Saipan had been secured and our

company was living in foxholes with the CP in the center. It was a defensive position because there were still plenty of well-armed hostile Japanese troops on the island. We were all on 50% alert. We'd been going out on daily patrols mopping up guerrillas and stragglers while waiting to invade Tinian. Occasionally, the Japs would try to penetrate our perimeter at night. They were looking for food, weapons and of course hoping to kill a few Americans.

On one particularly quiet night while sitting in their foxhole waiting for it to get dark, Shanghai looked at PFC Yancey and quietly said, "You've wanted to know about my interest in the Japanese for a long time. Now that you've told me all about your adventures with them in the jungle, I guess the only way I'm going to keep you from asking so damned many questions is to go ahead and tell you my story.

"You probably are not going like what you are about to hear and it may surprise you to hear it but you asked for it. If you ever tell this to anyone else I'll kick your ass right up between your shoulder blades and I'll never forgive you. I want you to know that I have not discussed this with anyone since my court-martial. I didn't think I would ever be able to talk about it again, but it's eating me up inside and you seem to be interested. I just can't forget what happened.

"I was given a bum rap; was reduced in rank, lost my security clearance and was transferred out of China, yet I did nothing that any other Marine would not do under similar circumstances."

He talked all through his watch and through Yancey's watch. It took the whole night, but the sergeant related his moving story just as it had happened. Yancey was thankful it was a dark night, too dark to look Shanghai in the eye. He knew the salty old sergeant was deeply moved and from the sound of his voice, there had to be a tear coursing down his cheek from time to time when he spoke of his Lillian.

Though Shanghai may never have told anyone the story before the young Marine could sense that he was haunted and tortured by his memories; he must have re-lived it all a thousand times. The salty sergeant and the young PFC sat in their foxhole and watched the darkness fade away to gradually be replaced by the tropical morning sunrise.

Prologue

This night would not be spoken of again yet neither of them would ever forget it. Shanghai had talked of his great love that knew no bounds and of how it had filled his heart and brought him great happiness. Paradoxically, it was that same love which caused the tragic consequences over which he had no control. He spoke of his lost love as one who knew he would never love again.

The young Chic Yancey tried to understand but he had never really been in love. He knew he could not reveal Shanghai's story yet he would never forget it. Few men are privileged to share the innermost secrets of another. Yancey felt honored. He was beginning to realize just how tragic and unfair life could be. Shanghai has now been dead for over 68 years and Yancey true to his word had never told the story. Now the time had come, it needed to be told.

A Chinese opium den in Shanghai.

American troops—Shanghai Volunteer Corps.

Marines man a street emplacement, Shanghai.

Acknowledgements

Many people have provided encouragement and technical assistance to the author. He would be remiss in not mentioning just a few to whom he feels especially thankful. They are as follows:

Mr. Blair Gluba
Former Assistant Director, NCIS, retired

Lieutenant Colonel John Hoy (Hsu Chao Ju 许超儒)
Defense Intelligence Agence & US Army, retired

Dr. John Brunner, PhD formerly with OSS China
Distinguished author and historian

Dr. Michael O'Shea, PhD
Marine, collector and historian

Lieutenant Colonels Phil and Chris Wagner
United Stated Marine Corps, retired

Christine Simmons for her artistic and computer expertise

Sam Sheng for his design talents

and

Memebers of the Privates Mess
The Honorable John Schuh, President

Acknowledgements

The Unpaid Docents at the National Muesum of the Marine Corps are the very heart and soul of that magnificent museum and must be acknowledged for all they do in perpetuating the history and traditions of our beloved Corps. The author is especially grateful to the Docents mentioned below for their patience and encouragement in helping to make this book a reality.

Colonel Rich Blanchfield — Pam Flynn — Lieutenant Colonel Andy Trainor — Cheryl Duff — Lieutenant Colonel Rich Duff — Lieutenant Colonel John Hoy — Marshall Stewart — Al Adler — Sergeant Major Pete Ross, Marine Gunner Alex Carrillo, Amber Carillo and last but not least "Queenie" Carole Quinn — Lasser.

SPECIAL ACKNOWLEDGEMENT

Special acknowledgement must be given to my good friend Jim Phillips. Lest the reader think of him merely as a publisher, I must mention that this remarkbale man is a retired Law Enforcement Professional, a collector of and noted expert on edged weapons and firearms and a true friend to the Marine Corps and the perpetuation of its long and colorful history.

A Chinese bandit en route to his beheading.

Part I

Nicaragua

The 2nd Nicaraguan Campaign lasted for nearly six years. The Marines had initially come to Nicaragua to aid in the establishment of a new democratic government and protect the lives and property of American citizens and businesses. They had stayed on to save lives in the civil war; disarm the contenders, chase bandits and hold an election, and the legacy they left behind in the end was a country peaceful and independent. It was a long, difficult job but gave the Marines experiences that would prove invaluable during World War II. The 2nd Nicaraguan Campaign was the last of the Caribbean expeditions that were known as "The Banana Wars."

Private Paul Pooley was a recent graduate of "Boot Camp" a training program conducted at the Marine Corps Base in San Diego, California. It was an intensive program of training and indoctrination designed to transform mere civilians into United States Marines. The teachers, referred to as "Drill Instructors" in the Marine Corps, were, for the most part, veterans of the fighting in France during the World War. They took their jobs seriously.

In Boot Camp Pooley qualified as an expert with the service rifle and he qualified as a first class swimmer. He showed an aptitude for military

subjects and scored high in all of the subjects taught. None of this was as impressive to Sergeant Major McIvor as what he learned from screening record books. McIvor had seen in Pooley's records that he was a high school graduate and had taken four years of Spanish.

The Sergeant Major was pleased. He had been looking for men with special qualifications that could serve to advantage in the 2nd Marine Brigade currently fighting in Nicaragua. He found that he had two privates that spoke Spanish. He would see that both were assigned to the brigade.

Upon graduation from Boot Camp Paul Pooley's orders directed him to report to the Marine Barracks at the US Navy Yard, Mare Island, California for further transportation to the 2nd Marine Brigade in Nicaragua.

Once aboard ship, Pooley climbed down to the troops' berthing compartment where he slung his hammock and was stowing his sea bag and field equipment when he met the Marine whose hammock would be next to his.

He was a powerfully built man who Pooley had seen a time or two in San Diego but he'd never had occasion to speak to him. Pooley smiled then stuck out his hand saying, "Hi, I'm Pooley, Paul Pooley, I guess we're going to be sailing together." The big man looked at Pooley and said, "Chief, just call me Chief, everyone else does." He then took Pooley's outstretched hand and firmly shook it.

Paul Pooley and the Chief were soon to learn that much of Nicaragua was composed of swamp, jungle, banana plantations, mahogany forests and a few gold mines. Its highways were rivers and footpaths and its inhabitants, mainly peaceable Mosquito Indians.

The 2nd Battalion, 5th Marines, of the 2nd Marine Brigade was currently enjoying the sunny climate, lush jungles and picturesque hills of Nicaragua.

Most Marines had joined the Corps for travel and adventure; or perhaps they were just down on their luck and, with the Great Depression in full swing, needed a job or a place where they could get three meals a day and a place to sleep. For those lucky enough to be accepted, an enlistment in the Marine Corps provided an immediate solution to their problems.

The Nicaraguan air was clear and the morning sun bright as it leisurely climbed out of the east and warmed the countryside. Soon it would inten-

sify and to the new men, not yet acclimated, the solar heat would become brutally oppressive.

The formation of new replacements was marched to the company area and halted then told to ground equipment. They were then put at rest and informed that the smoking lamp was lighted. They were to wait outside the headquarters tent until the first sergeant was ready to see them.

The blazing sun overhead was a part of their initiation to Nicaragua. The "Top" had a heavy workload and couldn't stop now just to check in a gaggle of new privates. The company commander was waiting for a report the Top was working on and the "old man" was not known to be patient.

Chief deftly rolled a cigarette while Pooley was lighting his. Pooley spoke, "You know amigo, I don't mind telling you that the "Top" is gonna be mighty sore when he finds out about my Spanish." Chief answered, "Aw hell amigo, I wouldn't worry about it if I was you; the Top probably doesn't speak Spanish either. Besides, I think you speak it pretty good."

The Marines assigned to Nicaragua found that there were benefits they hadn't previously considered. They were receiving an education. Some amassed vast amounts of knowledge in a short period of time. Of course it was on subject matter they would rather have not been exposed to.

They were able to learn, first hand, a great deal about flies, fire ants, mosquitoes, poisonous and non-poisonous snakes, prickly pear cactus, potable and non-potable water, stubborn mules and burros and a myriad of other things that contributed to their general knowledge, and discomfort. Among the main contributing factors to the discomfort of the troops were Augusto Sandino and his band of cutthroats.

Sandino was a powerful renegade who had kept his country in a state of turmoil for nearly seven years while Marines and Guardias tried to restore peace. The icon on Sandino's personal flag was a white skull and crossbones. Indicative of the kind of man he was.

On May Day in 1930 a communist-attended meeting was held in Union Square, Manhattan, for the purpose of raising funds to buy arms for Sandino. Significantly, his main sponsor in the United States was the Anti-Imperialist League, an organization formed and directed by communists.

Part I

On the 19th of June 1930, near Jinotega, Sandino was wounded during a coordinated Marine air-ground strike. Although he was temporarily out of the fight, Sandino's men continued their pillaging, plundering and raping of the countryside.

On and after November of 1931, Sandino, now recovered from his wounds, began receiving arms from Honduras and Mexico, which he happily used against Marine and Guardia forces.

Paul Pooley had come to Nicaragua to learn. His experiences encompassed all of the miseries encountered by the other Marines but in addition, he was learning a language. His Spanish improved daily as did his knowledge of firearms and their functioning and employment. He learned tracking from the local Indians as well as the effective use of cover and concealment far beyond what he had been taught in Boot Camp.

Gunnery Sergeant Kelly who worked in the intelligence section commented on Pooley's ability to learn quickly and to properly use what he had learned. Soon the lieutenants were discussing him and Captain Williams, the Brigade Intelligence Officer, in particular remarked about his usefulness as his ability to communicate in Spanish had increased noticeably. "This young Marine may be destined for a commission in the *Guardia National* before long." The others agreed.

Paul Pooley worked with members of the Guardia on a daily basis and they spoke Spanish to him continuously. He came to the realization that his comprehension was pretty good and it kept improving.

During the campaign the Marines participated in many patrols, some were more successful than others and a few were really exciting. None were boring.

Private Paul Pooley experienced his baptism of fire in Nicaragua when crossing a freshly plowed field with a mixed patrol. Sandino's bandits took them under fire from just inside a nearby tree line. One of his Marine buddies, Private Bert Hoffman, and three Guardias were killed. It made an indelible impression on Pooley; he would never forget that first patrol.

The Marine lieutenant was the patrol leader and he was on the point with the Nicaraguan *teniente* as they started to cross the freshly plowed field. The unmistakable crack of a rifle shot whizzed low overhead. Marine

Nicaragua

Private Bert Hoffman slumped forward, slid off his mount and lay dead on the ground.

The men immediately dismounted, dispersed their mounts dropped to the ground, and started to return fire. Luckily, the ground was freshly plowed and gave the men some opportunity to burrow down until they were in semi-defilade.

A bitter fight ensued with rifle fire spewing forth from an unseen enemy just inside the tree line. The Marines and Guardia obliged the bandits by returning an even greater volume of fire. There were three Automatic Rifles among the patrol and their volume of fire was sufficient to overwhelm the unseen enemy.

The *banditos* had had enough and quickly fell back in retreat. Silence prevailed over the now peaceful field.

When the firing ceased, Bert Hoffman and three Guardias lay dead in the field.

The ground held four crude crosses that had been quickly constructed from tree limbs. The row of crosses would remain in Don Hernandez's field until a larger patrol could be guided back to exhume the bodies for proper burial.

Paul Pooley had known all along that something was seriously wrong with the way the patrol had entered and started to move leisurely across such a large field. If he had been in charge, he would have done things differently and he immediately formulated the plan he would have used. He was eager for the patrol to return that evening so he could discuss his plan with some of the more experienced Marines. Pooley was always thinking and always learning.

On one of the frequent early morning patrols Pooley participated in, the *banditos* had set a trap for the Guardia patrol near the juncture of two jungle trails. They were waiting a few yards into the bush for the last man to pass their position.

The Sandinistas often employed this technique, believing that it gave them a tactical advantage to attack the rear of a column. It almost assured them of inflicting a few casualties before they became invisible by melting back into the concealment of the protective jungle.

Part I

Pooley and Private De La Cruz of the Guardia were on the point. They were moving stealthily through the thick bush on a narrow trail when suddenly, Pooley was overcome by terror. He froze in his tracks and his blood ran cold. A large snake was rapidly slithering across the trail not three feet in front of him. Paul Pooley did not like snakes; especially if they were twice as long as he was tall.

A shudder of fear crept up his back and he silently cursed himself for fearing such a creature. It obviously had no interest in him. The snake was determined only to move quickly across the trail. De la Cruz saw it and his native instincts were immediately awakened. He knew, through instinct and the way the snake disregarded them as it moved rapidly across their path that something or someone had disturbed or frightened it.

De La Cruz observed some small broken branches on the right side of the trail and showed concern as he looked down seeking footprints or further evidence of human intruders. He silently moved his finger pointing to other signs indicating to Pooley that they were not alone.

Pooley immediately understood what De La Cruz was telling him. He slipped his .03 Rifle off his shoulder and working the bolt, seated a round in the chamber as he turned and reversed his position. This alerted the other members of the patrol who became immediately aware of a possible enemy presence

From the enemy's point of view, the ambush was a dismal failure. How, they wondered, could the *Americano* know where they were hiding when he opened fire on them? The bandits lost three men and the Guardia patrol was unscathed. Paul Pooley thus developed a significant respect for the creatures of the wild and would devote many hours to the study of their habits

A few weeks later when Pooley was awarded the Nicaraguan Cross of Valor he marveled at his good fortune. His fear of a snake had helped turn a potential disaster into a victory and saved a patrol from possible annihilation.

Like a Branding Iron

Sitting on his folding canvas cot, Paul laced up his leggings then standing up, he strapped on his cartridge belt, reached for his rifle and stepped out of the tent. The Guardia were already having breakfast.

Nicaragua

Ortega slipped into Pooley's tent and emerged with his mess kit. He handed the meat can and meat can cover to Pooley then turned, reached down and retrieved his own. They ate together as they discussed the coming day's activities.

Paul thought the *tortillas* were too dry and hard but the *frijoles* were hot and the *salsa* greatly improved, or perhaps masked, their flavor. He lied as he told Ortega they were delicious.

They were soon on the trail with the Guardias fed, alert and well armed. Each day and each patrol held the possibility of new adventures. This particular day became a long one and was uneventful except that the men were apprehensive and mentally fatigued from being constantly on the alert.

Sandinistas had been shadowing them throughout the day but had shown no inclination to engage; the men's nerves were jumpy. Small patrols, such as this could be highly vulnerable to a superior force. They dared not make camp without first eluding the Sandinistas that had been trailing them.

Pooley doubled back to the southwest on an old, seldom-used, trail and emerged in an overgrown and badly neglected orchard. They saw what was probably the farmer's casa but detected no sign of life. He told Ortega to have the men tether their mounts in a secluded area 100 yards from the casa as the sun slowly clawed its way toward the dimming sky in the west.

It was nearly dark outside when Paul surreptitiously slipped into the building followed silently by Ortega and the Guardias at five-minute intervals. The casa was deserted. Paul told the four Guardias to stay in the main room sit down and attempt to relax. He was going to look around and see if he could find anything of importance then he would establish a watch for the night and they could all get some sleep.

Paul located a kerosene lantern, lighted it and proceeded to explore the premises. Someone out in the darkness of the night spotted him by the glow of the kerosene lantern and fired a single shot through the open window.

It felt like a branding iron had seared his left arm and a powerful force spun him around and knocked him to the clay floor of the *casa*. The suddenness of it all caused him to be more curious than afraid until a split-second later he realized that he had been shot.

Still on the floor beneath the window he whispered loud enough to be heard by the men in the other room, "You men in there, stay where you are, lock and load and maintain silence. No talking among yourselves just listen to me and do as I say. Stay in the shadows, don't strike any matches and stay out of this room. Because of the lantern they can see everything that goes on in here through the window."

"Let's keep them thinking I'm alone until they move in. They know they hit me and they're probably closing in right now to see if I'm dead or alive."

Paul said a silent prayer of thanks that the kerosene lantern, still burning, had not started a fire. Then he directed,

"You men move cautiously toward the window and doorway and stay in the shadows, maintain silence. Look carefully out there and see if you can spot them. When you see them, aim in carefully but hold your fire. I want to be sure we get as many as possible with the first volley. I'll give the command to open fire when I think the time is just right."

The disciplined Guardias did as Pooley had directed, each selecting his intended shadowy target in the pale moonlight. They aimed and carefully scrutinized the area immediately around their intended targets to see if others were close by. Then waited patiently, nervous fingers on their triggers, each wondering if Pooley had forgotten to give the order to open fire.

The wary Sandinistas stealthily approached seemingly transfixed by the window from whence the light was showing. They cautiously moved closer with each passing breath. From their crouching positions they slowly began to walk upright as they gained confidence. No firing had come from the casa. The Americano they had seen and shot through the window must be inside alone, perhaps already dead. If there were anyone else inside they surely would have extinguished the light. Finally, at the last possible moment Paul Pooley knew the time had come. He gave the Guardias the order to open fire.

At daylight the bodies of six of Sandino's bandits were dragged to a spot beside the casa where their erstwhile *compadres* could retrieve them should they decide to return. The patrol moved on.

Nicaragua

Action at Agua Carta

The long patrols were usually larger than the local patrols and an officer generally led them. Guardia companies varied somewhat in size but were usually composed of not more than 50 Marines and Guardias. When M Company went out on patrol, both the commanding officer and the executive officer would go along. They were close friends who shared the same values and each was as professional as field Marines get. They made a great team in the field.

The company commander took his executive officer, Lieutenant Bill Lee, 40 men and 18 pack animals on a patrol that he knew was going to be significant. A few days before, he had been reconnoitering the mountainous area northeast of Jinotega and had stumbled across a previously unknown trail 15 feet wide and freshly cut. It was a remarkable find.

M Company departed Jinotega on the 20th of September 1932. Paul Pooley was pleased; he wanted to make this patrol and knew it may be one of his last as his two years in Nicaragua was coming to an end. The captain had listened to the lieutenant and decided it would do no harm to take Pooley along. After all, it meant an extra rifle. Paul felt that he had been confined to the headquarters area much too long. His wound was healed and he wanted to get back to being a field Marine at least for a while before returning to the United States.

The captain mused, "So this is how they're doing it." "Doing what?" the lieutenant asked, "Moving down from the heavy wilderness; the deep jungles of the upper *Coco* River east of *El Jipote* into the populated areas surrounding *Jinotega*. Good grief, old man, there must be a whole squad of those bastards out there on our flank." "They've been trailing us for the past couple of days you know."

"Yes, Lewis," the lieutenant answered, I do know and I also know that we don't dare open up on them because in addition to outnumbering us, God knows how many to one, they have every tactical advantage over us.

The captain wondered how his lieutenant could be so sure they were outnumbered, but said nothing. He felt the same way and he somehow sensed that the bandits were just waiting for the right moment to attack.

Part I

The captain turned to his executive officer and asked, "Bill, Where's the Indian?" The Lieutenant answered, "I'll pass the word for him to get up here Lewis."

When Chief reported to him the captain, taking his corncob pipe from his mouth and pointing the stem at Chief said, "Indian, I'm not going to call you Chief. Everyone else might but as far as I'm concerned Old Man, there's only one chief on this patrol and that's me." Returning the pipe to the corner of his mouth he went on; "The responsibility for this "lashup" is on my shoulders. This world has far too many chiefs in it and not near enough Indians. Do we understand each other?" Chief answered, "Yes Sir, when you call for the Indian, I'll be here."

"Okay, Indian, I want you and one of the Guardias, one that you personally know and can trust, to go out ahead of the point a couple of hundred yards or so. Just ride along as though you are a couple of Nicaraguan *camposinos* with nothing better to do. See how much you can learn. They may try to make contact with you. Hell, they might even try to recruit you; you know there are plenty of them out there on the flanks, I'd like to know what they're up to. They aren't likely to fire at you, wouldn't want to give themselves away just to get two men, so I think you'll be all right."

Chief and the Nicaraguan scout did a useful job of locating a remarkable number of deserted enemy campsites, which were waiting to be put to use by Sandino's army but were subsequently destroyed by the patrol. Puller turned to Pooley who was riding beside him and proclaimed, "Look here Old Man, as you can see, there's lots of evidence that Sandino's cutthroats have been spending a lot of time around here. This trail is headed right for Jinotega and it is wide enough to accommodate one hell of a lot of men."

The captain was proven right when; in addition to the wide trail, the Patrol located and leveled 18 campsites along 12 miles. On the following day they continued through the mountainous jungle trail. As the elevation intensified and the distance from friendly forces back at Jinotega lengthened they found and destroyed an additional 9 campsites along 16 miles of trail. Sandino was planning something really big.

The massive attack they were planning was obviously aimed at *Jinotega* and it's nearby villages. The wide trail was to be their main route of ingress and egress and the many campsites they found were assembly and staging areas. The Puller Patrol would find a way to subvert Sandino's grandiose plan. They remained uneasy about the growing number of enemy scouts out to their flanks.

It wasn't much later when Chief and his Guardia partner came cantering in from the point. Chief hailed, "Ahoy Skipper!" Puller responded, "Ahoy Indian!" Then Chief said, "There's something fishy going on up ahead Captain." Sanchez and me noticed that there's a lot more of them now and they're on both sides of the trail.

"There's a pretty good-sized river up ahead and they are on both sides of it too." I recon if they are going to put up a fight, that's as good a place as any to do it." Puller looked at Chief and asked, "Do you think they saw you? Chief answered, "Of course they did but they left us alone just as you told me you thought they would." Taking his pipe from his mouth, the captain said, "Indian, you're a good Marine. Thanks, that's just the kind of report we needed." Time continued to pass slowly as the patrol continued moving silently up the trail.

They crossed a stream at a place noted on the captain's map as *Agua Carta*. By now they were an estimated 75 miles from *Jinotega*.

Lieutenant Lee rode up alongside the captain and said, "Louie, I don't know if you've noticed it or not but them little bastards that have been shadowing us for the past couple of days disappeared about an hour ago. I've asked some of the men and they haven't seen any of them either."

The captain responded, "Well Bill, it's their country, I guess they can come and go pretty much as they please as long as they behave themselves. You know the rules of engagement as well as I do. We can't do much unless they start shooting at us.

After considering what Chief had reported was up ahead of them and now that the scouts out on their flanks had vanished Captain Puller decided that the time for decisive action was nearing. He directed that half the patrol dismount and move out on foot in a skirmish line on each flank; the

mounted men and pack animals were to continue in a column along the trail. The going would be slow and difficult for those who were dismounted but he had to get the men off the trail and spread them out to engage the enemy if his calculations were right.

The main body continued slowly along the trail. Every man was cautioned to be especially alert. As they approached the river, rifle shots were heard followed by a burst of machine gun fire. The firing ended abruptly and the patrol cautiously resumed its forward movement as the captain was thinking to himself; seasoned troops wouldn't have opened up like that. It's a sign of inadequate training; they're trigger happy and nervous

Suddenly, Pooley was appalled! Right in front of Captain Puller, Hernandez seemed to be blown apart. He went down hard and was motionless. The captain was standing facing him, his chest and torso covered in blood. Pooley exclaimed, "Captain! Captain Puller! What can I do to help you? You're hit!"

Puller retorted, "Don't concern yourself about me old man. I'm not hit; I'm just covered in someone else's blood that's all. It's your Guardia friend Pedro Hernandez that's been hit. Don't waste your time on him now; nothing can be done for him. We'll bury him later when this fracas is over. Stop wasting your time Pooley! The only thing you should be doing now is looking for the enemy and directing carefully aimed fire at those sons-of-bitches! They are going to kill us if we don't kill them first! Don't be fooled by their cease fire, they'll open up again just as soon as it suites them."

It was the morning of the 26th of September. The Sandinistas did open fire again. The whole ridge to the right of the patrol seemed to explode with dynamite bombs, musketry, hand and rifle grenades and automatic fire from machine guns and automatic rifles.

The Guardia immediately returned fire on the ridge and then pressed forward in the attack as the bandits melted back into the bush. Three Guardias and Lieutenant Lee fell wounded. Lee was desperately trying to slash an automatic rifle (Lewis Gun) from a pack mule when he was hit a second time. Exerting all of his strength, Lee managed to free the Lewis Gun and get it into action.

Another force of bandits opened up from the opposite ridge, now the patrol's rear. When the Guardias topped the first ridge, they turned around and raked the opposite high ground with musketry and rifle grenades. After more than an hour's desperate fighting the bandit's firing slackened then it ceased. The patrol had won. Sixteen dead bodies were found with evidence of more that had been dragged off. Because of his wounded, Captain Puller was forced to return to Jinotega. In ten days they had marched more than 150 miles, destroyed numerous enemy camps, killed at least 30 bandits by actual count and probably killed many more that thy hadn't seen.

The captain's old friend and executive officer, Lieutenant William A. Lee, was flown to Managua for hospitalization and treatment of his wounds. He received his third Navy Cross for the action at Agua Carta making him the first individual ever in history to receive three Navy Crosses. Captain Puller received his second Navy Cross for this action. Later, in World War II and the Korean War, Puller would exceed Ironman Lee's distinguished record. Lewis Burwell Puller became the most highly decorated Marine in the Corps, earning a total of five Navy Crosses and an Army Distinguished Service Cross.

On their way back to Jinotega, Pooley heard Captain Puller say, "In the days of wooden ships and iron men, Bill Lee surely would have been an Iron Man." The nickname "Iron Man Lee" stayed with him for the remainder of his life.

The government of Nicaragua, on The 22nd of February 1934, executed Augusto Sandino.

Paul Pooley had not liked Nicaragua but he felt that his time had been well spent. He'd arrived as a private and with only two years in country he left as a corporal. His command of the Spanish language had improved remarkably in two years and he felt confident speaking it.

He was looking forward to a stateside assignment with the Sixth Marines upon his return to the Marine Base at San Diego, California.

A Saipan Marine studies his former foe.

Japanese surrender their weapons in China.

Part II

Office of Naval Intelligence

The newly arrived Marines were lined up at attention as the roll was called by a salty platoon sergeant. When he came to, "Pooley, Paul," Pooley responded with, "Here!" The platoon sergeant looked up from his clipboard, saw Pooley, nodded his head toward a gentleman wearing a three-piece suit and a fedora, then said, "Fall out and report to Mister Robbins over there, Pooley." The platoon sergeant then resumed calling the roll.

Paul Pooley was not accustomed to meeting people attired in three-piece suits and wearing fedoras. As he pitched his sea bag off his shoulder he looked at the blue suit and asked, "Are you Mr. Robbins?" The impeccably attired gentleman answered, "Yes I am Corporal, "Rob" Robbins. I'd like you to accompany me to the DIO if you don't mind. We've got some folks who'd like to talk to you."

Part II

As they drove off of the Marine Base and turned right a confused Paul Pooley asked, "Mr. Robbins, what the hell is a DIO?" Robbins answered, "Its Rob, Pooley. Just call me Rob; I'm a Marine just like you are." I'm wearing civilian clothes because my job requires it, I'm a technical sergeant assigned to the Office of Naval Intelligence and to answer your question, DIO stands for District Intelligence Office.

The black lettering on the frosted glass window in the office door proclaimed, "Office of Naval Intelligence, 11th Naval District."

When they entered the office Robbins pointed down to his left and said, "Sit on that bench over there Pooley. Have you got your orders?" Paul, looking down at the folder in his hand, answered "Sure." Robbins reached out saying, "Let me have them. I'll get 'em endorsed for you. Be sure you pick them up before you leave." Pooley, not really sure of what was going on, muttered, "Okay."

Paul Pooley had suddenly been catapulted into a world he hadn't even known existed. From the rugged mountains and jungles of Nicaragua to this clean, efficient businesslike office. He was learning that there was much more to being a Marine than he had ever imagined.

The sign painted on the office door he was escorted through had proclaimed, "Commander Anthony Mancini, USN." The office was impressive. It had a map of the world so large it covered nearly the entire south wall. There were multi-colored tacks all over the map. The commander was a senior officer yet he was friendly and spoke to Corporal Pooley almost as an equal.

"There are a couple of other folks who'd like to talk to you Pooley and then we'll let you know what we have in mind for you."

Pooley next found himself standing in front of a desk occupied by Captain Sullivan who he remembered as being on the brigade staff in Nicaragua. The captain was speaking,

"It became obvious to me in Nicaragua that you had some of the qualities we are looking for. Some of the officers, myself included, thought that you should have had a commission in the *Guardia National*. The only thing that prevented it was your rank. To hold a commission in the

Guardia National, a Marine had to be an NCO or an officer in the Marine Corps.

"You never got the commission but you did get the Nicaraguan Cross of Valor and you made corporal before returning to the States. That's pretty significant, and Pooley, you also showed me that you have an excellent aptitude for languages. How much Spanish did you actually know before you joined the brigade?"

Pooley replied, "Well Captain, I took it in high school for four years but never actually had a chance to use it. I guess I had a pretty good understanding of grammar and sentence structure and I had some vocabulary. I never actually spoke the language until I had to in Nicaragua. Frankly, I really felt good about the way it came to me. I know I can improve my vocabulary a lot if the job you have in mind for me entails speaking Spanish."

A slight smile graced the captain's lips as he said, "Well Pooley, we are interested in your ability to learn languages and we can use some of your other talents as well, but first, you will have to start learning something about sabotage, espionage and counter-subversion and paper shuffling. That's what the ONI is all about." He smiled then added, "We'd like to observe you for a while just to be sure you are the right man for the job we have in mind for you, so you will start off performing routine security duties around the DIO."

Paul Pooley considered his new job as little more than glorified guard duty, which he performed at the San Diego Field Office on 32nd Street. He was generally posted at a desk to screen visitors to the office.

After Pooley had been assigned to ONI for two months Captain Sullivan sent for him and counseled him on his performance of duties and informed him that he was being enrolled in classes three nights a week. Attendance was mandatory and would be considered a part of his military duties.

Sullivan had a twinkle in his eye as he informed Pooley that the classes would please him. He knew how much interest Pooley had in foreign languages and was pleased to let him know that his class would be a language class. Pooley responded by saying that his Spanish was a little rusty at the moment.

Part II

Captain Sullivan's expression turned serious as he looked at Pooley and informed him that he may as well forget about Spanish. The language he would be studying from now on would be Japanese.

Paul was more than a little surprised. He had never thought of himself speaking Japanese. In fact, he didn't know of a single Marine who spoke Japanese. His life was about to undergo another dramatic change.

After two years with the ONI, performing routine security and administrative duties, Pooley was sent on Temporary Additional Duty (TAD) to the Office of the Chief of Naval Intelligence in the Main Navy building on Constitution Avenue in Washington, DC for further training and instruction.

During his time at Main Navy, he spent two weeks away in New York at 90 Church Street aboard the "USS Concrete" (a tongue-in-cheek term of endearment for the Third Naval District, District Intelligence Office). He met some very interesting people and received more instructions on covert operations. ONI personnel taught some of his classes but members of the New York City Police Department taught several others. Paul considered his mentors to be among the best in the business. After his time in New York Sergeant Paul Pooley was posted back to the DIO in San Diego.

Feeling that he was not making sufficient progress in Japanese, Paul considered asking Major Sullivan to allow him to drop the language courses. He quickly changed his mind when he learned that his Japanese classes would henceforth be with a private tutor, Professor Keiji Shimada and he would now have classes five nights a week. Studying became more intense and included Japanese history, culture, customs and many of the intricacies of Japanese life that would not normally be taught in a classroom devoted to studying the Japanese language. Paul's interest in all things Japanese increased remarkably.

When he was not working in the field office or studying with his teacher, Shimada Sensei, Pooley was encouraged to make weekly visits to the "Little Tokyo" sector in East Los Angeles where he attended Japanese movies and frequented Japanese restaurants.

Pooley was in the Field Office on 32nd Street reading a Form 119, it was an ROI (report of investigation) on a case that he had heard about and was

interested in. Since being promoted to sergeant, he had been expected to familiarize himself with most of the ROI's generated by the San Diego Office. He was neither qualified nor expected to work any actual cases; but reading through the reports and sometimes talking about them to the agents who generated them was helpful in furthering Pooley's education.

By 1935 Pooley had achieved a reasonable level of fluency in spoken Japanese and he felt comfortable using an ink block and brush. He had progressed through the *hirakana* and *katakana* "alphabets" and could read and write a respectable number of *kanji* ideograms. Shimada Sensei, who by now thought of him almost as a surrogate son, was pleased with his progress. He was sure Paul would do a good job at the American Embassy in Tokyo, where he felt certain Paul was to be assigned.

It had been a pleasant afternoon. Shimada Sensei and his American protégé were sitting in a booth in the front part of the *Yamato* restaurant in Little Tokyo, in Los Angeles. Later, they were going to attend a Japanese movie together then drive back to San Diego.

Paul looked up surprised as Major Sullivan walked through the front door and approached their booth. The major greeted them and standing beside their table made small talk until Shimada Sensei graciously invited him to sit down and join them. The major sat down beside Paul and when approached by a waitress he greeted her then placed his order in perfect Japanese.

As a Marine, Paul Pooley had learned not to be surprised by many things but this was exceptional. Major Sullivan's command of spoken Japanese came as a complete shock. He stumbled over his words as he stated, "Sir, you never mentioned to me that you knew Japanese. You speak it fluently."

The major smiled as he stated, "We've known each other for some time Paul but there are still many things about me that you don't know." Paul mumbled, "Yes Sir, I guess not." For the balance of their time in the *Yamato,* Shimada Sensei and the major spoke only in Japanese.

After they had finished dining and consuming two bottles of Kirin beer apiece, Shimada said, "Well Paul San we must be going now if we are to make it to the theater in time for the beginning of the movie."

Part II

As they were taking their leave of Major Sullivan three Japanese gentlemen at another booth, who obviously knew him, hailed him and speaking in Japanese they asked him to join them.

It was a sad day for Paul Pooley when Major Sullivan asked him to come into his office and introduced him to Lieutenant Commander Farragut. Mr. Farragut was Sullivan's replacement. The major said some kind words about Pooley to Mr. Farragut then extended his hand to Paul and said he wished him well and was pleased with the progress he had made thus far. Paul asked the major where he was going and the major replied, "Wherever the Marine Corps sends me Sergeant, that's what makes being a Marine so interesting."

Major Sullivan's statement took on more meaning when, a few months later; Mr. Farragut sent for Staff Sergeant Pooley and informed him that his orders were in. Pooley was delighted; he had been looking forward to going to Japan. All of his hard work and studying would finally pay off for him now. Mr. Farragut reached across his desk and handed the orders to Pooley with the admonishment, "You'd better read them now Sergeant."

Staff Sergeant Paul Pooley was flabbergasted. As he read the orders he simply couldn't believe what his eyes were seeing. He was directed to report to the 6th Marines for a period of 90 days for DUINS (Duty under instruction) and FFT (For Further Transfer) to the 4th Marines, Asiatic Fleet. The 6th Marines were right here in San Diego! The 4th Marines were under the operational control of the Asiatic Fleet and were stationed in Shanghai, China.

Pooley exclaimed, "Commander Farragut!" (He almost never referred to Mr. Farragut as commander) "These orders, what the hell do you know about them? They are obviously a mistake! The Navy and Marine Corps have invested a fortune training me to go to Japan. I've worked my butt off for years preparing to do my job over there and now I get orders merely transferring me across town and then out to China."

The lieutenant commander gave Paul a compassionate look and said, "Staff Sergeant Pooley, I am not a Marine, you are, and so you should understand things like this better than I do." I can remember Major Sullivan saying something to the effect that he would go wherever the Marine Corps

sent him, and then he told you that that's one of the things that make being a Marine so interesting.

"I will tell you what I can about your assignment but the only way you are really going to know what the hell its all about is to execute the orders and see what happens." Farragut leaned back in his chair, clasped his hands behind his head and said, "When your orders came in yesterday I thought it was very unusual that they would send you to the 6th Marines prior to having you depart for China so I called a couple of Marine friends; they couldn't tell me a thing but; speculation is that you have been away from the real Marine Corps for so long that you needed to get back with troops and spend some time in the field for a while before joining your regiment in China. The Corps doesn't want to send s Staff NCO out there and embarrass him in front of his men. Let's just surmise that you're joining the 6th for a brief refresher course on how to be a Marine.

In the years prior to 1940 and war mobilization, most of the Marine Corps were unmarried. In the regular Marine Corps second lieutenants were not permitted to marry during their first two years of duty. The lower ranking enlisted men could not afford to be married. There were no family allowances for any but senior ranking staff NCO's and sergeants with seven or more years of service. Most sergeants were bachelors who lived in the barracks with their men. With the mobilization of Reserves, many married Marines of all ranks came on duty.

Paul Pooley had resided in the Bachelor Staff NCO Quarters at the Marine Base in San Diego off and on for the past few years. In fact, even when he was transferred from ONI to the 6th Marines, he kept the same quarters. This time it was different he was really leaving. He held a thorough field day in his room and packed his belongings. Pooley didn't mind moving out of his quarters, in fact, he always looked forward to new adventures but he was furious about the orders he had received. Prior to departing Pooley had agreed to have a couple of drinks with two of the Staff NCOs he had been serving with in the 1st Battalion, 6th Marines.

He strolled down the base arcade to the Staff Non-commissioned Officers' Club, went through the door and approached the bar. Surprised to see

Part II

his two friends already at the bar, he asked, "Hi Simms, Scotty, I'm not late am I? According to my watch, I'm right on time." Technical Sergeant Tim Simms looked at Gunnery Sergeant Mac Pherson and asked, "Scotty, Is the staff sergeant late?" Mac Pherson looked at Simms and, with a straight face, answered, "Timmy, I'm a gunnery sergeant in the Marine Corps and you are a technical sergeant, we are at the bar waiting for this lowly staff sergeant to arrive and he asks if he is late." Turning to Paul he barked, "Marine! We are 2nd pay graders you are a 3rd pay grader, nothing but a lowly staff sergeant. Any time you are to meet with seniors and they arrive before you do, you are late!" Gunnery Sergeant Mac Pherson then addressed the bartender, "Sully, my good man, set us up with a couple more of the same and you may as well give one to this staff sergeant since he is buying." Turning to Paul Scotty proclaimed, "That's penance for keeping your betters waiting."

Scotty looked at Paul and stated flatly, "You know Pooley you are the first Marine I've ever known who was pissed off about getting orders to the 4th Marines. There is no better duty in the Corps than a tour with the "Millionaire Marines" in Shanghai." Pooley answered, "Scotty, you just don't understand, I've really worked hard to learn Japanese and I've read everything I could get my hands on about Japan. The Marine Corps spent a lot of money training me for a job in Japan and I feel that it is all wasted now that they're sending me to China. I really don't care how good the duty is." Scotty smiled as he reminisced, "Too bad you wasted so much time learning Japanese Pooley but don't worry about it anymore. When you get to China you can get along just fine by speaking Pidgin English like all the other Marines."

It was Sims's turn to chime in and he did by stating, "Wait until you get a look at some of those Chinese and Eurasian sing-song girls wearing their high-collared silk *cheong-sams* with slits that go all the way up their thighs. That'll change your mind. I wish it was me going aboard ship tomorrow, by God I'd be glad to go back to Shanghai anytime." Scotty chimed in with a hearty, "Yeah, me too."

As the night wore on, Sims revealed that Pooley had to be the luckiest Marine in the Corps. Not only was he going out to the old Asiatic station

but a message had been received late in the afternoon that was being attached to Pooley's orders. The message directed that he be promoted to gunnery sergeant on the first of the month. "That means that you will be promoted while aboard ship with a bunch of strangers and since there is no liquor permitted on board ships of the US Navy, you won't even be obligated to pay for a wetting down party."

Scotty said that it was perfectly all right since the first of the month was only a couple of days away and they were already in the Staff NCO Club. Pooley could celebrate early by buying a round for the house; then they would permit him to continue buying their drinks for the rest of the night. That would be a preliminary, though modified, wetting down party.

Paul Pooley had always liked the crisp clear sounds of bugle calls but on this fateful morning he was not pleased when the field music broke the precious silence of the early morning darkness by sounding first call. It was the first time Paul had ever thought of first call being not unlike the determined crowing of a pesky rooster. He disliked roosters that crowed in the night.

Paul rolled over and fell back into a deep slumber. Within five minutes the bugle's brassy blast shattered the peaceful morning silence again and reminded him that in the Marine Corps, Staff NCO Clubs were not always a safe place to frequent. He had a throbbing headache. It was reveille, time to heave out and trice up.

Paul reported to the Officer of the Day's office and picked up his orders from the Sergeant of the Guard who arranged for transportation to take him over to Pier B in San Diego where the mighty "Hendy Maru" was tied up. The USS Henderson, PA-1 had just come from Quantico on the east coast. San Diego was her first port of call in the Pacific after transiting the Panama Canal.

Paul went up the accommodation ladder smartly, his hangover-induced headache now nearly forgotten. He arrived on the quarterdeck, saluted aft then inboard and requested permission to come aboard. The Junior Officer of the Deck returned his salute, took his orders, made a notation in the deck log and asked a quartermaster to show him below decks to the Marine office. As Pooley and the sailor stepped away from the quarterdeck, the ship's

bell struck a four-part sequence of two bells each. It was eight bells, eight o'clock in the morning. Attention was sounded and everyone on deck and on the pier beside the ship froze to a respectable attention and saluted. As Morning Colors was sounded Paul Pooley, facing the ensign and saluting smartly proudly decided that he still liked the sound of bugle calls after all.

The ship's bell aboard USS Henderson PA-1 was important to Marines throughout the Corps during the 20's and 30's, as most of them had set their watches by it. The Henderson was one of two Navy transports (the USS Chaumont PA-2 being the other) that had transported Marines from Quantico and San Diego to the Far East for decades. She was named for Archibald Henderson, "The grand old man of the Marine Corps" who had served as a Marine officer for a period of 59 years, 39 of them as commandant.

Following the decommissioning of Henderson, her bell was rescued by the late Colonel F. Brooke Nihart, USMC, who had served aboard her in the early days of World War II. Colonel Nihart presented the bell to the Marines of Henderson Hall in Arlington, Virginia.

As visitors to Henderson Hall, or passers-by out on the streets of Arlington, hear the traditional bell time struck they are hearing the sound of the original bell from the "Galloping Ghost of the China Coast," the USS Henderson. Marines of today are aware of their heritage and the traditions and customs of the Corps. The sound of an old ship's bell continues to play its part in perpetuating and adding strength, character and color to the rich history and traditions of our Corps of Marines.

After leaving San Diego the Henderson stopped at San Pedro and San Francisco in California then she headed west across the vast Pacific Ocean to Pearl Harbor, Guam and the Philippines. She then headed for the coast of China, stopping at Chin Wang Tao near Tientsin and then proceeded south to Shanghai.

Part III

China

Before they had even made landfall, Paul could smell China. He did not consider it a pleasant smell. He had enjoyed the long trip across the beautiful blue Pacific, including the stops in Hawaii, Guam and the Philippines, but now as they approached the coast of China the sea had gradually changed until it was a dirty yellow color. He had always known that it was called the Yellow Sea but had assumed it was just a name, he hadn't imagined that the place was so dirty that even the seawater was actually yellow for as much as forty miles off the China coast.

He marveled at how many American servicemen claimed to like China. How could anyone be fond of such a place? He had read about the killings and kidnappings, the gang wars, the poverty and starvation, the scourge of opium, and the many natural disasters. He did not look forward to living in such a place.

In contrast, Japan, where he was supposed to have been assigned, was a beautifully landscaped, peaceful, law-abiding country with manicured terraces and practically no crime. In addition to speaking the language, Paul

Part III

had studied about the Japanese culture and had greatly looked forward to being stationed there.

He silently wondered to himself for the hundredth time, how could the Marine Corps have done this to him? And yet, everyone he had spoken to had told him how he was going to like China. He believed them wrong and wondered why he was so determined not to like it. He decided it was a mental block that he had developed as a result of the years he'd spent being groomed for an assignment in Japan.

He determined that he must not let his feelings show. He would report in for duty and would do his job with enthusiasm. He was a Marine and by God he had to stop feeling sorry for himself and act like one. After all, they had promoted him to gunnery sergeant, a coveted rank. Things couldn't be all bad.

The chief petty officer standing beside him at the rail was an old China hand; Pooley surmised this because he had seen the chief's tattoo. On his left arm was a classic dragon. Paul assumed it had been done in China. Just to make small talk Paul looked at the chief and said, "Well Chief, I guess you're pretty glad to be getting back to China."

The reply surprised Paul as the chief explained, "To me it's like coming home. When I go back to the States I sort of feel like I'm just a visitor on vacation for a while. You know Gunny, the same thing can happen to you out here if you're not careful, the Dragon of Destiny may reach out and grab you and you will never be the same again." Paul had never heard of the Dragon of Destiny and he had serious doubts about the chief's prediction.

From the Yellow Sea the ship had entered the mouth of the mighty Yangtze, (correct Chinese name of which was the *Cheung Kiang)* or "Long River" it has been aptly described as the lifeline of China with Shanghai, China's largest and most progressive city located just fourteen miles from its mouth.

Shortly after the pilot had come aboard and gone up to the bridge, the great river seemed to be narrowing. As they steamed closer to Shanghai there was more and more river traffic, mostly junks and sampans. Paul watched fascinated. It was as though they had gone back in time a century. They continued moving closer to the great city.

China

The city of Shanghai had grown from the mud flats of the Soochow Creek and the Huang-pu River. Soldiers of Fortune, Tycoons, Taipans and dreamers from the great western nations descended upon this rapidly growing city to contribute to its transformation from humble beginnings into the business and financial capital of the Far East. Shanghai was catapulted into the modern world as no other city before it. It grew rapidly, and was nurtured by the adventurous of many nations. As it grew, Shanghai took on a character and personality of its own, developing strength, culture, beauty, wealth and a very special cosmopolitan mystique that stood it apart from all of the world's great cities. It had also acquired the dubious title of crime capital of the world.

On the teeming Huang-pu River, lighters plied their way from luxury liners, freighters and the modern Men-O-War of the great western powers to the Shanghai Bund passing Chinese junks, sampans and houseboats from another time, almost from another world. These floating relics of the past were not yet ready to accept or even to acknowledge the great ships or the ways of the outside world. The smartly uniformed officers and crewmen on the modern luxury liners and men-of-war were in sharp contrast to the sunbaked men on ancient houseboats; using the huge web-footed cormorant birds to fish in a manner as old as time itself.

Pre-World War II Shanghai was where the cultures of old China and the modern western world met. They crashed headlong into one another like someone striking a Chinese gong and in spite of their vast differences, they came together like two exotic herbs that, when blended into an ordinary recipe magically bring it to life and make it a great one.

Some called Shanghai "The Pearl of the Orient." To others she was "The Paris of the East" but to everyone who beheld her she was magic and was at the very least one of the truly great cities of the world.

The USS Henderson dropped anchor ın the rıver and was soon surrounded by a small fleet of lighters and bumboats, the lighters would take her eager passengers ashore where they would be transported to their destinations. In Paul Pooley's case, it would be to the Regimental Headquarters of the 4th Marines.

Part III

As the lighter bobbed its way to the dock Paul could see the magnificence of the Waterfront, known as the Bund. The Bund was the very heart of Shanghai's Commercial district. It was what kept the port strong and active.

Shanghai was China's leading port. It was the gateway to the vast Yangtze River Valley. Soochow Creek was on the northwest and the Huang-pu River on the southeast. Some distance out to the west of the International Settlement was the Shanghai-Hangchow-Ningpo Railroad. The French concession was to the south. To the northeast was the densely populated Chinese quarter of Chapei.

Shanghai in the 1930's was considered the best possible duty for U.S. Marines, The rate of exchange was very favorable and Marines in Shanghai were sometimes referred to as the "Millionaire Marines" as their pay went a long way. The 4th regiment of Marines had been stationed in Shanghai since 1927 and Marines lucky enough to be assigned to the 4th were the envy of the Corps.

As Paul got out of the lighter and retrieved his sea bag and luggage he was confronted by a Marine technical sergeant that asked if he was Gunny Pooley. Paul answered in the affirmative and the technical sergeant stuck out his hand and said, "Hi, I'm Wilson Haigler, I've got a vehicle waiting to take us to headquarters where you can get checked in."

As they rode through the busy city Paul noted that in addition to the usual honking and clashing sounds of the city there was a hint of something else, something more exotic. Delicate wind chimes and other oriental sounds like the pat, pat, pat of rickshaw coolies soles on the pavement and the aroma of the foods of many cultures wafted through the streets of old Shanghai.

They turned off Hart Road onto Sinza Lu, parked and walked into the regimental headquarters compound where Paul presented his orders to the regimental sergeant major.

Blood Alley

Technical Sergeant Haigler was an old China hand. He spoke passable Pidgin and a little Russian and was on his second tour in Shanghai. When Paul first arrived he shared a room in the Staff NCO billet with Haigler. He

went out with Haigler a few times, drank some beer with him and considered these sojourns to be educational. The "Tech" sergeant knew his way around Shanghai and Paul considered him a good teacher.

One evening the two had been walking along the Quai de France on the Bund when they turned up Avenue Edward VII, which formed the border between the International Settlement and the French Concession. They had not gone far when Haigler turned right into an alley named Rue Chu Pao-san. Paul Pooley was 'astounded as he read the signs. There was: The Frisco, Mumms, the Crystal, George's Bar, Monk's Brass Rail, the Kit Kat Klub, The New Ritz and several others. In a stretch hardly more than a city block long, he counted 27 bars.

In this area there was action aplenty for the stouthearted warriors of a dozen nations. The proper name of the street may have been Rue Chu Pao-san but as Haigler explained; it was aptly known up and down the China coast simply as "Blood Alley."

The two Marines approached a group of drunken seamen in the middle of the street where they seemed to be having a riotously good time. As the two got close enough to see what was going on they observed that the seamen had commandeered a rickshaw and had knocked the coolie to the pavement.

Without hesitation, the two Marines strode up to the rickshaw and took it from the seamen. Haigler announcing in an authoritarian voice, "All right men, you've had your fun, it's all over now. Move along or you'll soon find out what a Chinese jail cell looks like—and it aint pretty, I can promise you that."

Paul went over to where the coolie was attempting to get on his feet and offered him a hand. My God, he thought, what a terrible smell! The coolie reeked of garlic. When he mentioned this to Haigler, the sergeant chuckled and asked, "Gunny don't you know the definition of a rickshaw coolie? Rickshaw coolies are the "garlic motors" that propel the rickshaws through the boulevards and back streets of Shanghai and provide newcomers, like you, with thrills and excitement. It's all done on garlic power. If you're going to live in Shanghai you'd better learn to put up with the odor of garlic."

Part III

Paul responded with, "Garlic motors, huh? Well, it smells like it's strong enough to propel a rickshaw, or something a helluva lot bigger than that."

The coolie was on his feet now and bowing his thanks to the two Marines. Paul reached into his pocket and pulled out a few Chinese coppers then pressed them into the coolie's hand. The "Garlic motor" bowed his thanks accompanied by a "Thankee Mastah, thankee!" Willie Haigler looked at Paul Pooley and said, "Shouldn't have done that Gunny, coolies don't think like we do. It is an idiosyncrasy of the coolie mind to mistake generosity for idiocy. What you just did will make him think you are nuts. They like money but they feel that they have to earn it. When someone gives them money for no reason, they assume he's crazy. You'll probably never see this coolie again, but if you ever do, he won't respect you."

Paul knew he had a lot to learn about China as he answered, "Well Willie, I don't know if I'll ever see him again, but he's not through seeing me tonight. I'm ready to go back to the billet, so let's flag down a rickshaw for you and I'll let this guy take me back. He needs to get out of this neighborhood before he runs into any more of those drunk merchant seamen." Paul walked around to the front of the rickshaw and told Garlic Motor he wished to be taken to *Mei-Kuo Ying P'an*, the American compound.

As the coolie nodded his understanding and muttered "Hokay Mastah" their eyes met briefly. They looked at one another with a frankness that transmitted an unspoken message of thanks and respect from the coolie to Paul and a message of friendly compassion from Paul to the coolie. They were two human beings from two different cultures with nothing in common to share except for a mutual respect that passes between two people and gives them a glimmer of understanding, each of the other. Paul sensed that Willie had been wrong about the coolie.

He noticed that his "garlic motor" had a spring to his gait as he propelled the rickshaw with a noticeable enthusiasm, which created a problem for Haigler's puller, who had to keep up or lose face.

Arriving at the compound, the rickshaws pulled up side by side. Haigler's coolie obviously a bit winded. Paul alighted and reached into his pocket for the fare when Garlic Motor spoke up. "No Mastah, alleddy pay." Shunsan

Wu reached into a pocket then stretched forth a dirty hand and opened it to reveal the coppers Paul had given to him on Rue Chu Pao-san. Paul Pooley decided that "Blood Alley" may be one of the most notorious places in Shanghai but for him it was a lucky place. He had found an honest rickshaw puller and he intended to keep him.

Morning Colors

A typical Shanghai summer heat wave blanketed the city. The air was sticky and as heavy as a steam bath. The Intelligence office windows were open and electric fans had been strategically placed to create a breeze that moved the air and helped to dry perspiration but did very little else to relieve the oppressive "tiger heat" of the Shanghai summer. Paul soon learned the value of paperweights. One had to be careful where he laid documents when the fans were oscillating. As he mopped his sweaty brow he thought to himself that it was no wonder that the more affluent residents of Shanghai always tried to be away from the city during the hottest part of the summer.

Paul looked over at the desk in the corner where Captain Hogaboom was wading through a stack of papers. He felt sorry for the captain who was hard-pressed to keep up with the mounds of paperwork in the intelligence office and still manage to fulfill his duties as a company officer and as an Assistant Battalion Training Officer. It was fortunate that Captain Robert E. Hogaboom was a workaholic. A lesser man would never have kept up the grueling pace.

The lilting notes of First Call had penetrated the screened windows just a few minutes before and now the brassy four notes of Attention were sounded. The captain pushed his chair back and in what remained of his Mississippi drawl he stood up muttering, "Damn its eight bells already." Paul said, "Yes Sir, time for morning colors." They came smartly to attention as the flag outside was raised and the duty Field Music sounded Morning Colors followed by the signal to carry on.

Standing at attention for colors while inside a building working in an office was certainly not required by regulations but it was a natural response

for Captain Hogaboom. Paul felt a deep respect for the captain and for the many other dedicated Marine officers like him

Handball

Shortly after his arrival in Shanghai Paul was surprised, but quite pleased, to see the name of Major William B. Sullivan on several documents in the intelligence office. He asked about the major and was told that he was "up country" and would likely be back the following Wednesday.

Paul was eager to see the major again. They had served together in Nicaragua and when Paul was assigned to the District Intelligence Office in San Diego. Sullivan had been his reporting senior and mentor. He knew that Major Bill Sullivan was responsible for his accelerated promotions and much of his special training.

Sullivan was a veteran of the fighting in France, as were most of the senior officers at that time. He worked for the ONI but spent much of his time in the R-2 (Intelligence) Office of the 4th Marines. He was unique for a Marine officer in that he could speak, read and write Japanese. While on a previous assignment in China, Major and Mrs. Sullivan rented and lived in the home of the Chinese Salt Inspector in Peking, an address that was quite prestigious in China and gained him many useful contacts. During his former assignment, as in the present one, Sullivan made occasional trips to Japan.

The major was an adventurous soul and a man of action who found it difficult to be comfortable spending more time than necessary in an office. He had friends in the Shanghai Municipal Police and along with a young captain, made it a point to go to the Municipal Police headquarters and "play handball" frequently when he was in Shanghai.

On Wednesday afternoon, Pooley stepped back into the office, after noon chow and was confronted by none other than Major Sullivan who seemed genuinely glad to see him. The major noted his chevrons and, pretending surprise, congratulated him on being a gunnery sergeant. Pooley knew that it was Major Sullivan who had been most responsible for him becoming a gunnery sergeant.

China

The major spoke to a captain on the far side of the office who had obviously just returned from "up country" with the major. "Don, come over here, I want you to meet one of my special protégés; this is Gunnery Sergeant Paul Pooley." The impressive captain reached his hand out to shake with Paul and said, "I'm overwhelmed Gunny, you are the first of the major's protégés that he's ever admitted to. And he even called you special. I too thought I was one of his protégés but he would never admit to it and he certainly wouldn't claim me as special."

Major Sullivan smiled at Pooley as he stated, "Donaldson is a big windbag. Pay no attention to whatever he says." Paul Pooley thought to himself that Captain Donaldson looked like he should have been on a Marine Corps recruiting poster. His appearance was the epitome of military bearing and neatness.

The captain reached under his desk and retrieved a small handbag as Sullivan addressed Pooley, "Come along Gunny its handball time. The captain and I are going to introduce you to the Shanghai Municipal Police armory and compound."

The captain added, "Yeah Gunny, we're also about to introduce you to one of the most notorious intersections in Shanghai, the corner of Foochow and Honan Roads and if you're really lucky we'll take you down the street a block and let you see Hankow Road and "The Lane of Lingering Happiness." Reportedly home to 151 singsong houses, several opium dens and an assortment of other establishments offering the pleasures of the east to anyone who may be inclined to sample their wares."

The police compound was comprised of several three-story buildings that housed the Central Station, the administrative headquarters, the Special Branch, the armory, range, drill field for parades and inspections and everything needed to house one of the world's premier police departments.

Major Sullivan made it a point to introduce Paul to Assistant Commissioner William Ewart Fairbairn who had joined the Shanghai Municipal Police in 1907. He had been promoted to Assistant Commissioner after a series of monumental contributions to the department in particular and to law enforcement in general. Among his many contributions was the introduction of

Jiu Jitsu, unarmed combat for police. At that time, Jiu Jitsu had been virtually unknown in the west.

Paul had heard of Fairbairn, he knew Fairbairn had played a major role with a couple of young Marine captains in the development of a prototype of a fighting stiletto knife that would later become known as the Fairbairn-Sykes Commando Knife. Paul was impressed, he knew the original knives were designed and manufactured in this very armory.

Ramrod straight and the epitome of a professional, Paul wasn't surprised when the affable commissioner extended his right hand and explained that he too was a Marine; and then he said, "Once a Marine, always a Marine," which impressed Paul immensely. Fairbairn said that he had served in the British Royal Marines Light Infantry prior to coming to Shanghai.

With Major Sullivan's concurrence, Commissioner Fairbairn had a young constable escort Pooley around the three story buildings that comprised the police compound. It was an impressive tour taking the better part of an hour and at its conclusion there was a surprise for Paul. As Constable O'Reilly showed him into the armory's gymnasium he was somewhat taken aback. The "handball" game that the major and Captain Donaldson were to be playing turned out to be something entirely different than expected.

Both officers were on the mats attired in white *Gees*. They were sparring and to Paul's surprise he could see that they had obviously both been involved in Martial Arts for a long time. Paul watched them with a certain degree of envy. He had been to a couple of Dojos in the "Little Tokyo" section of Los Angeles and had gone to some jiu jitsu matches but had never thought of participating himself. All of the participants he had seen were Japanese.

On their way back to the office at the 4th Marines Headquarters building, Paul received a short briefing from the major and Captain Donaldson, then the major asked, "Gunny, when you saw Don and I out there sparring, what did you think?" Pooley responded with,

"Well Sir, at first I was really surprised that you weren't playing handball. Then I wished to hell that I'd had the initiative to take up jiu jitsu myself while I was back in the States. I just didn't know it was a sport a white

man would be welcome to participate in. All the matches I ever saw were Asians, mostly Japanese."

The captain told Paul that Assistant Commissioner Fairbairn was believed to be the first white man to study jiu jitsu. Years ago he had gone to Japan and studied at the Kodokan in Tokyo. He later returned to Japan where he earned the coveted title of master. Fairbairn introduced Martial Arts into the police training program in Shanghai. The major wanted Paul to understand that what he and the captain were doing was not really jiu jitsu or judo. It was a hybrid consisting of not more than 20% Jiu jitsu and encompassing bits of all the known disciplines in martial arts but mostly it is down-and-dirty street fighting. It was developed by Fairbairn himself and is absolutely lethal when employed by a skilled practitioner.

Whenever they were in Shanghai, Major Sullivan and Captain Donaldson worked out at the armory on as many days as their duties would permit. "Handball" was simply a code name for what they were doing at the armory. They chose not to voluntarily reveal to the others what they were up to in order to prevent a stampede of curiosity seekers.

Fairbairn never forgot his early years as a Marine. He was obviously proud of his prior service and truly believed, "Once a Marine, always a Marine." He was always willing to cooperate in sharing his vast knowledge and the Shanghai Municipal Police facilities with his brother Marines.

Detective Cahill of the SMP

Gunnery Sergeant Pooley, USMC and Detective Sergeant Cahill, Shanghai Municipal Police, were seated side by side at the long bar in the basement of the municipal police headquarters building with Sergeant Eric Anthony Sykes. Sykes was a sergeant in the Shanghai Municipal Police Reserve. He was also a big game hunter and a firearms expert who ran a gun and ammo shop in Shanghai. Sykes had brought Pooley and Cahill together at the suggestion of his friend and sometimes partner, Assistant Commissioner William E. Fairbairn. Within the first few minutes Sykes could see that the two Marines were getting along splendidly and felt that he was no longer needed.

Part III

Sykes wanted to get back to his full-time job, take care of some administrative matters and prepare for the next day's business. After a couple of brief stories about his adventures as a sniper during the war in France Sykes bid the two farewells for the time being. Looking at Cahill, Pooley stated, "Wow, he's quite a character, do you know him very well?" Cahill answered, "Not really, this meeting was the Commissioner's idea. He's always had a thing about Marines. He thought you and I should meet and Sykes was the conduit. You're right about him being a character though; I've heard all kinds of stories about him. In addition to being Fairbairn's pal and hunting partner, he commands the sniper unit for the Shanghai Municipal Police.

His full-time job is managing the local outlet for the S. J. David Company, they're importers and exporters of firearms and ammunition primarily. His main interest is in selling weapons manufactured in the United States by Remington and Colt to both China and India. He's really well known as a big game hunter in Asia and Africa."

Pooley, knowing that Cahill had been in the Marines just had to ask; "How long have you been in Shanghai Sergeant and whatever brought you here in the first place?" Cahill took a deep breath, looked at Pooley then seemed to be looking right through him as, in deep thought, he reflected for a moment then he made eye contact with Pooley, Paul detected a very slight impish grin as Cahill's eyes focused on him and he answered,

"Some of the finest restaurants in the world are in Shanghai Pooley and I just happen to like fine cuisine. Perhaps that's one of the reasons I stayed, but whatever brought me to Shanghai? Well it's a pretty long story but since you are a Marine, if you really want to know, I'll tell you."

"Its funny the things you remember about when you were young. Coming from the north, I had never seen grits before. I guess it was about our second day in Boot Camp at Parris Island and when we went to morning chow there were those grits. It was my first time eating them and they looked just like a breakfast cereal that we had back home, Cream of Wheat. I put liberal amounts of cream and sugar on the grits and started eating. I would have stopped after the first mouthful except that my Drill Instructor was from the

south and he seemed mildly amused as he approached me saying, "Take all you want Boy," and then he gruffly admonished, "But eat all you take!"

A few days later I tried grits again but this time I put butter on them. I've liked grits ever since."

Looking down the bar the detective caught the eye of the Chinese constable who had been assigned duty as barman for the month and beckoned, "Hey Boy, Lee, Sung-hua, let us have a couple more whiskies over here." The barman placed the single-malt scotch before his guests and with a look of near adoration uttered, "Here you are Sir," then continued about his business. Paul instantly surmised that there had to be something very special about this detective sergeant. His knowledge of restaurants, fine foods and his friendships with Shanghai's prominent chefs was only a part of his persona. They obviously opened doors to him and aided him during certain investigations but it was also important to know that Cahill was liked and respected by the Chinese constables with whom he worked.

Cahill started, "I was a corporal in Smedley Butler's Brigade. When we came over in '27, I was with the 6th Marines. They decided to keep the 4th Regiment in Shanghai and General Butler took the 6th up to Tientsin and Peking. They needed an NCO and a small detachment of Marines to stay in Shanghai and look after some of the brigade's equipment that was being left here. It was just a glorified guard post around a rented warehouse or as the Chinese call it, a *godown*, but they had my men and me wear MP brassards so we'd look official.

"Since we were members of the 6th Marines and the regiment was up in Tientsin and we'd been left in Shanghai we had to bum chow off of the 4th Marines. Some of their mess sergeants were pretty good about it but they really didn't do us any favors. They were always concerned about who was going to pay for our rations; even though I was always willing to sign their mess chits for my men and myself.

"Finally, one night a wonderful thing happened. Wonderful that is, depending on what part you played in the drama. It was a cold blustery night and it had been raining for hours. Private McDonnell was outside standing post; the other men had turned in for the night and I was finishing a letter to my folks back home.

Part III

"Suddenly, there was a commotion outside and Private Jerry McDonnell was shrieking, "Corporal of the Guard! Corporal of the Guard!!!" I ran out and saw a very upset Marine shaking his fist at two rapidly vanishing rickshaws. I grabbed the Marine by the arm and walked him into the little office we used in the corner of the warehouse. The Marine turned out to be a paymaster sergeant. He was muddy and dripping wet as he related his story to us, whom he thought were the real military police.

"He'd been out on liberty and after drinking more than he should have, he hailed a rickshaw but had a hard time telling the puller where his billet was. He then apparently fell asleep because the next thing he knew was he was on the ground in a muddy puddle with two rickshaw coolies going through his pockets. Luckily for him, it happened on the dark street practically in front of the warehouse we were guarding.

"The sergeant was sobered up, cleaned up and transported back to his quarters. As he was thanking me, I said, "You're welcome sergeant Lengyell and don't worry about a thing, we'll take it from here." He declared, "You'll never catch those sonsabitches Corporal Cahill, all these damned chinamen look alike. You'll never find them."

"Knowing Lengyell was right; our chances of finding the two perpetrators was like finding a needle in a haystack, I just had to say something positive to make him think we would pursue them relentlessly. After all, he did seem to believe we were the Military Police. And I had a very important favor to ask of the paymaster sergeant.

"As I departed I said "Just leave it to me, we'll trace them down and see that justice is done. I'll be checking back with you soon." I really did plan to check back with him soon but certainly not the way it happened.

"Over coffee the next morning Private Jerry McDonnell casually asked me, "Hey Don, are we gonna make a report of the incident with that drunk Marine last night or should I just throw the license number away?" Shocked I looked up, spilling a bit of coffee on my fieldscarf, and stared at McDonnell in disbelief.

"Jerry, do you mean to tell me that you actually got a license number off of one of those rickshaws?" McDonnell casually replied, "Sure,

but I could only get one, it was raining like hell and it was pretty dark you know. The one I got had a Shanghai Municipal Council license number."

"Handing me a piece of paper, McDonnell stated, "Here." I smiled and shook his hand and said, "Jerry old buddy, you're a much better Marine than you think you are. That Paymaster Sergeant is the NCO-in-charge of the Brigade Disbursing Office. He, my friend, is our ticket to gastronomic nirvana." I immediately started formulating a plan.

"At the Shanghai Municipal Police headquarters, I had the good fortune to actually meet your friend Chief Inspector William Fairbairn. He was always interested in talking to Marines and once told me how he had been in the RMLI himself when he was a young man. It took me a while to learn that the RMLI stood for Royal Marine Light Infantry.

"Fairbairn seemed impressed that we had gotten the license number of one of the rickshaws on a dark, rainy night and said he would dispatch a constable to locate and apprehend the perpetrators. Then he said I would be receiving a call from his department to bring the victim in for a positive identification. I assured him that I would give the SMP my full cooperation in this and all matters of mutual interest."

The Shanghai Municipal Police conveniently provided a car and driver for Corporal Cahill to go to the Brigade Disbursing Office and pickup Paymaster Sergeant Lengyell and transport him to Central Station at Fuchan and Honan Lu where the Shanghai Municipal Police have their headquarters. Cahill triumphantly confronted Lengyell with his remarkable success and told him that he was turning the matter over to the local police who would take it from there.

During the lineup and identification, Cahill won the approval of the two Chinese constables by wisely suggesting to Lengyell, within earshot of the constables, not to press charges against the two perpetrators as a conviction may cost them their lives. Cahill further endeared himself to the two constables by suggesting they cultivate the pullers as informants. They certainly saw and knew much of what occurred on the streets of Shanghai. After all, the rickshaw men now owed their lives to the constables.

Part III

Lengyell felt that he owed a debt of gratitude to this MP corporal for the efficiency in which they handled his case and for saving him considerable embarrassment. The brigade paymaster sergeant found a way to convince the disbursing officer to put the Brigade Special Security Detachment on a subsistence allowance while they were on special duty in Shanghai. This pleased the battalion mess sergeants and forever changed the life of Donald L. Cahill who now had the privilege of dining in Shanghai wherever he pleased.

When the Marine Brigade was withdrawn from China in January of 1928, the 4th Regiment remained behind in Shanghai and the 6th Regiment returned to their home in San Diego. Corporal Cahill requested to be transferred from the 6th to the 4th Regiment where he served as an MP for the balance of his enlistment. When his time in the Marine Corps was up, Cahill accepted his discharge then joined the Shanghai Municipal Police.

Don Cahill had been promoted and, though he was reluctant to leave the mounted unit after five years, he was pleased to have passed the examination and been selected to be a detective. A conscientious and determined officer; he was ultimately promoted to detective sergeant.

Mission to Nanking

In the second story R-2 office on Sinza Lu, the major, leaned back in his chair, looked over the rim of his coffee cup at Paul and said, "Okay Gunny, you are going to take a little train ride on Thursday. We'll have a pouch made up for you to take to the American Embassy in Nanking. Your tickets will be waiting for you in Captain Sam Griffith's office at the consulate and he will brief you on your mission at 0815 Thursday morning. He or "Banks" Holcomb will ride with you to the North Station and see that you get safely aboard your train. Your point of contact at the Embassy in Nanking will be the Assistant Naval Attaché, a Marine major by the name of Edward G. Hagen. I'm sure Sam Griffith will remind you that the North Station is not the safest place in the world; but then, very few places in Shanghai are safe these days. Keep that in mind and guard yourself accordingly." Paul replied, "Aye aye Sir, you can count on me." Then he wondered to himself just what the major was getting at.

Delivering a pouch from Shanghai to the American Embassy at Nanking could have been accomplished by any of the commissioned officers that travelled to Nanking on a regular basis. Captain Holcomb made the trip almost weekly. Paul decided that it was a combination training exercise and test for him. He was pleased as it gave him an opportunity to see the countryside from the train and to visit the Chinese Capital at Nanking.

Following his interesting but uneventful trip to Nanking, Paul immersed himself in his routine duties with a brief interlude in the middle of each day to spend time at the Shanghai Municipal Police Armory for "handball" practice in lieu of eating lunch.

He was grateful to Commissioner Fairbairn for the opportunity to use the police department's facilities and approached his newfound hobby with great enthusiasm but was a novice and knew that to achieve the martial arts skill he desired would take a very long time.

Paul's duties in the office entailed a lot of reading and translating. Among his current reading assignments was "Kokki" or Glory of Empire written in 1925 by a colonel Sakurai who was also the author of "Human Bullets." The Japanese War Office published Colonel Sakurai's work.

Victoria Printers and Engravers, Ltd.

The captain was speaking to Paul about the necessity of having an adequate cover for future operations, "Gunny, what do you know about the types, weights and finishes of paper? Or about monograming, sealing waxes and the reasons for various envelope sizes and configurations, or what do you know about printing and engraving in general?" A surprised Paul answered, "Frankly Skipper, not a damn thing." The captain shot back with, "Excellent! Then you have no preconceived notions about the stationery business?" Paul responded with, "None whatsoever, Sir." "Good, you'll be able to learn something new and different. It should be interesting for you.

"I've got a couple of catalogs and a book I want you to look through this afternoon and tonight. Tomorrow morning, you are going to make the acquaintance of a very interesting gentleman who will be your teacher for

the next couple of weeks. He will show you how to order your new calling cards then he will walk you through the whole procedure right up until the plates are engraved, the cards are printed and finally delivered to you. This will provide you with an opportunity to see the business from your future customers' point of view.

"After that, he'll spend a week with you and then he's departing for a new life in the United States and you'll be on your own."

Pooley made the acquaintance of a distinguished Chinese gentleman by the name of Oliver Chan who had been educated in England and spoke fluent English with a slight British accent. He had returned to Shanghai to manage the Victoria Printers and Engravers, Ltd., a printing and stationery store on Kiangse Road just off Nanking Road where he had worked for the past several years. He was a charming man and a good teacher.

Oliver informed his employees that the American, Mr. Pooley had purchased the business and would expect it to continue operating just as though he was still there. Paul shook hands with each of the employees and told them that he would be stopping by from time to time. He told them that Mr. Fang-chu Ah Sam the assistant manager, would now fulfill the duties of manager at an increased rate of pay and would answer personally to him. He would be stopping by from time to time to ensure that things were progressing satisfactorily. Ah Sam smiled broadly, bowed respectfully and assured Paul that he would not regret placing him in charge, and Paul never did.

A Legitimate Address

The captain walked across the room and sat down beside Pooley's desk. Speaking softly, he said, "You know Gunny, sometimes I just can't understand this intelligence business. The Navy gives us the money to send you to schools and for you to travel around Japan like a tourist but when something important comes up, they're stingy as hell. It's taken a few weeks but the old man has finally gotten the authorization to move you out of your quarters."

Pooley was astonished as he asked, "What? Why should he want me to move, Sir? My quarters are just fine." The captain responded with, "Well, we've been pretty edgy about you living the way you do. We've been working on building a plausible cover for you just in case you ever need it, and sooner or later, you will, but you haven't even got a legitimate address. Sam Griffith is going to look around and he'll come up with a conservative apartment in the right neighborhood for you to use as an address and mail drop. I don't give a damn whether you actually live there or not, but I want people to think you do. It'll probably be in "Frenchtown" that's where a lot of western business people live. The major says you can maintain a locker here in the intelligence office and there's space for your footlocker if you need it but under no circumstances are you to have anything in the new apartment that can identify you as a member of the U.S. Marine Corps. Do I make myself quite clear?"

"Yes Sir, you certainly do. I hope this means I don't have to stand Staff Duty NCO watches or commander of the guard anymore." The captain was looking down as he answered, "Well Gunny, that's another matter, the major is trying to work something out with regiment on that right now." Paul explained, "You know Captain, it just doesn't make any sense. They give me a civilian clothing allowance, make me dress up in civvies and put me in a phony business and now they get me an apartment so no one will know I'm a Marine and then I'm told to go put my uniform on and pull the duty.

"As commander of the guard I have to ride through the settlement in a sidecar while checking posts at the various billets. Does that make any sense to you?" It apparently did not, but the captain only responded with, "Well Gunny, when ONI sent you out here they thought, for some reason, that you should show up on the Muster Roll of the 4th Marines and work, at least part time, here in the R-2. This precipitated an exercise in futility that has resulted in the powerful chains of bureaucracy temporarily tying our hands. We are shackled by a system that doesn't always work as well as intended. The captain obviously had other pressing matters to attend to so he stood up and went back to his desk.

Part III

The City

Paul liked to drop in at the Victoria Printing & Engraving Company from time to time to help maintain the effectiveness of his cover. He found it useful to show up at different times of the day. Leaving the office for the Victoria shortly before sunset one late afternoon Paul declined to be transported in Shunsan Wu's rickshaw and decided to enjoy the spring evening by walking.

In many ways it was like being in any big city in the West during the evening rush hour. Paul was strolling along on the sidewalk enjoying the sights and looking very much like a businessman. He secretly enjoyed his role in life. Grinning to himself he wondered if anyone who saw him would ever guess that he was a Marine gunnery sergeant.

The clanging of trolley car bells and the restless honking of horns punctuated the usual humming and buzzing sounds of the busy city. Busses, taxis and trolley cars conveyed their homeward-bound fares to their various destinations as the glow of streetlamps coming on blended with a variety of multicolored signs and lights to race the setting sun and turn the impending nightfall into an artificial daylight that was a bright kaleidoscope of electric illumination.

In passing, Paul casually glanced at the beautifully executed displays in the large windows of a modern department store. The latest in men's' and women's' fashions were attractively displayed on mannequins. He continued to walk past other windows filled with clothing and the perceived necessities of modern western civilization. Passing the stately main entrance he noted a large polished brass plaque bearing the numerals 570.

The Sun Company at 570 Nanking Road was one of the city's largest and most prestigious department stores. When he arrived at the corner, Paul waited for the signal lights to turn green before stepping off the curb and crossing the street.

This could easily have been San Francisco, New York, London or Paris. The street sign on the corner brought him back to reality as he read, "Nanking Road" and a nearby rickshaw coolie in the street was loudly imploring him in pidgin, "Mastah, Mastah, No wantchee walkee. Takee rickshaw." He was again aware that this was Shanghai, the world's most remarkable city.

The Intelligence Office

Colonel Charles F.B. Price stepped out of his office and walked down the 2nd floor passageway. When he came to the door marked R-2 he reached for the handle and attempted to turn it; knowing full well that it would be locked. He heard a buzzer sound from within and could sense that someone was looking at him through the small peephole at the center of the upper portion of the door. A small red light over the door had commenced flashing. Inside the office, drawers were quietly opened and documents that had been on the desktops were placed in them and the drawers closed.

A sliding metallic sound was heard as a bolt slid back and the door opened. Sticking his head in the door the colonel slowly looked around, a sly grin on his face as he said, "Okay all you spooky cloak and dagger types; got everything official out of sight? Your poor old uninformed commanding officer wants to come in. Damn! I just can't understand how this system works. They issue me a Top Secret security clearance, send me half way around the world to Shanghai then give me command of the best damned regiment in the Corps and then they tell me that I can't even enter my own intelligence section's office without everything being put under wraps. Things are so secretive around this place that it sometimes makes me think you men must be running a bookie joint or some major criminal activity out of this office. I hope you're not trying to go into competition with the Green Gang. They've had a substantial head start you know.

"Tomorrow, I'll probably get a call from Asiatic Fleet telling me there's going to be a top secret briefing on the flagship and when I get there, it'll be my own intelligence officer who conducts most of the briefing. When it's over, the admiral will say, as he almost always does, "Your intelligence people have done a superb job on this Colonel Price; be sure and give them a special bravo-zulu for me. I really appreciate their fine work."

The colonel neglects to relate that later the next night in a third floor drawing room of a beautiful Edwardian mansion on Rue Foch he, the

admiral, his Fleet Intelligence Officer and a few other close associates will sip brandy while smoking their fine Cuban cigars and discuss everything covered at the briefing and a great deal more. The admiral will lament that for some reason, he can't get the Navy Department to seriously consider or act upon the many complex problems facing the Asiatic Fleet or the International Settlement and its inhabitants. Someone may mumble something disparaging about the Navy Department being unduly influenced by the State Department's lack of understanding about such matters after which the subject will quickly be changed.

The Liberty Experts

The Marine Privates' Club was an imposing structure situated at 722 West Nanking Road in the center of Shanghai. Modern and up-to-date, it was equipped with a gym, bowling alley, swimming pool, soda fountain, bars, billiard rooms, reading, writing and dining rooms. Here Marines were allowed credit the amount depending on their rate of pay. When that credit was exhausted the Club's cashier stamped the book closed until the next payday. Paydays were twice monthly and there was scarcely a private whose book was not closed within the period. Of all the services and amenities offered by the club, Privates Brinker and Cosgrove were especially interested in the bar. It was the perfect place for meeting new arrivals to the regiment.

During their first week in Shanghai, newly arrived Marines below the rank of staff sergeant were restricted to the regimental area for briefings and indoctrination. The one exception to the restriction was the Marines' Club.

Privates Brinker and Cosgrove were seated side by side at the bar in the Privates' Club as three new arrivals from the States freshly disembarked from the USS Chaumont entered the club for the first time and were listening to the words of wisdom graciously offered by the two professionals, who they assumed to be "old China hands." One of the new men generously bought Brinx and Coz a round of cheer in hopes of keeping them talking. He didn't want to miss a word of their vast knowledge on the subject of Shanghai liberty.

As they expounded on the virtues, and pitfalls, of liberty in Shanghai a list of bars was mentioned and the top five were ranked in order of preference. Some mention was made of Asian ladies and their Eurasian and White Russian sisters that seemed to arouse the interest of the new men. Private Cooper was listening so hard that he knocked his beer over as he leaned forward to better hear what was being said. This wasteful act caused considerable chiding and Cooper was coerced into buying another round. Brinx and Coz drank free for the rest of the night.

New arrivals were permitted to go on liberty only after their first week of familiarization and indoctrination in the regiment and they eagerly solicited Brinker and Cosgrove to accompany them on their first liberty as special advisors or "liberty experts." The two looked at one another then answered that they weren't certain they could agree to such a plan as some of their secret hangouts and pleasure palaces may be discovered. They alleged to have always closely guarded their choice liberty spots and weren't at all sure they would be willing to let a bunch of boots, fresh from the States learn their secrets.

The new men eagerly offered to subsidize the venture if Brinx and Koz would only agree. The dynamic duo was careful not to show their enthusiasm but they were delighted with the prospect of having the newcomers subsidize their liberty. When the eagerly awaited day finally arrived they reluctantly had to decline. Unfortunately, the two "liberty experts" were burdened by two weeks unofficial restriction that had been imposed by Corporal Nelson as a result of their having been late for a formation due to a slight overindulgence in alcohol consumption while out practicing for the indoctrination liberty with the new men.

Terror on Hung Hua Lu

The major asked Paul if he would like to take a little trip over to 181 Kiangse Road. Paul responded, "The American Consulate? Sure Major, I'd be glad to. It's always good to get out of the office for a while and move around the city." The major explained that he had some material to be delivered to the consulate then he said, "By the way Gunny, after you deliver

these documents why don't you take off for the rest of the afternoon. You've been putting in a lot of time lately and I know you could use a break." Paul thanked the major declining to comment that the entire staff had been putting in a lot of time lately and probably all needed a break.

It was a beautiful day in downtown Shanghai. Paul had just delivered the documents to Captain "Banks" Holcomb at the Consulate and then spent a few minutes chatting with the captain and his friend Captain Sam Griffith with whom Holcomb shared an office. Captains Holcomb and Griffith were two of the very few Marines Paul was aware of who were fluent in the Chinese language. They were talented officers in many respects and Paul was certain their jobs at the consulate consisted of a bit more than the unimpressive title on the door of their office, "Language Officer" implied. He later learned that the remarkable Captain Holcomb was also fluent in Japanese.

Completing his business sooner than expected, Paul took advantage of the time available to go for a walk. He liked to "cruise" around the International Settlement whenever time permitted. He had learned that there was much more to this fascinating city than the many fine restaurants and the exciting nightlife that was so attractive to many of the younger Marines. On those rare occasions when he was able to be free during the day he would walk for hours going up one street and down another. He loved to go into the shops and stores and browse and often would engage shopkeepers in conversation. He found this educational and always thought it may be useful to him sometime in the future to know the city well. He could never be certain what sort of assignment they might think up for him.

The Wing On and Sincere Department stores were large, impressive emporiums and compared favorably with the best department stores in the great cities of the Western World. They had liveried doormen, uniformed elevator starters with castanets and each of the big stores was graced with a wonderful tearoom on the top floor. Paul had discovered the department stores when on a surveillance training exercise. They were challenging locations for training a novice to tail someone.

China

In the rooftop restaurants of the department stores there were always distractions including entertainment in the form of plays, operas and music, all, of them of course, in Chinese. The great department stores were located just off Nanking Road on the way out to the racecourse. They were easily accessible by streetcar.

Paul discovered a very fine British Store as well. It was the Whiteway Ludlow Store on Nanking Road and the Bund, about a block from the Palace Hotel. Paul understood, of course, that the big department stores were unlikely places for a Marine to spend his off duty time but to him they were educational and somewhat enjoyable.

On this particular day, he was strolling down Avenue Joffre past the Pastry Shoppe on the corner of Rue des Soeurs where one could always get an ice cream soda and fancy French pastries. He had been told by some of the old-timers in the regiment who were veterans of the World War that it was as good as any place in Paris, and he believed them.

When he thought about the veterans of the war in France, he couldn't help but think of his own past. What a contrast there was between his early years as a Marine and what he was doing now. In Nicaragua he had tramped through the hills and jungles in his sweat-soaked cotton khaki uniform wearing leggings and a hot, felt campaign hat. Here he was wearing a fine tailored suit and a Dobbs snap-brim fedora.

In Nicaragua he was invariably dirty, sweaty, hot and often hungry. Here, on this beautiful day he could go into any fine restaurant and eat whatever he desired and he had money in his pocket to pay for it. Life as a Marine was certainly full of contrasts and it was never boring.

The traffic was heavy as usual at the corner of Fong Pang Lu and Chung Wha Road. People were scurrying everywhere. Motormen on the electric trolley cars were clanging their bells furiously as Paul wondered how they kept from running over pedestrians on every block. The European driver of a highly polished Packard motorcar was honking his horn at the liveried chauffeur of a Cadillac limousine immediately in front of him. Neither driver could move. The pedestrians seemed to have been gathered from the four corners of the earth and deposited in this one intersection.

Part III

Paul quickly snapped out of his daydreaming as he heard a commotion nearby. Over the heads of the throngs of pedestrians he could see three dromedaries coming up Chung Hua Lu. The camels contrasted remarkably with the shiny modern black Packard and Cadillac motorcars and with the scores of rickshaws and the trolley cars to create a scene that could only be found in the great lady of the east, Shanghai. He was entranced by this exotic, exciting and colorful place.

Paul had developed a decided respect for the agile Rickshaw coolies who always seemed to find a way through or around the traffic. He smiled as he thought of Shunsan Wu who was so skillful he could maneuver his rickshaw through a maze.

Most of the Marines preferred rickshaws but there were many other modes of transportation in Shanghai including the red Double-decker busses similar to the ones in London. The busses were plastered with a combination of signs and posters in both English and Chinese with a smattering of French and other languages. As Paul watched, a trolley car spewed out passengers who quickly scrambled in all directions in their haste to get to their varied destinations.

He was crossing the intersection amid the teeming throngs and had nearly gotten to the far side when there was a clatter and the usual sound of shuffling feet was replaced by the sound of running feet as he heard screams of panic. He turned to see a horse that had broken loose from its wagon and was running wildly through the crowded intersection scattering pedestrians and bumping rickshaws. There was Terror on Hung Hua Lu.

Among the first casualties was "Johnny Sikh" who was knocked unceremoniously from his traffic control pedestal in the middle of the intersection. Miraculously he managed to somersault and land on his feet apparently unharmed. In old Shanghai the traffic policemen were Sikhs, tall, ramrod straight and their neatly bearded heads were adorned with red or maroon turbans. The swarthy, lantern-jawed, Sikh straightened his turban, remounted his pedestal and went back to directing traffic.

As Paul turned to continue on his way, a well-dressed Asian couple that had been walking toward him stepped off the sidewalk into the street. In the

flurry of activity and confusion, people were running to escape the frightened horse. Some simply got up, dusted themselves off and continued about their business. Others fled in panic.

The young Asian woman, obviously distracted by all the activity, stepped off the sidewalk and turned her heel. She fell forward and as she did so Paul reached out his arms and caught her to keep her from falling into the street. With his arms around her, he lifted her up and realized that she had broken the heel off of her western style shoe. He held her in his arms for a brief moment and looking into her pretty face, watched as it was quickly transformed from a delicate ivory to a blushing scarlet.

She was thoroughly embarrassed. The Asian man quickly grabbed her arm smiling and bowing and indicated to Paul that he had her. A quick glance into the intersection and Paul noticed that a smile had cracked the coarse brown face of "Johnny Sikh." The no-nonsense Sikhs usually took their job of directing traffic very seriously. This particular chap had a knowing twinkle in his eye that showed him to be more human than his authoritarian position and traffic cop's uniform would imply.

Instinctively Paul knew the couple had to be Japanese. The girl's total humiliation at something over which she obviously had no control and the man's way of smiling and repeatedly bowing was a dead giveaway. Paul spoke to them in Japanese and suggested that they step into the Maison Marcel, a nearby French Pastry Shoppe and Confectionery. Both were embarrassed and eager to agree to anything that would get them off the street and out of public view.

Inside, Paul beckoned the French manager and asked him in English to send someone out with the woman's shoe to have the heel repaired while they were dining. In Shanghai, anything was possible. The two Japanese giggled like children when they heard him speaking in English. The man explained that they both spoke English and told Paul that he sounded like an American then he asked Paul if he was an American. Paul, of course, answered in the affirmative.

Iwao Kurihara said he worked at the Japanese Consulate. His sister was introduced as Sumiko, her Japanese name, but she promptly corrected her

brother in English and laughingly explained to Paul that she had adopted the Christian name of Lillian. Many Japanese had difficulty pronouncing the "L" sound and she wanted to perfect her English pronunciation. If her name was Lillian, she knew she would have to pronounce it every time she met someone or answered the telephone. She spoke English nearly as well as most American-born Japanese. With her fine-tailored Western style clothing and her command of American-style English, she could have easily passed for a Nisei lady.

Inside this little pastry shop the world seemed cozy, intimate, and safe. Outside, all of Shanghai, perhaps all of China, and the rest of the world as well, seethed with unrest. Storm clouds were gathering and at this time in history, majestic old Shanghai, the "Pearl of the Orient" with her teeming millions was very close to the eye of the storm.

An Unlikely Friend

Gunnery Sergeant Paul Pooley had just come out of the Shanghai Municipal Police armory after a vigorous workout. Squinting through the bright afternoon sunlight he looked around and saw that there were plenty of other rickshaws waiting but at first glance no Shunsan Wu. Then he suddenly recognized the highly lacquered back of one of the rickshaws bearing a Shanghai Municipal Council license. He strode toward it and found Wu squatting down busily wiping the spokes with an oily rag. Pooley knew that ownership of the rickshaw meant a great deal to Wu and he respected him for it.

Wu first sensed Pooley's presence then glancing up he saw him approaching. Springing to his feet he uttered in his typical pidgin, "Mastah Pu Lee. Wu solly, you come chop chop, no 'spect yet." Paul smiled and gently scolded, "Wu dammit, I've told you I'm not your master. Now stop calling me that." Smiling back Wu dutifully retorted, "Hokay Mastah."

Paul Pooley considered Shunsan Wu to be incorrigible and with a smile on his face dismissed the matter. He told Wu where he wanted to be taken and Wu picked up the shafts of his rickshaw and moved forward. As they entered Hankow Road and headed left toward Kiangse Lu Paul thought

about how fortunate he was to have Shunsan Wu around. As far as he was concerned there wasn't a better rickshaw puller in Shanghai but more importantly Wu was more than a rickshaw coolie he was becoming, in spite of their vastly different stations in life, a friend.

A Scientific Study

Back at the B Company billet Corporal Nelson's voice demanded to know, "Dammit Cosgrove, are you hung over again?" The casual reply from Coz, "Oh, perhaps just slightly Corporal but it's nothin' a couple of aspirins and some black coffee won't take care of. I wasn't going to tell this to you now but I'm involved in a very important scientific study. I was going to wait and surprise you with it later. But, I guess I'd better tell you about it now just to ease your mind.

"Knowin' how upset you always get when I'm drunk Corporal, I think I've figured out a way to solve the problem scientifically. I certainly don't want to give up drinking, as it would ruin my reputation with the troops so I'm going to stay sober by building up my immunity to alcohol. If I can do that no matter how much I drink I'll stay sober and I won't embarrass you or the Marine Corps anymore. You see corporal, the hangovers seem to be the result of me tryin' too hard and drinkin' just a bit faster than I should. Now I'm taking it easy and just building up my immunity gradually by drinkin' a little more each night but as you can imagine; that takes time and a powerful lot of drinkin'. It's tough to do it on private's pay but I promise you, I'll keep tryin' just as hard as I can. After all, I'm not exactly proud of bein' a drunk. On the other hand, if I can build up my immunity to alcohol, I'll be able to drink all those other drunks under the table and still be sober and fit for duty."

Corporal Nelson did not see an immediate need to let Cosgrove know his opinion of such a brilliant and carefully thought-out plan. There would be plenty of time later to explain the fallacy of this masterful scheme to Cosgrove; right now Nelson's primary objective was to get him properly sobered up and fit to go on duty.

Part III

Rickshaw Boy

Paul Pooley realized that he knew little about the Chinese people yet he could not help but be curious about them and their way of life. They were visible and coexisted all around him but unless they were spoken to or confronted directly, they seemed just a part of the background like a stage setting or backdrop for the drama unfolding before him; they were almost like shadowy figures from a different world. Paul could see the many hardships the people faced and he felt compassion for them yet he noted that outwardly, they gave the impression of being content with their lot in life.

The only Chinese that Paul had personal contact with on a fairly regular basis was Shunsan Wu. He found that whenever he had need for a rickshaw Wu was nearby. He liked him and was curious about whatever had caused him to become a rickshaw puller? It was an especially demanding occupation. What did he expect from life? What were his hopes for the future? Paul had read that the average working life for a rickshaw puller was only eight years. He made a mental note to ask Wu about it someday.

The Dream of Shunsan Wu

Wu inhaled deeply; Yu Shih, the Master of Rain, had been lingering nearby and had just moved off. The smell of newly fallen rain was a clean smell, one that he had always liked. There had been more than enough rain to wash the dust from the Shanghai streets but the gloomy clouds that hung overhead threatened yet another shower.

He could hear the pat-pat, pat-pat of a rickshaw coolie's sandals on the wet cobblestone street as he approached the big double swinging doors of the rickshaw stable. The doors had been lacquered a rich, dark red and above the entrance way was a thick horizontal wooden plaque with the name of the rickshaw stable carved into it. The deeply carved characters were painted a shiny gold. These were the doors that the rickshaw men used in taking out their rickshaws or bringing them back.

Shunsan Wu looked at the sign and at the glistening bright swinging doors as the rickshaw man passed through. He longed for the day when he would be master of his own rickshaw stable.

China

Wu had started by pulling an old rickshaw that he had been able to rent cheaply. Quickly learning the streets and the important places of Shanghai he had gained confidence. He wanted to do better than the other rickshaw pullers, many of whom were lazy and most gambled away their earnings or drank too much. He rarely permitted himself to gamble or drink and he did not like haggling for prices and competing for fares with the other rickshaw pullers.

Most of the time, Wu avoided going to the rickshaw stands at the big intersections. He would put his rickshaw wherever there were no others. By being at these out of the way places, he found that he could often get better fares and was spared much haggling and competition.

In time, Shunsan Wu decided to exchange his rented rickshaw for a better one. The rent was higher by 22 cents a day, but it was a much nicer rickshaw with a rain cover for the top and a curtain for the front and two carbide lamps and a horn. With a rickshaw of this quality, he was sure to attract better fares and make more money and this would help him to realize his dream much sooner.

If he was careless and allowed one of the rubber tires of the rickshaw to run over a bit of twisted metal or broken glass the tube might blow out and there would be a sound like a firecracker exploding. The only thing he could do then was to return the rickshaw to the shed where he had rented it. If he got into an accident and damaged a rented rickshaw he knew that he would have to pay for the repairs.

He hoped to learn by being silent and listening to the older rickshaw pullers in the marketplace or in the little tea shops. They would often relate the experiences they'd had with arrogant or difficult fares and tell of little problems they had in traffic or with worn or broken parts. Vicariously, their experiences became his and Shunsan Wu learned much from them.

It was important for him to listen to the other rickshaw pullers and show interest in what they had to say but he must guard against adopting their bad habits. If he followed the life style of the others he would not be able to pursue his dream.

Wu had always been determined that someday he would be able to purchase his own rickshaw and not have to pay rent. With the rent money he saved by owning his rickshaw, he would buy a second and then a third

rickshaw, and by renting them out to others, he could eventually become rich and would be the owner of a rickshaw stable.

Shunsan Wu had worked long, tiring hours for the past four years and he had been very frugal. He made it a point to never pass up a fare, even during the blistering hot Shanghai summers or in the chill of pelting winter rains when other rickshaw pullers could scarcely be found on the streets. He saved his coppers parsimoniously until he had amassed over a hundred and thirty silver dollars and now finally, he had been able to purchase his own rickshaw.

He no longer had to worry about paying the rent each day. All he earned in fares was his to keep. He could rent out his services by the day or by the month to wealthy families or he could just pick up fares as he pleased. He finally had his independence.

Wu's new rickshaw meant more than just his independence; it was his pride and joy. The springs were soft and bounced gently as he trotted along and even the shafts vibrated a little in his hands as though they had lives of their own and were telling him that they too were proud to be a part of so fine a rickshaw. On the outside, the back the rickshaw was black lacquer and shined brightly it contrasted with the soft tan seat cushion inside.

When he squeezed the rubber bulb the sound of the horn pleased him but the smelly kerosene lanterns used for headlights concerned Wu as they were of poor quality and did not reflect the dignity of such a fine rickshaw. He would have preferred carbide lamps but they cost too much money and he had important plans for every copper he could save. Sadly, Shunsan Wu and his rickshaw would have to do without carbide lamps.

He gently kicked the spokes of one of the wheels and listened to its sound, the vibration caused it to hum briefly like a musical instrument of some kind being tuned up. He could see a reflection of his face in the bright surface of the rickshaw's lacquer as if he were looking in a mirror. He sat down on the carpeted footrest, his eyes on the burnished yellow brass of the horn on the shaft. Shunsan Wu knew this was a time he would always remember. He was finally the owner of his own rickshaw. He no longer had to worry about the rental money at the end of the day.

China

It was not long after he had become the proud owner of his own rickshaw that he began to feel as though every part of it was alive and had feelings of their own. When he came to places where the road was smooth and the people few the soft whisper of the rubber tires on the pavement behind him, like a favorable wind, would carry him along evenly and at a fair speed.

He was fast but he was not careless in the way he sped along with his rickshaw. The rickshaw was his life and he knew he must be careful of it. With great care and courage he became more and more self-confident until he was convinced that both he and his rickshaw were invincible. Shunsan Wu felt that for him to earn his rice by pulling his own rickshaw was the very best thing he could do. It gave him much to look forward to.

Speed was important to Shunsan Wu. With every fare that he picked up, he would act as though getting them to their destination rapidly was of the utmost importance. He believed that he must become one of the best and fastest rickshaw pullers in all of Shanghai. When he reached the destination of his fare, he would often be dripping with perspiration. He would feel tired but very happy. It was the kind of tiredness of which he could be proud. He knew that with every copper he earned and could save he was just a little closer to attaining his important dream, the rickshaw stable.

Shunsan Wu knew that he could only achieve his goal by much hard work and perseverance yet; he also had to show courage and occasionally take chances. He knew that some of the big nose foreigners were lavish with their money and could be very generous but pulling them was risky as many of the *die bay low* drank strong spirits to excess.

It had not been a good day for business and Wu had few fares. He decided to take a chance when a fare wanted to go to Rue Chu Pao-san where there were many bars mostly frequented by foreigners. He hoped that when he dropped his fare off he could pick up another quickly and leave the potential dangers of Rue Chu Pao-san.

The big foreigner stepped out of Wu's rickshaw, paid him then headed directly into the Kit-Kat-Klub just as an unruly group of foreigners was coming out. They hailed Wu and another nearby rickshaw puller and were determined to have a race. Shunsan Wu was fast and he knew he could beat

the other rickshaw puller but the *die bay lows* didn't want Wu to pull his rickshaw, they wanted to pull it.

A chill went through him and he was overcome with a feeling of hopelessness. It had taken four long years of hard work and much sacrifice for him to buy his rickshaw. Rickshaws were delicate and had to have special care. He tried to defend his treasured rickshaw but was thrown to the pavement by a drunken seaman. It was during this time that he met and was rescued by Pu Lee an unusual *die bay low* with a Chinese name that spoke but little pigeon and no Chinese.

Guard Mount

Gunnery Sergeant Paul Pooley stepped off the curb. Crossed Hart Road, rounded the corner onto Sinza Lu and walked into the regimental headquarters compound. He didn't like being assigned as Commander of the Guard or standing duty with the regiment. Time spent in uniform could compromise him in the performance of certain of his other duties. The regimental sergeant major thought otherwise.

Paul went up the steps two at a time then walked directly to the sergeant major's office and reported his presence aboard. In spite of his misgivings about standing the duty he couldn't help but admire the crusty old sergeant major for taking the position he did. It was the Marine Corps way.

Pooley was a staff NCO and he was carried on the Muster Rolls of the 4th Marines; every man would pull his fair share of the duty. It mattered not that Pooley worked for ONI and the Asiatic Fleet. In fact, the sergeant major didn't have the slightest idea what Pooley did for the Asiatic Fleet and if anyone had told him, he wouldn't have believed it. Enlisted Marines just didn't do that sort of thing. When Gunnery Sergeant Pooley's turn came for duty with the regiment, he stood the duty.

First call had just been sounded in the compound and the men were straggling out. The field music bugler would sound Guard Mount in five more minutes and they all wanted to be near the place where they were to form up. Mounting the guard was serious business in the Marine Corps of the 1930's and no one wanted to be late for formation. The oncoming

commander of the guard had been reading through the logbook and taking note of what had transpired in the past few days. As he closed the book and stepped out of the guard office he overheard Corporal Nelson speaking to Private Brinker.

"What the hell are you doin' at guard mount? You just got off the guard!" Brinker replied, "I'm standin' in for ole Cosgrove he's not feelin' well this morning." Nelson asked in a somewhat hostile manner, "Is that sonofabitch malingering again?" Brinker looked at the corporal and stated, "No Sir Corporal, he aint malingerin' he's just under the weather that's all." Nelson exclaimed, "Under the weather hell! He's more than likely under the bar. Is that bastard drunk again?" Nossir Corporal. Cosgrove's a fine Marine and a good man, he just doesn't feel very good today so I'm standin' his watch." Nelson snapped, "A fine Marine and a good man huh? Well don't you tell me about Cosgrove, I know that bum a hell of a lot better'n you think I do."

"Corporal Nelson, Cosgrove would give his bottom dollar and his last cigarette to a shipmate if he was asked and that's a fact. He's loyal to his buddies and he's loyal to the Marine Corps. So what if he does drink a little more than most of the guys? He's still my friend and I'm stickin' by him." Nelson spoke quietly, "All right Brinker but if you fall asleep on post, it'll be your ass, not his. Do you understand me?" "Yessir. I understand."

Corporal Nelson was more understanding then his gruff mannerisms implied. He was glad to see his Marines sticking up for one another and he respected their loyalty to each other. He suggested to Gunnery Sergeant Pooley, the oncoming commander of the guard that Private Brinker be assigned as supernumerary of the guard, generally the easiest job available. Nelson respected Brinker and Cosgrove. Each was decidedly a liberty risk but on duty they were good men and when they were right they would stand their ground like Marines. The dynamic duo of Brinx and Coz were the kind of Marines who, when they were right, had the nerve to look the rest of the world in the eye and tell it, individually and collectively, to "Go to Hell!" He wished there were more men like them.

Pooley was glad that Captain Piper was assigned as the oncoming Officer of the Day. He was a good man and Pooley always enjoyed talking with him.

Part III

The Captain was a distinguished officer. Although stern of expression and a strict disciplinarian he was fair in all of his dealings with the men and they liked and respected him for it. Once the guard had been posted, it was a part of the captain's routine duties to inspect all posts. Like all of the O.D.'s, he made his rounds in the sidecar of a motorcycle.

"Hurricane" Haggerty, Captain Piper's usual driver was standing by. Driving a motorcycle through the slick, usually crowded, streets of Shanghai after a rain took considerable skill and expertise and the kind of talent generally possessed only by a Hollywood stunt man or of course "Hurricane" Haggerty.

Haggerty's perennial grin, sunny disposition and immaculate appearance did little to belie the fact that he was somewhat intellectually challenged. A brave, nearly fearless and slightly reckless driver Hurricane had a special flamboyance about him when engaged in carrying out his professional duties. A Marine of great determination, he would tear up to the Headquarters Building with motor roaring loud enough so that everyone knew that Hurricane was in the compound and on duty. He pulled up with a roar and stopped, sitting at attention all the while, with the motor running.

The captain was always ready and always immaculately attired in his freshly pressed green uniform with its knife blade creases, glistening Sam Browne belt, breeches and highly polished puttees. The captain, pistol at his hip, would step into the waiting sidecar whereupon Haggerty would pull out and charge down the street. All this was done in what seemed like one continuous motion. Haggerty's wide jaw was fiercely locked and his eyes stared straight ahead. Leaning back in the sidecar, the captain always maintained his composure.

Haggerty was an impressive figure as he sat erect and easy on his motorcycle. Paul was always amazed as he watched him leave the compound, banking sharply to avoid the Post 2 sentry box as he hurled like a steeplechaser onto the paved Ferry Lu Road.

Paul often wondered who or what Hurricane would eventually collide with. At some time during the first watch he would summon Hurricane to take him on the rounds of the compounds to check posts and inspect the mess halls. He would have preferred to ride leisurely in the rickshaw of

Shunsan Wu or to drive the motorcycle himself rather than be chauffeured by the daredevil Haggerty but that was not to be. Paul must maintain the dignity of his position as Commander of the Guard by being driven in a proper Marine Corps vehicle.

Shih Tien-wei

It was during the time of *Ta-han*, and was a bitter cold January night. Shunsan Wu did not want to go indoors, that would mean spending money. To achieve his dream, he must be frugal and if that meant waiting out in the cold he must attempt to do so. As Shunsan Wu waited the temperature continued dropping and the night grew colder. An arctic wind penetrated right to his bones. When he had waited but a half-hour Wu was already trembling from the biting wind and cold. Finally, he knew he would have to seek shelter.

There was a little teahouse in the alley beside the theater that was frequented by rickshaw men. He stepped into the teahouse. Because of the cold night the doors and windows were shut very tight. The place was full of coal smoke, the smell of sweat and the odor of cheap cigarettes. The panes of the windows were covered with frost. The tea drinkers were mostly rickshaw pullers. Shunsan Wu, finally resolved to the fact that he must spend a few coppers, went inside and joined them.

A disgruntled rickshaw puller whom he knew as Shih Tien-wei was sipping rice wine and complaining to anyone who would listen about the "monkey men." His master was Japanese and had treated him cruelly since before bringing him to Shanghai from Nanking. Wu thought to himself how fortunate he was to be independent and not to belong to one master like Shih Tien-wei.

He reasoned that if circumstances were such that he did have but one master, it would not be a monkey man, Wu disliked them and he could not understand them. If he had but one master Wu was sure it would be a *die bay low*. He would especially like it if Pu-Lee were his master.

As time passed, each of the rickshaw men told his story. Shunsan Wu sipped his tea and glancing over his cup to the left and right knew when his time to speak had come.

Part III

He told the others that he was independent and took whatever fares he could get. He had occasional fares and several masters but all of the masters were only part time. One of his part-time masters he wished to tell them about. He was a good man and fair but something about him was quite unique. Shunsan Wu confided that one of his masters was a *die bay low*. He was a *Mei-Kuo* (American) with a Chinese name; it was Pu-Lee.

They all agreed that this was indeed unusual and each confessed that he had never before known of a *Mei-Kuo* to have a Chinese name. "Perhaps" suggested Chan Loo, "He was sired by a Chinese and is proudly using his father's name." But "No." Wu stated, "He is all *Lo-fan*." Then hastened to add with a touch of pride, "He is a very good master."

Shih Tien-wei lamented that he wished he had a master like Shunsan Wu described or a Chinese master or anyone but a monkey-man. Wu wondered how Shih could have gotten into such a situation. If it were he, he would simply leave and find another master. His curiosity about Shih Tien-wei would not be satisfied this night as a puller opened the door, letting in a chilly blast of air, and announced that the theater was letting out. There was an immediate scramble for the door and each puller headed for his rickshaw.

Mission to Japan

Paul had received a few hours of instruction and then had been left on his own with his new camera for the past three weeks. He was pleased with the quality of the photographs he had been taking. The major and the Fleet Intelligence Officer were briefing him on what was expected of him during his upcoming trip to Japan. He had been looking forward to seeing Japan for a long time and was pleased at the prospect of traveling as a vacationing Shanghai businessman. He was to travel incognito with a group of Canadian and American tourists on an excursion that covered the principle sights and major places of interest on Honshu and Kyushu including the Nagoya World's Fair. The ONI paid his expenses in full and his duties were not only minimal, they were certain to prove interesting and fun. He was required to keep an extensive diary and photograph everything he wrote about. He was to attempt to make friends with as many of the American businessmen as

possible with the objective of maintaining a running correspondence with certain of them after their return to the United States.

He was to endeavor to ascertain the reasons his American companions were interested in Japan. In his "After-action" report, he would submit a list of their names, photographs, addresses and a short biography of each of them gained from his conversations with them during the two weeks they were to spend together.

The Fleet Intelligence Officer ended the session with, "So that's about it Pooley, you know what we're after. Your mission should be fairly simple and the major and I can't see any reason why you shouldn't really enjoy the assignment. There are a couple of things I want to remind you of; the first of which is, your travelling companions have no need to learn that you speak or understand any Japanese, secondly, you are a businessman so be sure you take a few samples of your printing and stationery with you and enough of your new personal business cards to exchange with whomever you meet.

Remember, everyone in your party gets photographed multiple times; close-ups of their faces will be especially helpful. Don't overlook such things as scars and distinguishing marks like tattoos. Jewelry, especially fraternal rings and lapel buttons will be helpful. Do you read me?" Pooley responded, "Loud and clear Sir, I can hardly wait to get started." The major interjected, "Don't be too eager to get started, you've still got a couple of weeks of work ahead of you right here before your departure date." Pooley responded with the usual, "Aye aye Sir."

The Monkey Men

Shunsan Wu entered the teahouse and saw Shih Tien-wei sitting at a corner table slowly sipping rice wine. Shih felt the warmth of the wine inside him and he could have been very content if only he could get the thoughts of the monkey-men, especially his master, out of his mind. Shunsan Wu wondered how long Shih had been sitting there and how much wine he had consumed. It was not long before Shih confided to Shunsan Wu,

"Younger Brother Wu, you are more fortunate than you know. You have your own rickshaw and may come and go as you wish. You are independent

and belong to no man. With me it is different. The Dragon of Destiny has dealt me a very poor hand indeed."

Wu replied, "Elder Brother Shih, you must play the hand you have been dealt and when it has been played, the Gods will smile on you and you will be much favored by them when the next hand is dealt."

The wine had caused a slight bleariness in his eyes and was thickening his tongue. As Shih asked, "How can you say such a thing? Are you a fortuneteller? Do the birds speak such things to you younger brother Wu?"

"No elder Brother Shih, I am no fortune teller but I am a gambler as all rickshaw pullers must be and I know, as you do, that the odds favor you greatly after so much bad luck. Your time will soon come."

Shih Tien-wei crushed out the stub of a cigarette he had been smoking, looked at Wu, took a sip of his wine and started to air a full report of his grievances with the monkey-men. He was speaking not only to Wu but also to anyone who would listen. Shunsan Wu quietly listened with rapt attention.

Number 31 The Bund—NYK

In the R-2 office Captain Hogaboom asked Pooley, "Gunny, do you know where the NYK Office is?" Paul responded with, "No Sir, but between Shunsan Wu and me we shouldn't have any trouble finding it." The captain looked up and asked, "Who the hell is Shunsan Wu?" Paul answered, "He's my rickshaw man Sir." Hogaboom asked, "What! You've got your own personal rickshaw coolie?" Paul responded with, "Well, in a manner of speaking, yes Sir. He doesn't work just for me only Sir but whenever I need him, he manages to make himself available. I'm helping him to learn a little English and he helps me to learn about Shanghai and the local people." The captain seemed satisfied as he said, "Okay Gunny, the NYK office is down on the Bund at number 31. The major wants you in civilian clothes; go down there, buy your ticket and book your passage for Yokohama."

Paul got out of the rickshaw and told Wu to wait for him. He glanced up and read the sign over the door that proclaimed *Nippon Yusen Kaisha* in Japanese: under the Japanese characters smaller lettering proclaimed

in English, Japan Steamship and Mail Company. He entered and booked round trip passage for himself on the *Wakasa Maru* bound from Shanghai to Yokohama.

As the young woman behind the counter stamped Paul's ticket and handed it to him she looked up into his face and recognized him as the Japanese speaking American who had been helpful on the day she had broken her heel. They smiled their recognition of one another and she innocently said that she hoped he would enjoy his trip to Japan and would tell her about it when he returned to Shanghai. He smiled at her and said he would but they were just being courteous to one another as it was unlikely that they would ever meet again.

Saturday Morning in Shanghai

The 1st Battalion, Seaforth Highlanders magnificently represented Great Britain. They were trained to perfection and made a colorful and impressive spectacle when parading on the streets of Shanghai; their colorful tartan kilts moving in rhythm to the skirl of the pipes and the rattle of drums. Their white gloves and leggings moved with a snappy military precision and the spectators were much impressed with the military pageantry of this old British regiment of the line.

Between the Seaforth Highlanders and the United States' 4th Marine Regiment, a friendly rivalry existed. It was a continual struggle for dominance in athletics and while on parade; with the Marines having a slight edge in uniforms and equipment.

Colonel Charles F.B. Price was the regimental commander of the Marine regiment. He proudly commanded what he considered the sharpest military outfit on the Asiatic Station; everything was custom tailored for his men, even their shoes. Their helmets were smooth and polished and their bayonets were nickel-plated. Even the brass keepers on the men's rifle slings were highly polished. A tan *Blanco* on all web gear added to the brilliance of their parade uniforms.

For the 4th Marines, the regimental parade and inspection took place on Saturday mornings and was held at the Racecourse. The racecourse was in

the heart of Shanghai's International Settlement, covering an area of some two and a half miles. Within the track was a manicured oval of beautiful green lawn. Dotted about on either side of the track were numerous small buildings. They were the clubhouses owned by companies such as the Standard Oil and British American Tobacco Company, by the Consulate Generals of various countries, and by several local organizations. Here were tennis courts, soccer and rugby fields and a baseball diamond. It was a rendezvous for the elite Shanghai society of both sexes and of all nationalities. The British were the most predominate.

Down Bubbling Well Road, through the heart of the International Settlement and just a bit over a mile away from the Race Course a US Marine field music bugler shattered the Saturday morning quiet as he sounded First Call. Before he could follow it up with Assembly, just five minutes later, the billets were emptied of Marines.

In the shadow of the second story windows, several pairs of almond eyes were peering down at the ranks being formed. The Marines' trousers had knife-blade creases and their cordovan leather shoes glistened mirror-like. The houseboys smiled down with satisfaction at the appearance of "their" Marines. It was Saturday morning in Shanghai.

The troops were streaming out of their billets into the morning sunshine and forming up ranks for a cursory inspection by their platoon sergeants and the company first sergeants. Web belts and canvas covered bayonet scabbards as well as the men's canvas leggings were blanco'd a light tan so that all were uniform and contrasted with the men's forestry green uniforms. The morning sun sparkled when it struck the glistening helmets, bayonets and the shiny brass rifle sling hooks.

Privates Cosgrove and Brinker were turned out as well as any parade-ground soldiers could be. This, in sharp contrast to their appearance at the Privates' Club the previous night when the jovial, rollicking pair were poured physically into rickshaws by concerned squad mates and dispatched home to the company's billet where a thoughtful corporal of the guard and supernumerary rendered assistance in getting them up to their bunks.

When assembled for parade the regiment extended over three city blocks. The forty-piece regimental band was augmented by a drum and bugle section comprised of the field music drummers and buglers from each of the companies. At the head of the band was Technical Sergeant Rauhauff, the popular and ever colorful drum major. Next came the regimental staff and headquarters company followed by the 1st and 2nd Battalions. The regimental motor transport company would bring up the rear.

Complete silence reigned. The men were at right shoulder arms and standing at attention—not an eyelash flickered. Suddenly, as if from some faraway place, one could hear the preparatory commands passing down from regiment to battalion to company and finally, close at hand, a familiar voice pierced the air with "Squads right!—March!" With the drums beating out a military cadence, squads of Marines stepped off with mechanical precision, wheeling to the right and four abreast. The United States Marines were on parade.

The glistening sun reflecting off the highly polished helmets turned the column into a moving stream of silver—as the regiment columned onto Bubbling Well Road. Co-operating to the fullest extent, Johnny Sikhs and Chinese *Shimboos* stopped all intersection traffic. Running interference, and astride a spirited horse of fifteen hands, martingaled and prancing, rode Jack Mills of the Shanghai Municipal Police. A former U.S. Marine well over six feet tall and weighing 200 pounds, he was proud to clear the way for the men of his old regiment.

The Saturday morning spectacle never failed to impress the thousands lining the pavement along the fourteen blocks to the racecourse. Arriving there, Colonel Price and staff broke away from the main body to form themselves in front of the grandstand, already filled with spectators from many nations. The regiment, continuing to march, maneuvered into a regimental front by battalions.

The four-man color guard wheeled onto line between the 1st and 2nd Battalions with a precision for which Marine color guards were well known. To the left of the red, white and blue flag of the United States was "Old Blue" the regimental standard of the 4th Marines. The embroidering on

the red ribband over the eagle, globe and anchor read: "Fourth Marine Regiment" and under the emblem was another which read, "US Marine Corps."

The regiment is now on line with the Marines at order arms, as the adjutant marches out halts, executes a sword salute and addressing the colonel states, "Sir, the parade is formed!" Colonel Price returns the salute and commands, "Receive the report Sir!" Whereupon the adjutant turns about and commands "Report!" Having received the report, the adjutant again faces about, presents sword and states, "Sir! All present or accounted for." The colonel directs, "Take your post Sir." Then addressing the assembled regiment, he orders, "Port Arms!" then "Left Shoulder Arms!" and in a custom as old as the profession of soldiering, the Marines of the regiment execute the manual of arms.

The command, "Publish the orders Sir!" rang out across the field. A Marine field music snapped his brass key of G bugle up to his lips, as the scarlet and gold bugle tabard rippled and flourished with the movement. He then sounded the six-notes of the bugle command, "Attention to Orders." The adjutant's booming voice repeated, "Attention to orders! Officer of the Day, Captain Hogaboom." He went on with two or three other brief items of importance to the regiment and the orders were published.

Next came the command "Sound Off!" and the Band stepped forward and paraded down the field, countermarched, then swung into position before the reviewing stand. The colonel ordered, "Pass in Review!" Then a voice from somewhere out on the field, "Sound Adjutant's Call!" Intermingled with the brassy notes of the bugle sounding Adjutant's Call could be heard the command "For—waaard"—then, on the final note of the call, "March!" The cymbals clashed and drums and bugles blasted a prelude to the *Semper Fidelis March*. All the instruments of the band soon joined the drums and bugles as they continued playing *The Semper Fidelis March* followed by the 4th Marines' own tune, *The Song of The Marines*.

Standing beside the bleachers inconspicuously attired in a business suit and hat, Gunnery Sergeant Paul Pooley silently hummed along as the band played:

China

Over the sea let's go, men!
We're shovin' right off,
We're shovin' right off again;
Nobody knows where or when,
We're shovin' right off,
We're shovin' right off again.
It may be Shanghai,
Farewell and goodbye;
Sally and Sue don't be blue;
We'll just be gone for years and years and then,
We're shovin' right off for home again!

As the troops passed smartly in review the commands for eyes right were accompanied by a flourish of the guidons and the flash of the platoon commanders' swords being presented as each platoon passed the reviewing stand in succession.

The command, "Officers, center march!!" resonated across the field and the officers and guidons marched to the center of the regimental front then halted, faced to the front and resumed marching. They halted again and presented swords and the colorful guidons to the regimental commander who addressed them briefly in a subdued voice, then commanded, "Officers, Post, March!"

In the shade of the stands, Paul Pooley snapped a number of photographs during the parade but of greater importance were the photographs he was taking of the Japanese officers who usually attended the parades in uniform. He looked out at the troops with a practiced eye and made mental notes that he thought would be beneficial when passed on to some of his Staff NCO friends.

A command resonated from on high, "Battalion Commanders--Inspect your Battalions!" as a succession of commands and movements steeped in military tradition cascaded through the formations of troops.

The instructions passed down the line as "Company, Prepare for Inspection!" was heard. Men rigidly at attention carried out the orders. "Open

Ranks March!" Inspecting officers trooped down the ranks to martial music as the rifles rippled up to inspection arms.

Finally, the inspection being concluded, the regimental staff led the parade from the racecourse as they headed back down Bubbling Well Road. The sound of the music was gradually muffled and swallowed up by the city of Shanghai 'till only a faint drumbeat could be heard reverberating off the buildings in the distance as the regiment continued moving. Those lining the streets along the route of march were treated to a rendition of the old Spanish American War tune, *The Raggedy Assed Marines*.

The regiment continued moving away and Paul could soon hear little more than a faint drumbeat echoing off the distant buildings along Bubbling Well Road. Brimming with pride, he wondered to himself what life would have been like if he had not chosen to be a Marine. He shuddered at the thought. The Marine Corps was his life and he could think of nothing he would have liked better.

The God of Wisdom

It was early evening and Paul had just come from a visit to the Victoria Printing and Engraving, Ltd. It was one of those occasions when he had taken advantage of Commissioner Fairbairn's offer to use the Shanghai Municipal Police bar. The fellow standing next to him was an Englishman who was a detective on the SMP. They made small talk for a while and then "Reggie," after he had learned that Paul had only been in China for a few months, decided to show his vast knowledge of all things Chinese. He commenced talking about the many childish superstitions of the Chinese people. Pooley, always curious about such things, wondered if there might be something he could use in his work. He asked for a couple of examples. Reggie responded with, "Well, for one thing, they're very big on the God of Wisdom.

"I once had a Chinese acquaintance tell me that if anyone gets to the God of Wisdom and taps his knowledge, the God of Confusion is brought into play. When they leave the God of Wisdom's lair he directs them out through a garden; the garden leads to a maze where they get lost. While they're in the maze they get waylaid by the God of Confusion who resides

in the maze and by the time he finishes with a human, they act like victims of dementia; they are confused. Not only do they forget what they've learned from the God of Wisdom but they hardly remember their own names. How's that for a crazy superstition?"

Paul responded, "Well, maybe its not really so crazy after all Reggie. You don't believe in their Gods do you?" His immediate response, "Of course not, that's a ridiculous question!" "Well maybe they don't either but they don't want you to know it they'd lose face having westerners find out that they have Gods that they don't even believe in. If the God of Wisdom isn't really what he purports to be they have to have a way of neutralizing him while still letting him be a God just for the sake of tradition and face saving thus the God of Confusion." Reggie Chuckles, "Damn clever, these Chinese. Let's have another drink." Paul agreed then wondered how he might use such information in the future when dealing with the local people.

The Arrival of Feng Po

Shunsan Wu had just dropped off a fare and was trotting along the Bund seeking a lucrative spot where he could pickup another. It was then that he first sensed the arrival of Feng Po. It pleased him as the Count's arrival was gentle and felt good to the sweating Wu. Rickshaw pullers generally liked Feng Po the Count of Wind when he was friendly but they all knew that he had an irritable temper and if disturbed by the arrival of other Gods he often became violent.

Shunsan Wu glanced skyward and watched as dark clouds began to gather and now he felt a stronger gust of wind as often precedes a rainsquall and indicates that Feng Po is becoming disturbed. Wu was disturbed as well as he sniffed and could now smell rain in the air. Lei Tsu, the Ancestor of Thunder, was chasing Tien Mu, the Mother of Lightening across the sky and he knew instinctively that Yu Shih, the Master of Rain nearly always accompanied them. Wu set his rickshaw shafts down, pulled up the top and quickly put up the isinglass rain guards. He knew that when it is summer and the time of *Li-hsia* the Shanghai rain comes the instant Lei Tsu tells you it is going to and it gives no further warning.

Part III

A downpour such as this one was no time for man or beast to be out. Looking through the isinglass rain guard, Wu saw a rickshaw coolie splashing along through the downpour with a very irate fare yelling at him and hurling insults in a language Wu did not understand. He immediately recognized the coolie, as Shih Tien-wei and then he knew that the man doing the scolding was Japanese.

Fujiyama

The time had finally arrived. Paul was embarked aboard the *Wakasa Maru*, on his first trip to Japan. She was bound for Yokohama. The *Wakasa Maru* was a 5,500-ton steamship owned by NYK, the Japan Steamship Company. His fellow passengers were Americans and Canadians. As best Paul could figure, some were businessmen curious about the opportunities Japan had to offer; the others seemed to be schoolteachers and tourists. He wondered about them and what they expected to find in this exotic land. As for himself, he had a few preconceived ideas based upon the training he had received during the past few years but mostly based upon his observations of the Japanese on the west coast of the United States and, more recently, in Shanghai. This was a trip Paul had wanted to make for a long time.

The chill morning wind blowing across the deck was no deterrent to Paul he had waited too long for his first glimpse of Japan. He searched for the shoreline as the shroud of darkness slowly lifted and was gradually replaced by a delicate morning lightness. A gray cloud hung in the distance as though floating just above the water. It was bathed in the early morning sunlight and as the ship moved closer the cloud gathered clearness of outline, and its gray brightened into hues of pink and pearl. The early morning sunlight teased it into a magnificence Paul had rarely seen. Continuing to increase in size the now huge cloud formation rose majestically into the blue sky above, and it's pink hues bathed by the morning sun softly melted into the gray beneath.

Dramatically thrusting upward through the cloud was the uppermost snowcapped tip of Fujiyama, the divine mountain. Paul realized that the

other passengers had silently joined him on deck. They too seemed captivated at the view materializing before them. When the clouds about the great mountain's base had resolved themselves into land Paul was surprised that Fujiyama was even larger than he had expected.

The ship steamed slowly into Tokyo Bay, passing imposing navy warships and many other ships large and small flying the ensigns of a score of nations. The *Wakasa Maru* tied up at the *Nippon Yusen Kaisha* shipping company's buoy off Yokohama. Lighters bustled alongside to take passengers to the Customs House on the Bund.

From the train that took them the eighteen miles up to Tokyo it was possible to glimpse at a tidy countryside, with vegetable plots growing onions, cabbage and white radishes, and the Verdant banked-up terraced rectangles of green rice paddies.

To some, Japan was a fairyland with landscaped terraces, beautiful gardens, quaint temples and an almost elflike people. The women were especially polite, gentle and graceful. In the words of the American writer Lafcadio Hearn, who wrote back in 1891: "But how sweet the Japanese woman is! All the possibilities of the race for goodness seem to be concentrated in her." Paul was curious and wondered if he would agree with Lafcadio Hearn's assessment of Japanese women.

He saw about him the green hills of an almost artificial wonderland. He had come to a land even more beautiful than he'd been told to expect, an island empire of quaint customs and fine silks and porcelains. It was the land of *Geishas,* delicate fans, cherry blossoms and chrysanthemums. His first sight of Japan was enchanting—and quite disarming.

Once the train entered the suburbs and passed the fine municipal gasworks it reached the Tokyo terminus and Paul discovered that fairyland was on a wartime footing.

He had seen the travelogue accounts of this land of quaint clothes, fragile houses, wooden temples, tripping, doll-like, women in their colorful silk *kimonos* and *obis* wearing *geta*, and a terraced green countryside of thatched villages. Now he was here in person and could see it all for himself; it really did exist.

Part III

As he looked about, he was impressed with the efficient railway system that covered the nation. Its trains were always on time. Its clattering textile mills and its vast well-trained army were immediately apparent to the newly arrived military observer. As were the arsenals belching smoke into the sky as they turned out gun barrels and other implements of war. Japan's shipyards were sending new destroyers and cruisers down the slipways at an alarming rate. It was Paul's opinion that Japan was rapidly becoming a formidable military power.

As he looked down a country road to his right, he saw something much more formidable than what he'd seen printed in the travelogues. It was a column of soldiers in mustard-brown uniforms with wrapped leggings wearing helmets and carrying their long *Arasaka* rifles with fixed bayonets as they marched in formation to a distant field where they would hone their skills as soldiers of the Emperor—and as killers of men.

He noted with some concern that along with the Arcadian fantasy that most of his fellow travelers saw and admired, another Japan was emerging, a newer radical warlike nation whose people were caught up in a fanatical military frenzy. He was fast becoming aware of this other Japan. It was emerging as an industrial giant, determined to catch up with the West seemingly at any cost. In spite of Paul's fascination with the myths, culture and dignity of "Old Japan," he knew that it was also the land of *Bushido*! It was this new Japan that he was here to learn about.

At the *teishaba* (railroad station), lines of little Japanese flags were strung above the approaches, and every few minutes the dense crowds at the roadside broke into repeated shouts of "*Banzai*!" It was a poorly kept secret that the throngs of soldiers at the station were bound for adventure somewhere across the sea. Paul feared that he knew just where that somewhere was; it almost had to be the China coast.

Strolling alone in the late afternoon, Paul saw an old man sitting on a bench in a small park. He had not spoken a word of Japanese since arriving in Japan and felt that speaking to the old man could do no harm. No one else was within earshot. His travelling companions were all busy shopping. It would give him a chance to test his language skills.

Paul bowed respectfully to the old man and asked if he might join him on the bench. The man graciously invited Paul to sit. They spoke of the weather and other things mundane and the old man complimented Paul on his ability to speak conversational Japanese. He wanted to know where Paul was from and learning that he was an American, the old man seemed pleased. He had encountered Americans before.

Paul's companion turned out to be a veteran of the Boxer Uprising and the 1904 war with Russia. The old man talked of the past and of the great Japanese general Baron Fukushima who had been his commander in China and Manchukuo and who had actually been to America. He spoke of wearing the blue army uniforms of the time while in China and was chagrined that the new, modern Japanese army had changed such a proud uniform for one that had little color and no combat heritage.

The old man had been a member of the first Japanese participation in a multi-national force comprised of troops from eight of the great western nations and Japan. He spoke of the Chinese rabble they fought from Tientsin along the Pei Ho River and beside the railroad tracks up to Peking and of two Japanese soldiers that had been caught by the Chinese and crucified. They had been spread-eagled and nailed to the side of a wooden building. Their bodies impaled by large spikes. There had been retribution for this but the Chinese atrocities were an insult the Imperial Army would not soon forget. Paul wondered if this incident, that had occurred thirty-five years before, had not played some small part in the continuing infusion of hostile Japanese troops into China.

Listening to the old man, Paul instantly recognized his deep feelings of patriotism and the great pride he had in having served in the Imperial Army. He thought of the flags at the *teishaba* and the throngs repeating "*Banzai!*" and he knew that the old man's feelings were a reflection of the Japanese people in general. His brief sojourn in Japan was proving to be enlightening.

Paul returned to the hotel before the others and made some observations in his diary. He dutifully obeyed the major's admonition to carefully check for signs that someone may have tampered with his luggage or looked through his things but his luggage and all of his personal effects were exactly as he had left them. He reset his indicators for the next day feeling confidant that he would again find things exactly as they should be. He had studied enough about the Japanese people the past few years to believe them to be very honest and trustworthy.

Over in Shanghai most of the Marines he'd spoken to just didn't like or trust the Japanese. Paul found it disturbing to continually hear their views as they spoke disparagingly of the Japanese; after all he probably knew more about the Japanese people than any other enlisted Marine in Shanghai and he trusted them. He made a mental note to put in his report some of the observations he had made concerning the character of the people in general. Two of the things that stood out most clearly as different from life in the United States or China were that at the *teishaba,* commuters left hundreds of bicycles unattended and unlocked while they went off to work. When they returned later their bicycles were there waiting for them. The other, very significant difference from the United States was that Paul had noticed no locks on the doors to people's homes. Honesty seemed to be a national trait among the Japanese.

A knocking on the door broke Paul's chain of thought as he heard George's distinctive voice proclaiming loudly, "C'mon Mr. Pooley, we're supposed to meet in the lobby, Mary Lou is already down there with the others. It looks like these people are finally gonna feed us." Paul was ready and as he swung the door open he could see that George had a Martini in hand; he was getting off to an early start.

As they entered the lobby, Albert was sitting at the little bar off to the right side smoking a big cigar that gave off a strong odor. The ladies were in the central part of the lobby relaxing in the overstuffed chairs and chatting about the wonders they had seen and the bargains they'd found while shopping.

Albert, the only customer at the small bar, was doing his best to describe to Kato the bartender all of the things he had seen during his first 24 hours in Japan that he thought needed to be changed. Kato, the inscrutable Japanese, was a good listener and from time to time he would smile approvingly as though he had understood every word and agreed with Albert's words of wisdom.

China

George approached the bar and taking a stool beside Albert he put his martini glass on the bar and addressed Kato, "Boy, make me another one of these." Albert told George that he had been advising Kato how to get Japan straightened out. George looked at him incredulously as he responded, "Albert, your wasting your breath. These people don't want to change. They aren't going to amount to anything as long as they've got the form of government they have. That little pipsqueak with all the medals the fancy uniform and the big white horse; Emperor Hirohito is running this country and they'll let him do it as long as he can keep 'em thinking he's a God of some kind.

"What the Japanese need is to send a delegation back to Chicago so we can teach them what politics is really all about. We can show them how to have a real active democratic system where everybody votes. And they vote the way they're told dammit, if they know what's good for them." A smiling George spoke up addressing Kato as he advised, "Kato, you come back to Chicago with us and we'll show you how to become a rich man after you return to Japan. We'll show you how to organize a really effective political machine that will help you overthrow your present system of government. You've got to drop this emperor. Every now and then, the leadership at the top has to change. Hirohito's got your whole country right in the palm of his hand. The Japanese Diet does just what he tells 'em. That power should be passed to the people."

Paul cringed hoping that Kato understood little of what George and Albert were saying. These two were anything but ambassadors of good will. In fact, Paul considered them to actually be dangerous. He wanted to admonish them and tell them how much harm they were doing to American-Japanese relations but dared not alienate the two at this time. He was here on a spotting and assessing mission and that included befriending his traveling companions and getting to know what had motivated them to come to Japan and what their expectations for the future were. He did feel very sensitive to the loud conversation and tried to do something to quell it by inserting himself between Albert and George at the bar and joining in their conversation in order to change the subject. He ordered a drink and spoke

to Kato in a courteous manner hoping he would realize that all Americans were not so offensive.

Before leaving, Paul placed a slightly more than generous tip on the bar as Kato bowed his thanks with a, "Sanku berry mutchee Mistah Pooree." As Kato leaned forward to bow, the underside of the left lapel on his white cotton mess jacket flapped down slightly; it seemed to be weighted down by something. Paul recognized it as a little gold-colored chrysanthemum pin and wondered why the *kempeitai* even bothered to wear it if they were always going to place it where it was not supposed to be seen. Practically everyone in Japan knew the *kempeitai* wore their chrysanthemum insignia behind a lapel or pinned on the inside of a coat.

Paul stood up, hoping the other two would follow suit but was disappointed until he acquired an unexpected ally in the person of Louise. She strode across the lobby and in her piercing voice uttered, "Albert! You men are keeping us all waiting. Come on, we want to go eat. Then looking at the bartender she said, "I'm sorry Mr. Kato but your buddies are coming with me. You've had them long enough." Paul smiled to himself realizing that Kato was overjoyed to have Louise remove these two objectionable characters from his presence.

George's wife, Mary Lou spoke very little unless someone spoke to her. Courteous to everyone; she seemed like a sweet lady who was lost in thought most of the time. Louise stayed close to her and looked after her as best she could, as George was generally too preoccupied to be bothered.

The dinner was exquisitely served and was delicious. Paul sensed that the two schoolteachers were a bit reserved as they joined in quiet conversation with Lucy the Canadian lady. George and Albert monopolized the evening talking mostly about the fortunes that could be made by selling steel to Japan. Mary Lou appeared ambivalent while Louise glared disapprovingly at the two husbands. By the time dinner was over, Paul noted that Mary Lou had quietly consumed four martinis. He wondered how many she had while they were waiting in the lobby before dinner.

Albert and George were old friends who had known each other and done some business together back in Chicago but Ole Swenson and the Müllers

from Canada, were strangers to them. Olaf (Ole) and his wife Lucy were from Omaha. Ole had worked in Public utilities in Minneapolis for several years but relocated to Omaha when he saw an opportunity to become a private contractor and with the encouragement of a few friends that had deep pockets, he seized upon it.

Ole's trip to Japan was more than just a vacation. He hoped to make some contacts while in Japan that would be helpful to him when he got back to Omaha. The Japs wanted to buy steel and Omaha was about to come into a large surplus of steel. Streetcar tracks in Omaha were being torn up and removed to make way for the transit system's new busses that were replacing the trolley cars. Omaha, like most other American cities, was converting to busses. After all oil was cheap and in spite of the diesel fumes and pollution, the busses were more comfortable and quieter than the old fashioned streetcars. If he could find a cheap way to transport those steel tracks out to the west coast, the Japanese could then ship them from California to Japan. American cities were converting to busses and would have to find an economical way of disposing of the steel tracks. If he could find a way to corner the market on old tracks, he could make millions. Many big cities were merely covering the tracks over with asphalt paving instead of pulling them up and removing them. Ole was appalled at the thought of all that steel being lost. He was eager to find someone in Japan that would be willing to finance him in recovering and shipping the steel.

Ole was a good listener but was cautious about revealing his knowledge of the Omaha Transit System's steel to his two exuberant companions. He listened to the two with rapt attention hoping to learn what they actually knew and how much was mere speculation. Paul knew nothing about the steel industry or about trading with Japan and said so. He could tell, however, that Ole had a reason to listen and participate whenever he could do so without tipping his hand.

The Canadian couple kept to themselves, quietly conversing with each other and the two teachers. The Canadians gave the impression of being genuine tourists with no ulterior agenda other than seeing the Nagoya World's Fair and satisfying their curiosity about Japan. The two school-

teachers Madeline Fry and Stella Smart were partially subsidized by the Board of Japanese Tourism and were on the trip to see Japan's social, cultural and economic achievements.

Paul was pleased when the dinner was over, as he wanted to get to his room and work on his report for the day. When he had finished the report he stepped out onto the veranda and leaning over the railing drank in the beauty and serenity of the night. The soft glow from colored lanterns dotting the little homes scattered throughout the valley below cast an almost magical spell. As a big bright moon played peek-a-boo with drifting clouds overhead that intermittently masked the moon's brightness only to have it emerge again and bring back a view of the trees and quaint little Japanese houses. The whole scene before him was a picture of the beauty of a Japanese night that he would long remember. He could hear the exotic strains of classical Japanese music drifting up from one of the nearby houses in the valley below.

He'd only been there a short time when a slight giggling down the veranda to his right interrupted his reverie. Knowing that it was none of his business, he did his best to ignore the muffled sounds.

Suddenly, he heard, "Oh no Mr. Jameson no, you shouldn't!" Then he heard a sighing and cooing that told him that "you shouldn't" had obviously been the wrong choice of words. Paul felt trapped. If he remained where he was, he would be eavesdropping; but if he moved to leave, he knew they would hear him and be embarrassed. Paul had a mission and at this time, he did not want to embarrass or alienate anyone. He stood silently in the shadows and waited.

Paul's mission was to keep an extensive diary, photograph everything he wrote about and do his best to befriend the American businessmen among his travelling companions with the objective of maintaining a running correspondence with them after their return home. Periodically, he was to send his reports and film back to ONI in Shanghai.

The next day promised to be interesting as they were to go to the island of Kyushu where they would visit the city of Beppu in Oita-ken and see The Nine Hells of Beppu. Beppu has nine major geothermal hot spots, which are

sometimes referred to as the "nine hells of which they all enjoyed immensely except for Mary Lou Jameson who had a nagging headache causing her to stay in her room.

George was eager to experience the communal baths at *Beppu* as he had heard that both sexes bathed together and was eager to satisfy his curiosity about Japanese female anatomy. The water temperature turned out to be almost more than George or Albert could stand and the only females in the bath were the attendants, who were clothed. This was somewhat of a disappointment to George but once he became acclimated to the scalding water, even he seemed to relax and enjoy himself. The enjoyment and relaxation stopped abruptly when they emerged only to have little wooden buckets of cold water poured over their heads, a shocking experience for the unsuspecting Americans. The ladies in their party, including Madeline Fry and Stella Smart had declined to bathe while the men were present.

The Tattoo

When they were in the baths, Paul noticed a tattoo on George's left Shoulder. It was not unlike other tattoos he had seen on sailors. The tattoo was an anchor with USN superimposed over it. That was the insignia that chief petty officers in the US Navy wore on their caps. During the trip Paul had refrained from mentioning anything military. He felt that his cover as a Shanghai businessman was sufficient and he did not want to open any avenues that may lead to a probing of his true identity but the tattoo had aroused his curiosity so he asked, "Mr. Jameson, I didn't know you were a navy man, you've never mentioned anything about it."

George promptly answered, "Well, no Mr. Pooley, I'm not. It's a little embarrassing to talk about, but since you asked, I'll tell you. I was never in the US Navy. Albert here is probably tired of hearing me tell the story but when I was a young man some friends and I thought we'd join the service. You know how kids are; Pershing and the US Cavalry were down on the Mexican border fighting Poncho Villa and America's participation in the war in Europe was becoming inevitable. We didn't want to miss any of the action but I didn't like horses so instead of the army, I chose the navy. I went

down to the recruiting office and filled out all of the necessary paperwork and was proud as a peacock. The boys and I went out and had a few drinks after leaving the recruiting office to celebrate my going into the navy. We drank too much and in a stupid burst of temporary insanity, I decided to get this damned tattoo. The following day when I took my physical they found out I had flat feet and rejected me. And that was the end of my Navy career. Only one day in the Navy and there I was, stuck with the damned tattoo for the rest of my life, I was disappointed but it's really the best thing that ever happened to me. You know the war started in April of '17 and I would have been right in the middle of it. I wouldn't have made a very good sailor Mr. Pooley, I'd rather give orders than take them, I'm good at that." Paul smiled and nodded his understanding as he thought to himself how difficult it was to be friendly to someone he had so little respect for.

As they were leaving the baths to return to their rooms Paul noted with great interest that Mr. George Jameson's wet footprints on the smooth floor showed no signs of flatfeet. The arches of his feet seemed as healthy as his own. Was there a cure for flat feet? Paul thought not and wondered if this was of sufficient interest to put in his daily report. He had developed a distrust of George from their first meeting. His intuition made him include everything in the report; it contained the facts including photographs of a man's left shoulder bearing a tattoo of an anchor and the letters USN and a set of footprints on a concrete floor and a brief synopsis of Paul's opinions.

Japanese authorities had classified numerous areas of its coastline as 'strategic zones' and forbade the taking of photographs. Many foreign tourists were detained for hours of questioning and confiscation of film because they unwittingly used a camera in one these zones. Paul wisely obeyed the rules. He also transmitted his reports and the rolls of film he had legally been able to shoot as frequently as he could. The others thought he was sending back ideas and paper and stationery samples to his subordinate managers in the engraving shop as he always addressed his packets to the Manager, Mr. Fang-chu Ah Sam at the Victoria Printing and Engraving Co, Ltd. In Shanghai, China

China

Following their visit to Beppu they continued touring Kyushu and visited the beautiful port city of Nagasaki then on to Kumamoto to tour the ancient Kumamoto Castle. One of Japan's three great old feudal castles that still remained intact. The large medieval castle seemed like something right out of a storybook. From the outside they looked up and their eyes followed along the high, smooth stone wall that seemed to curve outward near the top making it impossible to scale. They looked beyond the wall and could see the decidedly Japanese architecture of the great medieval castle that played such a significant role in the 55-day siege during the final stages of the Satsuma Rebellion back in 1872. They visited the ancient and beautiful Suizenji Park and then traveled to Mount Aso where there was another famous hot spring and an opportunity to climb up to the rim of the smoldering volcano. Louise and Mary Lou declined to climb with the others so they remained back at the hotel where Mary Lou continued to enjoy her martinis. George stayed close to miss Fry to assist her in climbing Aso Yama and protect her from falling into the abyss of the volcano or from any other hazards, real or imagined, that she may encounter.

The night spent at the hotel on Mount Aso was much like the previous nights with George spending considerable time after dinner expounding on his business schemes with Miss Fry who seemed inordinately impressed with his plans for future wealth by exporting steel to the Japanese. She also expressed an interest in possibly leaving her teaching career and moving to Chicago.

Albert and George were sitting in the hotel lounge at the Yadoya Aso Yama enjoying their scotch and Cuban cigars. The ladies and the other members of the party were still in their rooms getting ready for dinner. Albert leaned over to George and said, "George, we've known each other for a long time. We've done a lot of things together and we've usually been pretty successful. I think one reason we get along so well is that it's always been business. I've never inquired about your personal life and you've never asked about mine."

George had a concerned look in his eyes as he asked, "Albert, what the hell are you getting at?" Albert snapped back, "It's Miss Fry George, it has become too obvious to all the others what's going on between you and Miss

Fry. Of course, it doesn't make a damn to me what you do with her in fact she's not a bad looker, but don't forget, my wife is on this trip. She has been giving me hell every night about what's going on between you two and she keeps nagging me to get you to have Mary Lou committed to a hospital before she gets any worse off. She's a pretty sick woman George and if she doesn't get help pretty soon, she may not make it."

George snarled, "Well, I'll be damned. I never thought I'd hear anything like that from you. For your information, Mary Lou doesn't want to go to a damned hospital in this god-forsaken country. I've already asked her and she refuses. She says she will see a doctor after we get back to America so tell Louise to back off and stay the hell out of it.

"As far as Miss Fry is concerned, I'm really quite fond of her Albert and I'm doing my best to talk her into coming to work for us. I think she's nearly convinced. All we've got to do is get her a little apartment close to the office. She's just what we need when we get back. If we've got someone like her to answer the phone for us and type our letters it will give us more leverage with those skinflints we have to deal with. It will make our business look a lot more prosperous and legitimate if we have a receptionist."

Albert was amazed as he asked, "Okay, wise guy, how do you propose we pay her? We've expended most of our resources on this boondoggle to Japan."

George, taking a long draw on his cigar and blowing the smoke out slowly contemplated it for a moment, then answered, "She's pretty naïve Albert, if we match what she's getting now as a schoolteacher and pay for a little apartment for her she'll think she's really moving up in the world. We might even give her a title of some sort, you know, like Administrative Assistant to the President. As far as the pay goes, we'll just pay her what a schoolteacher would normally get, that can't be very much. I'll have Mary Lou pay her."

Albert, stunned, looked at George and asked. "Mary Lou? How can you justify a thing like that?" George's immediate response was, "I offered her a dual position as our administrative assistant and as companion to Mary Lou. Mary Lou doesn't even have to sign the checks; I can do that for her. After all, she is sick you know." Albert knew.

China

When they got to Nagoya on the Pacific coast of south central Honshu to attended the "World's Fair" they were deeply impressed. His Imperial Highness, Prince Higashikuni Naruhiko, whom none had ever heard of before, was chairman of the fair. Paul Pooley noted with interest that there were no restrictions on taking photographs at the fair. He promptly took some good shots of His Imperial Highness and the few other Japanese dignitaries that he could identify. The fair was called The Nagoya Pan-Pacific Peace Exposition. Nagoya turned out to have a population of well over 2 million people and is one of Japan's major ports. It is also the center of Japan's third largest economic and industrial region, known as the Chūkyō Metropolitan Area.

There were so many things of interest that Paul felt should be reported. He found it difficult to keep up with his daily diary entries, which were becoming quite lengthy. Japan was turning out to be more than just a quaint little "Island Empire" that was emerging from the dark ages; it was a thriving industrial nation populated by a people determined to expand their empire and catch up with the west. Japan's growing military might was obvious to Paul and he wondered if all that he was seeing was simply to consolidate their holdings in China, Chosen (Korea) and Manchukuo or was something more sinister afoot? The Japanese needed more land to feed their people and more raw materials to feed their voracious industrial and military appetites.

Paul decided that George and Albert, and Ole as well, were not so crazy after all. They probably could make millions selling steel to Japan. He shuddered at the thought and feared the outcome. If the civilized world allowed them to continue unchecked, this charming and delightful people were in danger of becoming monsters. (The Second Sino-Japanese War erupted in China only two months after the close of the "Pan-Pacific Peace Exposition).

The voyage back to Shanghai was mostly uneventful except that a noticeable change had come over George and Albert. They spoke softly to one another and were constantly discussing things that had occurred in Nagoya. Apparently, they had made some important contacts that they felt would be useful to them and were planning their future strategy. Mary Lou Jameson

was taken aboard the *Wakasa Maru* on a stretcher with Madeline Fry, her new "companion" in attendance. Stella had attached herself to the Canadian couple and was planning to take her next vacation at their home in Alberta where she was hoping to meet a handsome member of the "Mounties," the Royal Canadian Mounted Police.

Lost luggage

The *Wakasa Maru* dropped anchor in the Huang-pu River on a sunny Shanghai morning. Bumboats and sampans circled nearby eagerly hawking their wares but the passengers, impatient to go ashore, paid little heed to them and queued up on the starboard side to shake hands with the captain and go down the ladder into a waiting lighter that was to ferry them over to the NYK landing on the bund. The ship's purser rushed up to the captain and jabbered something in Japanese that Paul could neither hear nor understand. The captain pursed his lips, bowed and stated that all passengers should remain right where they were for the moment.

Two gentlemen climbed the accommodation ladder and stepped onto the deck addressing the captain and showing him their official credentials. Paul immediately recognized them both. They were ONI Special Agents Smith and Yablonski. He had met them both on several occasions. Each of the agents looked past Paul showing no recognition and acting as though they'd never seen him before.

Mr. George Jameson, an American passenger, was taken into custody, placed under arrest and promptly removed from the ship. The other passengers were then permitted to disembark.

The passengers' luggage had been staged on deck on the portside while waiting to be sent ashore and delivered to them at the NYK Office on the bund. Most of the passengers had planned to remain in Shanghai overnight, and then they would go their separate ways home, with the very obvious exception of George Jameson. There was much anxiety and hushed conversation among the passengers as they discussed the arrest of Mr. Jameson. Mrs. Jameson sat in a wheelchair dabbing her eyes with a lace handkerchief, her loyal and devoted companion Madeline Fry, attending to her every need.

China

The Wakasa Maru passengers were soon notified that their luggage was ready to be picked up.

Paul was eager to get his things and drop off several rolls of film to be developed and printed then go to his apartment where he wanted to start working on the final installments of his report of the trip. Paul's luggage was nowhere to be found.

He was more than a little upset. Everyone else's luggage arrived intact but there was no sign of his. He wanted to go back out to the ship and conduct a search but was advised that it would be out of the question to do so. He was told that he would have to come back the following day and that his luggage would probably be waiting for him then.

Not willing to accept this, Paul was relieved to see a familiar face and he approached Lillian Kurihara's desk and told her of his plight and of his lost luggage. She showed what Paul thought was genuine concern and politely referred the problem to her supervisor, Mr. Morio Saigusa. Saigusa-san had been the manager of the NYK offices in San Francisco when Lillian had worked there. Like Lillian, his English was very good. He seemed to be fond of the United States and of Americans. Saigusa-san needed to have an address and a telephone number where he could contact Paul just as soon as his luggage was found.

Paul silently breathed a sigh of relief as he scribbled his apartment's address and telephone number on the back of his phony business card. He was grateful for the major's foresight in having Sam Griffith find him the apartment and build a suitable cover for him. He continued to realize just how much he still had to learn about the intelligence business.

Saigusa-san smiled and presented one of his cards to Paul. Saigusa was mortified that Paul's effects had been misplaced on the ship and told Paul that he would take personal charge of the case. Incidents like this were very rare, but when they did occur, they were an embarrassment to the NYK Shipping Company. He would recover Paul's things and have them delivered to his apartment as soon as possible.

Saigusa-san noted that it was nearly lunchtime and told Paul that he must make a couple of brief calls concerning the lost luggage. They should take less than five minutes. He told Lillian Kurihara to please make Mr. Pooley comfortable until he returned at which time he wished Paul to be his guest for lunch. It was the least the company could do for the inconvenience.

At first, Paul declined the invitation to lunch but realized that if he persisted in refusing it may become an embarrassment to Saigusa. Paul accepted Saigusa's kind invitation. He was pleasantly surprised that Saigusa's invitation included an English-speaking member of his staff, Lillian.

Paul realized that inviting a foreign stranger to lunch and including a female employee may have seemed normal in western society, but it was highly unusual for a Japanese businessman.

They had a brief but pleasant lunch at a nearby Cantonese restaurant where Paul relayed some of his observations about Japan, the Nagoya Pan-Pacific Peace Exposition and the things he'd seen while there. Both Saigusa-san and Lillian spoke fondly of their years in San Francisco.

Returning to the NYK office Saigusa-san was informed of the status of Mr. Pooley's effects. Turning to Paul with a smile, he said, "Mr. Pooley, I am delighted to inform you that when you get home, you will find all your things are waiting there for you. Then, in typical Japanese fashion he inhaled audibly through his teeth, bowed from the waist and said, "So Sorry."

Paul hailed a taxi and went home where he carefully inspected all of his belongings. It could not be just a coincidence that only his luggage had been lost or misplaced. Paul's belief in the absolute honesty of the Japanese was commencing to wear thin. He noticed that his belongings had been gone through and carefully repacked. The perpetrators could not have known the measures Paul had taken to insure that he would know if anyone had gone through his things. The lost luggage and its recovery would play a significant role in Paul's after-action report.

Embezzlement

The Fleet Intelligence Officer, Charles Morgan was having a cup of coffee and looking at photographic prints with Major Sullivan when Paul Pooley was ushered into his office. The two special agents who had arrested Jameson were sitting quietly side by side on a sofa along the west wall. They

both acknowledged Paul with a smile and a nod. Mr. Morgan looked up and exclaimed, "Oh, Pooley. Thanks for coming. I've been looking forward to asking you how your trip to Japan went. Nice piece of work you did over there, very professional." Paul thought to himself about what Morgan had said, "Thanks for coming." And wondered if he'd had any choice in the matter, then he looked at Morgan and stated, "Thank you Mr. Morgan, glad I could be of help." The major looked at Pooley and said, "Paul, your friend George Jameson has been wanted by US Naval authorities for years. He was wanted for desertion and embezzlement. The embezzlement case was quite significant. Special Agents Smith and Yablonski here," the major nodded to the two agents on the sofa, "got a confession out of the big blabbermouth within ten minutes of taking him into custody. He was singing like a canary before they even got him to the brig."

A concerned Paul Pooley asked, "What about his wife Mary Lou, Mr. Morgan, she's really sick, what's going to become of her?" Morgan stretched forth his open hands in a gesture as he answered, "I haven't the vaguest idea what's going to happen to her Pooley, but I can tell you that at the moment, she is being looked after in the best hospital in Shanghai and will be detoxified before they release her to her companion Miss Fry to take passage back to the States." Paul just shook his head, as he thought to himself; Madeline Fry is always going to be a winner no matter how the game is played.

The Luncheon

Paul had invited Morio Saigusa and Lillian Kurihara to lunch as his guests. He felt that making a few contacts among the Shanghai Japanese community could be helpful to him and he thought that it was time he reciprocated for the lunch Saigusa had hosted on the day he returned from Japan. He had spoken to Detective Sergeant Cahill since he was purported to be an expert on restaurants and asked him to recommend a restaurant that would be suitable for the occasion. On the Wednesday they had agreed upon, Paul arrived promptly at the NYK office at number 61, The Bund. He had come in a taxi, which was a bit pretentious but seemed appropriate for the occasion.

Part III

Paul entered the office and was met by a smiling and he thought slightly embarrassed Lillian Kurihara who explained that Saigusa-sa*n* had been summoned to 25A Huang-pu Road on short notice and deeply regretted that he would not be able to go to lunch with Paul. Saigusa, as far as Paul knew, worked for the NYK Shipping Company, not for the Japanese government. The address 25A Huang-pu Road was the Japanese Consulate. Normally if an embassy or consulate wanted to see one of their citizens they would notify him well in advance, not on such short notice. Unless he was in trouble of some kind or perhaps he was working for the Japanese government.

Paul looked at Lillian and said he hoped she could be spared from her duties at the shipping company for an hour as he had reserved a table in a nearby restaurant, had a taxi waiting outside and did not wish to dine alone. When she agreed to accompany him, he was pleased.

They made small talk while dining and Paul asked Lillian why she had left San Francisco and come to Shanghai. She explained that she had loved San Francisco and had made many friends there but her brother Iwao had been transferred from the Japanese consulate in San Francisco to the Embassy in Nanking, China. When he left the United States, she went back to Japan to care for her ailing father. Following her father's death she was alone in Japan. Iwao had received a promotion and was moved From Nanking to the Japanese Consulate in Shanghai. He invited her to join him and be the mistress of his household and she agreed so here she was.

Lillian told Paul that she had one servant to help her, her amah. Her amah's name was Yuang, Siao-sung. Lillian was very impressed with Yuang and told Paul that she played an important role in her life and was not only a servant but also at times, she thought of Yuang almost as a friend. Paul confided to Lillian that he had similar feelings about Shunsan-Wu, a rickshaw puller who worked for him. Paul and Lillian found that they had a mutual interest in music and agreed to meet on the following Sunday afternoon for a concert in Jessfield Park. Paul was pleased that he had this opportunity to get to know Lillian and was glad Saigusa-san had been unable to join them.

China

The Green Gang

Paul could hear commands drifting up through the screened windows. The troops outside had just secured from Morning Colors and were marching off. It seemed like it was going to be a routine morning in the R-2 office. Captain Hogaboom and a new lieutenant by the name of Krulak entered the office; having just turned their troops over to their NCO's following the morning colors formation. They sat down at their assigned desks and started right to work. Lieutenant Krulak was new to the regiment and Captain Hogaboom seemed to have taken him under his wing. The lieutenant shared the captain's interest in horses and was another workaholic. Paul thought to himself, the lieutenant couldn't have been better assigned; just about everyone in the R-2 Office was a workaholic. Paul was about to open the safe to retrieve the project he'd been working on the previous day when Captain Donaldson came in. Paul was always pleased when the captain was in town. They worked out together at the SMP Armory whenever time permitted.

Captain Donaldson was not as convinced as Paul that war between the United States and Japan was inevitable. His belief was that the State Department might be right. If Japan got what it wanted, through diplomatic negotiations, there would be no need for it to fight the United States. Donaldson was more concerned about what Japan would do if the communist threat continued to grow. If the Chinese Nationalists and communists were to continue fighting each other the communists with the help of the Soviet Union, would present a serious threat to the Chiang government. While the Chinese factions were busily engaged in destroying each other, the Japanese, with their Kwangtung Army comprised of several hundred thousand trained and disciplined soldiers, already in China, could be the ultimate victors without having to fire a shot or to commit their troops to a major war. They could simply occupy the areas they wanted. Lieutenant Krulak addressing Captain Donaldson stated, "Captain, you'd better give it some serious thought before you express your opinions around Colonel Price. He's pretty convinced that we are going to fight the Japanese and soon. I hate to say it but I think he's right. It's becoming more obvious every day." Having done his

best to warn the captain the lieutenant went back to work on the papers confronting him. Captain Donaldson had been monitoring Shanghai's notorious Green Gang for some time and had inherited, then vastly expanded, a sizeable dossier on their history, organization, activities and connections to agencies representing other governments and crime syndicates. The Green Gang was sometimes known as Ch'ing Pang or The Green Dragon Society.

Wang Ching Wei who controlled the Green Gang was a former War Lord that lived in a castle-like mansion nearly half a block square on Yuyuen Road that was entirely surrounded by a thick wall. The massive iron entrance gate was flanked by two large, fourteen-foot high sentry boxes. Shanghai in the thirties was known to be a hotbed of intrigue and corruption and Wang Ching Wei was the cancer from whence the tentacles came that ensnared the opium trade, gambling, prostitution, organized crime, political assassinations and all manner of evil and corruption. The Green Gang was not simply a criminal gang in the normal sense; it had grown and prospered to the extent that it possessed a small army. With the aid of the Japanese, the Green Gang was well supplied with military arms and munitions and had organized its uniformed military elements into companies and battalions.

Wang Ching Wei's officers were easily bought but intelligence garnered from them was not always reliable although on some occasions it was startlingly accurate. Paul wondered if there were not other factors involved. "Could the *Kuomintang* be using the same informants as the U.S.? And, could someone be feeding them misinformation interspersed with solid intelligence on occasion? How do the Japanese control Wang Ching Wei and how great a roll do double agents play in the scenario? What is the communist connection?" The captain answered, "Well Gunny, you first have to understand the Green Gang and few people really do.

"Misinformation is part of their stock-in-trade but that doesn't mean they don't come up with some rock solid intelligence on occasion. It is an unusual organization; going back over a hundred years, Chiang Kai Shek himself was once a member and his chief intelligence and law enforcement advisor, Colonel Dai Li is said to still exercise a great deal of influence over

many of their leaders. One faction pays them yet some of their officers remain loyal to other factions, the old ones that they used to work for. They all want to be paid, of course, so they do their jobs but there are some who would not be adverse to slitting a few throats or passing secret information, especially if it meant picking up a few *yuan*. They were closely affiliated with the *Kuomintang* for many years and now, as you know, they are on the Japanese payroll. It makes you wonder where their loyalties really lie."

Among the areas patrolled by Wang Ching Wei's band of armed henchmen was Ferry Road. The gate to the B Company compound faced Ferry Road. Captain Donaldson had frequently cautioned, "Any private can provoke an incident that might lead to war. Men, you must be constantly on your guard." Paul Pooley was surprised, not only by the magnitude of the Green Gang but at the extent of Captain Donaldson's knowledge of it.

Donaldson excused himself saying that he had to complete his after action report so he could leave early to get ready for a formal affair at the French Club that evening. Paul soon learned that Captain Hogaboom and Lieutenant Krulak would be attending the same affair. He was thankful that he was an enlisted Marine and not subject to the grueling social life the commissioned officers were constantly subjected to. He had once expressed his sentiments about the officers' many social obligations to the major stating that he couldn't understand how they managed to keep up with all of their duties and responsibilities and still be out nearly every evening and every weekend. The major simply responded with, "There are twenty-four hours in every day Gunny." Then he added facetiously; "If that's not enough time they can work nights."

It was Saturday and still early. Paul wanted to rush through his routine projects so he could break away this afternoon for a while. He was going to check things at the Victoria Printing and Engraving, talk to Ah-sam, read his mail and return to the R-2 office. He had a couple of unfinished projects in the safe that he needed to spend some time working on before submitting them to the major. More than anything else, he was looking forward to completing all the pending projects so he could be off on Sunday to go to the park where he looked forward to spending some time with Lillian.

Part III

The Amah

As previously planned, Paul met Lillian Kurihara in Jessfield Park on Sunday afternoon. As they casually conversed Lillian mentioned that she had attended a splendid formal affair at the French Club the previous evening. He smiled and said he hoped she had a good time. He couldn't possibly let her know what he was really thinking. Captains Donaldson and Hogaboom and Lieutenant Krulak were all at the same party. What was Lillian doing there? Then he quickly realized that Iwao was stationed at the Japanese Consulate and like Lieutenant Commander Ari Nishiyama he was probably required to attend a number of social events. Since Iwao was not married, Lillian, his sister, and the mistress of his household would be expected to accompany him. She probably accompanied Iwao to many such events. Paul wondered if his officers had much contact with Iwao and Lillian at these social affairs. He knew they considered Nishiyama as a source of low-grade intelligence when he was sufficiently lubricated. What about Iwao? If our officers extracted tid-bits of intelligence at these functions the Japanese must be doing the same. Could it be possible that Lillian was involved in such activities? Her fluency in English would certainly be an asset.

Bubbling Well Road and the Great Western Road Extension flank Jessfield Park. It was a beautifully maintained park and was similar to what one would expect to find in a city in the United States. The park reminded Lillian of Golden Gate Park in San Francisco. There was even a little Chinese tea concession in an ancient garden setting that in some ways resembled the famous Japanese Tea Garden of Golden Gate Park. Beyond Jessfield Park were the Shanghai Golf Course and the airport.

Across from the park on the Great Western Road Extension was Joe Farron's nightclub, dance hall and gambling casino. Considered too expensive for the Marines, limousines with liveried drivers were often seen discharging or picking up passengers at Joe Farron's. Paul was determined to go there someday if for no other reason than to satisfy his curiosity.

Farron's was situated just outside the jurisdiction of the International Settlement and the Shanghai Municipal Police. Considerable revenue was

generated from the gambling tables. Farren, an Austrian/Greek/Jew was paying protection money to the Green Gang of Wang Ching Wei and was in close contact with the head of the Japanese *kempeitai* in Shanghai who entertained his friends there frequently.

Lillian and Paul enjoyed being together and made their visits to Jessfield Park and the band concerts a regular Sunday routine.

On one of their Sundays in the park they were discussing the Chinese people and the topic eventually turned to Lillian's amah, Yuang, Siao-sung whom she had previously mentioned to Paul. Lillian explained, "Yuang was born into a very poor family in the ancient capital city of Nanking. When she was a young girl her father Yuang, Chen-Hua could not support her but he was very fond of her and did not have the heart to sell her as so many poor Chinese families were forced to do with their daughters. He instead hired a broker to find her employment. Yuang, Chen Hua had no money of his own but he agreed to pay the broker a fee based on a hefty percentage of Siao-sung's earnings. The broker agreed and for the first few years placed her in temporary positions to observe her and note her progress. She had a sharper wit than most of his other clients and learned very quickly. Yuang, Siao-sung was a diligent worker."

Lillian went on to explain to Paul that, "Chinese social strata are quite complex, with almost infinite gradations and levels of influence. Yuang, Siao-sung was close to the bottom level and thus caused much consternation for the broker. He was finally able to obtain employment for her as a char-girl on the custodial force at the Japanese embassy. A position that would normally be considered above her social level but she was a very good worker and it was financially beneficial to the broker to place her in a foreign embassy."

Yuang showed a talent for languages and she was soon speaking passable pidgin Japanese. By the time she had worked for ten years at the embassy, her language became good enough so that she was able to carry on limited conversations in rudimentary Japanese.

"She was offered a new position, one of considerably more trust and responsibility when my brother Iwao was newly arrived. He offered her a job

as cook and housekeeper in his quarters. She considered this to be another important elevation of her status in life far above what one of her level in Chinese society should normally expect. The crafty Yuang, Siao-sung arranged with my brother, her new master, that when she left the embassy, her wages no longer would be shared with the broker. During her year of service to him Yuang proved to be invaluable. She managed his household with care, skill and enthusiasm.

"Following a busy but pleasant year Iwao informed Yuang, Siao-sung that he would no longer need her services. He was leaving Nanking as he had been assigned to the big Japanese consulate in Shanghai. She was crushed to learn that he was leaving and her employment was to end. Sensing her disappointment Iwao told her that I would be joining him in Shanghai and he may need someone to serve me as an *amah*. This would be a position of considerable trust and responsibility.

"Yuang was apprehensive about working in a strange city; she had heard of Shanghai but had never been there. It was nearly 200 miles from Nanking. She was also greatly concerned about working for a Japanese lady whom she had never before seen but agreed to try very hard as it would save her the disgrace of going back to a menial custodial job which would entail considerable loss of face. She was cautiously optimistic as she accepted my brother's offer."

With their daughter working for the family of an important foreign consular official in Shanghai, Yuang Siao-sung's parents gained much face in their neighborhood and considered themselves, as well as their daughter, to be very fortunate.

"When I arrived in Shanghai I found that Yuang anticipated my every need. There was an immediate bonding between us. Shortly after arriving from Japan I confided to my brother that he could not have found me a better *amah* had he scoured the whole of China."

Riot Drill

Paul noticed in the R-2 Office checkout log that Captain Wally Greene had been checking out each morning to visit the SMP headquarters. He was there himself nearly every day to use the gym facilities but had no idea what

the captain's interest in the SMP was. Finally, he and the captain were alone in the office one afternoon and Paul's curiosity got the best of him. He had to ask. "Skipper, I notice that you have been going over to the Municipal Police compound pretty often but you always seem to be gone by the time I get there around noon. What's going on in the mornings am I missing something?" Greene answered, "Well, yes Gunny, in a way you are missing something, riot drill." Paul responded, "Riot drill? Is that what all those constables are doing out on the parade deck?" The captain answered, "You bet it is, Commissioner Fairbairn has been working on it for some time now and he's finally perfected it and has been introducing it to his men. We think it's important for us to learn this riot drill and adopt it for our Marines. In fact, I'm going to put it on the training schedule for B Company starting next week. The commissioner has been good enough to share his ideas with us and he's let me observe the program from the first day he started teaching it to his men.

"If your Japanese friends become too aggressive with the Chinese, we'll certainly need to be able to control large crowds. The International Settlement will look like a safe haven to them and they could easily overwhelm us with thousands or even millions of people trying to get in where they would hope to have some protection from the Japs." Paul looked at the captain and asked, "Sir, what makes you think a situation like that would ever occur?" The captain stood up, walked across the room to Paul's desk and looking down at him quietly said, "Several things, including your own report. When you returned from your first trip to Japan you indicated that the whole nation seemed to be on a wartime footing. Our intelligence reports speculate that their troop strength in China gets larger every month and from the way their soldiers conduct themselves up north in Manchukuo, they have little regard for the lives of the Chinese people. Pooley, some of us believe that it's only a matter of time before they try to take over the whole China coast." Paul looked up at the captain as he stated, "Sir, you're probably right but I didn't think you took it all that seriously." The captain replied, "How else could we take it? The Japs are becoming more aggressive every day."

Part III

Li-chun

Yuang, Siao-sung stepped into an open rickshaw and leaning back opened her parasol. She was on an important errand for her mistress. There was an almost regal air about her as she sat upright, her big black parasol shading her from the rays of the noonday sun. She was very much aware of her station in life, which was far above that into which she'd been born. Yuang reveled in her position as a foreign lady's amah and she had a look of dignity and authority about her as the rickshaw coolie pulled her through the streets of old Shanghai. Feng Po, the count of wind, was in a benevolent mood as he made his presence known as a gentle breeze caressing the wind chimes and causing them to emit a delicate tinkling sound. The sky was blue with puffy white clouds and birds nervously pecking at the pavement fluttered out of the way to safety as the rickshaw approached. It was the time of *Li-chun*; the beginning of spring and it was a beautiful sunny day. Yuang had such a regal aura about her that she looked as though she might be a recreation of the late dowager Empress herself.

The Moodmasters

Not all of the Marines in Shanghai spent their off-duty hours at the Privates' Club or the YMCA. There was action and adventure aplenty for the stouthearted warriors in Shanghai. US Marines, although not always recognizable as such, could be found anywhere from the depths of Blood Alley to the ballet, the opera, the racetrack and even the finest hotels and restaurants. Their off-duty interests varied remarkably.

During duty hours it was routine military training, guard duty and spit and polish. Each unit within the 4th Marines had a team for every sport and there was much athletic activity and serious competition. After working hours or when off duty, every Marine followed his own interests. There was plenty of activity for all, whether it was educational, professional, athletic or just plain curiosity about this great city, the fourth largest in the world.

On a mid-summer Wednesday evening Privates Brinker and Cosgrove were eager to "go ashore." It had been a long day in the field and they

looked forward to a couple of "cool ones" at the Privates' Club and later, maybe they would introduce Private Cooper to a favorite singsong house. Their rickshaws were side by side as Brinx and Koz climbed aboard. Koz, leaning forward, looked over at Brinker and asked, "Hey Brinx, look at those guys, I've seen 'em all duded up like that before. What do you suppose they're up to?" Brinker looked in the direction indicated by Cosgrove and said, "Beats me Koz, why don't you just ask them sometime?"

The men Cosgrove was curious about were four Marines casually standing together in front of the Headquarters Company billet. They were all wearing white dinner jackets and black bow ties. Cosgrove exclaimed, "Geeze Brinx, if I didn't know they wuz Marines, I'd think they were all gentlemen of some kind." Brinker answered, "Yeah Koz, maybe they got hired by some movie company to play the parts of gentlemen. They really look sharp dressed up like that."

The four in evening attire looked up to see the Regimental Communications Chief leaving the headquarters building and walking toward them. He was also in black tie. When he got up to where they were standing, he said, "Okay men, I won't delay you any longer, I've been on the phone talking to your nutty saxophone player "Mad Mike." He's composed another comedy monologue that he insisted I listen to over the phone. How did you boys ever get tied up with that oddball anyhow?" Without waiting for an answer, Technical Sergeant Ivan Buster waved his arm, indicating a taxi he had waiting for them. Luckily, it was a large cab with jump seats so all five managed to squeeze in.

Their destination was an unlikely place for four privates and a technical sergeant; it was the Cathay Hotel located on the northeast corner of Nanking Road At #20 the Bund just beside the Garden Bridge. It was believed by many to be the finest hotel in the Far East. The bandsmen were always curious as they passed through the revolving doors into the lobby of pink and gray marble and black pillars and ceilings, then walked past the long mahogany reception desk and passed The Horse & Hounds Bar on the main floor near the Nanking Road entrance. Walking through the lobby they always glanced toward the bar but knew that patronizing such a place was well beyond the means of Marines.

Part III

Boarding the caged elevator they rode up to the 20th floor. Their destination was the Ballroom, 20 floors above Shanghai. It was a beautiful ballroom with a marvelous view of the city and for those who arrived early enough to appreciate it in the afternoon sunlight, a lavish roof garden. Designed and laid out by Sir Victor Sassoon himself, reportedly the richest man in Shanghai.

When they arrived they went to the bandstand and started setting up and tuning their instruments. Buster adjusted the microphone and tested the sound system. They conducted themselves in a professional manner, as this was a routine they were all accustomed to. The "Moodmasters" broadcast over Shanghai's radio station, RMOK 269 on the dial, every Wednesday evening.

Marine Technical Sergeant Ivan Buster, the Regimental Communications Chief suddenly became smooth-talking Ivan the ever popular announcer and the four privates from the regimental band were now transformed into 4/5ths of "The Moodmasters," a popular quintet that entertained Shanghai every Wednesday night with easy listening or "music from the clouds" as Ivan often said; alluding to the fact that they were broadcasting from high above the great city in the rotating rooftop ballroom of the Cathay, Shanghai's finest hotel.

Once they were set up and nearly ready, the 5th member of the quintet burst into the ballroom and hurriedly approached the bandstand. Seemingly out of breath and with a look of great apprehension he grabbed Ivan and asked, "How's my bow tie Buster?" Ivan's response, "Terrible, it looks like hell! You look as though you've never tied one before in your life, here, let me retie it for you." Ivan looked at the panting musician and wondered whether he had been drinking to excess or was ill. Then a glimmer of understanding descended upon him as he remembered that on the previous Wednesday Mad Mike Madigan had shown up to play the piano with his right arm in a sling. Ivan Buster shook his head; he knew that Madigan was an incorrigible comedian. Ivan snarled under his breath, "Get over to that piano so I can introduce you. And, by the way, what made you so late?" The answer, "My rickshaw." Ivan's eyes widened as he asked, "What! You took a rickshaw all this distance, and dressed in a tux? No wonder you look like

something the cat dragged in." The response, "Sure, I was afraid of getting caught in traffic and a good rickshaw puller can always get around it." Ivan responded, "You're nuts you crazy squid." The response; "How did I know the coolie was gonna get a sprained ankle and I'd have to pull the rickshaw?" Ivan winced. He should have known better than to ask Madigan a serious question about anything. He was a consummate joker.

A few minutes before broadcast time, Ivan spoke to the crowd in the ballroom to get them in the right mood and then he introduced the renowned pianist, Michael Madigan. A slightly disheveled and seemingly disoriented Madigan bowed to the audience then sat down at the grand piano. Placing his hands awkwardly on the keys he started to play. The ballroom fell silent as all noted that he had taken complete control of the keyboard at his fingertips. The man, perfectly composed and relaxed, played brilliantly. He started with a couple of classical tunes to warm up. Proving himself to be a true virtuoso he held his audience spellbound. At show time, he left the piano and walked over to the bandstand and picked up his sax.

Once they were on the air, couples got up and commenced dancing. Ivan periodically would interview dancing couples and of course from time to time throughout the evening he would make commercial announcements. Michael now seated with the band and playing the saxophone, would glance at Ivan from time to time anxiously waiting for Ivan's familiar signoff.

"A very good goodnight to you ladies and gentlemen from the stunning Ballroom in the clouds—atop Shanghai's most glamorous hotel—the Cathay. Thanks for listening and come dance in the clouds to the enchanting music of the Moodmasters next Wednesday evening, or if you can't be with us in person, tune in same time, same easy-listening station. RMOK, number 269 on your dial, the English language station that has everything you want to hear. So long folks."

Once off the air, Mad Mike would put down his saxophone and casually walk back over to the piano. His stern expression now replaced by an impish grin. He would stand looking at the audience for a moment then would quickly plop down on the piano stool and start singing and playing some of the best comedy routines Ivan and the Moodmasters had ever heard.

The first time this occurred, the hotel management approached Ivan stating that this was not in their contract and that they hadn't budgeted for the additional entertainment. Once they were assured that there was no additional charge, they were happy to let "Mad Mike Madigan" continue. Mike needed no further pay than to be allowed to entertain, it was what he had been born to do. The smiles, laughter and applause of the public were the greatest reward Mike could receive; he wanted nothing more.

The Fourth Marines' Church

Lillian learned that Paul had been attending church services on Sundays before meeting with her at Jessfield Park. She told him that while living in San Francisco she had attended a Japanese Christian church, with some of her Nisei friends. A surprised Paul exclaimed that he hadn't known that she was a Christian. Lillian explained that she was not a Christian, at least not yet, but she was curious about Christianity and had enjoyed going to the Pine Methodist Church in San Francisco with her Japanese-American friends.

Paul thought it would be interesting for Lillian to join him some Sunday morning for church. In fact, he decided to invite her the very next Sunday since the 4th Marines' Band had a noted soprano, Marie Pavlo, who would be singing with them. Paul considered The 4th Marines' Church to be the most unique Christian church in the world; It had no building of its own so they congregated in the Grand Theater at 216 Bubbling Well Road. The services were open to everyone in Shanghai. Services were broadcast over radio station RMOK commencing at 9:45 on Sunday mornings. Each Sunday more nationalities gathered under the shadow of the American Flag to worship in the 4th Marines Church than in any similar church in the world. Since Lillian had told Paul that she was "not a Christian yet" he felt the sermon to be delivered by the chaplain, Reverend Dr. H.R. Trump on the following Sunday would be most appropriate for her. Dr. Trump's sermon was titled, 'Why I Am Not A Christian'. Paul's identity as a Marine was never disclosed to Lillian during their attendance at the Fourth Marines' Church. Of the 400 plus attendees on Sundays most wore civilian clothes and came from all walks of life in Shanghai; they were by no means, all US Marines.

China

Shina no Yoru

It was nearly sunset on a beautiful Shanghai evening. They had enjoyed a delightful Hungarian dinner impeccably served in the true tradition of old Budapest just as Detective Cahill had described. Neither was ready to go home and both were too full to just sit and talk so they walked along the park on the Bund. An enchanting place with boats and ships from round the globe moored in the Huang-pu River. They walked past the stately old buildings that lined the bund and they remarked on the sampans and junks in the river. The sun left an orange glow over the western sky as it dropped over the horizon to illuminate another part of the vast Asian land mass and the Pacific ocean beyond. The pale moon was full and in the darkening sky was ready to replace the vanishing sun and rule over the China night. Paul spoke softly, "Lillie-chan, look at the sail of the junk passing to the right over there. The sunset makes the sails appear to be almost purple." She looked at him surprised, "How strange that you would say that Paul. There is a new song that has just come out called *Shina No Yoru*, China Night. I do not know all of the words because I've only heard it a few times on the radio but I like it very much. The girl who sings it is called Rikkoran, she has such a beautiful voice. It tells a story about a China lady watching as her lover sails away at twilight on a junk with *murasaki* (purple) sails. Perhaps the composer of the song was here on the bund and saw that same junk that we see drifting down the Huang-pu with it's purple sails."

General Kurihara

It came as a distinct surprise to Paul when he was first invited to the Kurihara's for dinner. Paul considered it somewhat irregular, but a pleasant surprise. Enroute, he stopped at the Chinese florists at 832 Yuyuen Road and purchased a bouquet for the Kurihara's.

Arriving right on time, Paul removed his shoes and stepped through the open door. He was pleased to see that Lillian was wearing a traditional kimono and obi. Previously, he had always seen her in western clothing. Iwao wore a black *yukata* (men's *kimono)* and had one laid out for Paul. Paul

handed Lillian the colorful bouquet of flowers, which she promptly passed to Yuang to be placed in water. He then presented Lillian with a gift-wrapped phonograph record of *Shina No Yoru,* which he knew she would like.

Paul studied the miniature Bonsai tree with interest. He knew the Japanese treasured their Bonsai and since this one occupied the most prominent location in their living room he suspected it might have some special significance to the Kuriharas. Lillian stated proudly that Iwao had cared for the Bonsai tree since their late father's death. The general himself had grown it. "The General?" "Yes Paul, our father was Major General Tatsuhiko Kurihara." Lillian and Iwao may have said more about their late father but were interrupted by Yuang, Siao-sung as she bowed respectfully and announced that dinner was served.

Paul clasped the rim of the delicate porcelain teacup with the thumb and index finger of his right hand, gently supporting the bottom of the cup on the outstretched fingers of his left hand. Briefly glancing at her he lifted the cup to his lips, first savoring the delicate aroma. He sipped the tea, looked fully at her and smiled. Just a hint of a smile graced her lips as she glanced downward lowering her eyelids. Her expression told him that he was one small step closer to acceptance.

Carefully filling his rice bowl with a small wooden serving paddle Lillian placed two scoops of steaming rice into the bowl and passed it to Paul. As he picked up the *ohashi* (chopsticks) placed beside his dish, Paul looked at Lillian then at Iwao and softly said "*Itadaki masu.*" Lillian responded with '*Itadaki nasai.*" They then proceeded to enjoy a delightful dinner that had been skillfully and artfully prepared by the faithful Yuang, Siao-sung.

The sake was excellent, as good as anything Paul's sensei had previously introduced him to, or as good as any he had tried on his trips to Japan. Lillian knelt down to pour the warm sake for Paul and her brother. He watched her hold back the sleeve of her Kimono with her left hand and pour with her right in the traditional Japanese manner and realized that he was participating in something that had not changed in centuries. He was very pleased that Iwao had accepted a foreigner into his home and was al-

lowing him to maintain a friendship with his sister. Paul knew that this was not customarily done in Japanese families.

Iwao proved to have a low tolerance for alcohol. Paul was surprised at how quickly his face had become flushed and how he became more and more genial as he consumed the sake. Paul took it as a compliment that Iwao was able to relax, speak freely and treat him in such a friendly manner. Though, at times, his English became somewhat incoherent and he found it expedient to resort to his native Japanese.

Lillian was looking down and spoke very softly as she told Paul of her late father, Major General Tatsuhiko Kurihara. "He was a very good man Paul. I know you would have liked him and I think he would have liked you. When he was a young officer, he fought alongside the Americans and British against the Chinese rabble (Boxers) at the old arsenal just outside of Tianjin (Tientsin) and later at Beijing (Peking). He made many American and British friends because he spoke English and he was greatly respected by the Japanese because he proved to be a brave warrior. A few years later, during the Russo-Japanese War, he became famous in the Imperial Army.

"It was because he was so respected as a warrior and because he spoke English that he was assigned to be the Military Attaché at the Japanese Embassy in London. While assigned there, he was able to travel to the United States three times. On two of his trips to America, Captain Isoroku Yamamoto was the Naval Attaché in Washington. He and my father were friends and they traveled together visiting the battlefields of the American Civil War. It was during one of these trips that Yamamoto confided to our father that the Americans were a people to be feared if ever their country was in peril.

"Once in 1927 when my father was in America visiting Captain Yamamoto, Vice Admiral Osami Nagano made an official visit to Washington. My father and Captain Yamamoto went with him to the shrine of the unknown soldier in Arlington where the admiral placed a wreath at the tomb in a very special ceremony which was attended by many American dignitaries as well as the senior staff of the Japanese Embassy. My father knew that it was very important for Japan to maintain good relations with the

United States, our most important trading partner in the west. He learned much about the west and had great respect for the Americans. I suppose that is part of what influenced me to want so badly to go to America after my father's death.

"My father loved the Army but it was changing and he sensed big troubles were coming. The generals in China and Manchukuo had assumed too much power and sometimes they did not respect the wishes of the Tokyo government. At first, he was with them but they did much that he disapproved of and he tried to reason with them. They did many things that the Japanese government at home would not have approved of. My father had lived in the west and he knew that if the army in China continued their aggressive policies, they would be alienated from the western nations. He knew that if Japan was to prosper, she must use diplomacy and she must be friendly with the west."

Paul asked, "When they knew how your father felt, what did they say to him? Since he had so much knowledge of western ways and was a respected general, they must have listened to his opinions? It was the crimson-faced Iwao who, placing his sake cup loudly on the table before him, slurred the answer, "*Mokusatsu*!"

Paul understood enough Japanese to know that *mokusatsu* meant the general was ignored. This would have been interpreted by a gentleman, especially a samurai, as a serious insult. Paul wondered what the outcome of this insult had been but was too discreet to bring it up at this time.

He asked, "How could the Emperor have felt about what was going on in China and Manchukuo? He is very learned and knows much about the western world and how other nations might react to such aggression in China."

Lillian answered, "His Imperial Majesty could not have known all that was happening. Perhaps his uncle, Prince Asaka, who was an important general told him only the things he wanted his Imperial Majesty to hear."

Later that evening while riding home in Shunsan Wu's rickshaw, Paul made a mental note to learn more about the late Major General Tatsuhiko Kurihara of the Imperial Army. Perhaps Captain Holcomb at the American Consulate had something about him in his files.

China

Captain Donaldson

Major Sullivan confronted Paul as he entered the office following a brief sojourn up country. "Welcome back Gunny, You here to work on your after action report?" Paul answered, "Yes Sir." Standing up, the major looked at Paul and said,

"As you can imagine, a lot has been going on around here while you were away. I hate to tell you this, but you've got to hear it from someone, Captain Donaldson is dead." A shocked Paul Pooley asked, "What! What the hell happened to him Sir?"

The major responded with, "His body was found floating in Soochow Creek Wednesday. A "bumboat" man fished him out and there's an ongoing investigation but no details have been released as yet. I know how much you thought of him and I'm sorry I don't have more to tell you at this time." Pooley's eyes flashed with anger as he stated, "The Green Gang, it had to be that damned Wang Ching Wei! Those bastards would cut their own mothers' hearts out for a *yuan*! Who would benefit most from his death Major? The Japs, the *Kuomintang* or the Communists?" Sullivan replied, "My best guess would be the *kempeitai* but anyone of them could have done it or maybe "none of the above." Shanghai is a hotbed of intrigue and half the countries in the world have their agents working here. Some are fairly obvious but some are under deep cover and are damned good at what they do. Pooley, we've warned you before, now let Don's death be a lesson to you, stay alert, keep your eyes open and don't trust anyone. You never know when you are going to be in harm's way only that sooner or later you will be. Is that clear?" A saddened, but wiser Paul Pooley responded with, "Yes Sir, it is painfully clear.

Nantao

Siao-sung was pleased with her position in life and she had a deep respect for her mistress. One afternoon she told Lillian that she was happy that it was *Li-hsia* but she did not look forward to the time of *Ta-han*. Winter would then be upon them and she was concerned because a fortuneteller had recently told her that it would be an especially cold and turbulent

winter with much sorrow for the Chinese people. Lillian Kurihara tried to ease her fears saying that *Ta-han* was still months away but Yuan Siao-sung would not be consoled. She put a great deal of faith in the predictions of fortunetellers.

It was a bright Sunday afternoon and was still the time of *Li-hsia*. The heat of Shanghai summers reminded Paul of the time he had spent in Nicaragua but the heat was the only similarity. In all other ways the two were worlds apart. Lillian had mentioned wanting to enter the ancient Chinese city and visit a particular teahouse she had read about. Paul decided this beautiful afternoon was as good a time as any to do it. The ancient city was called by various names, the French referred to it as the, Ville Chinoise, to the British it was the Native City, but to those who lived there it was simply Nantao (Southern Market).

It was in Nantao in 1077, during the Sung Dynasty, that the name Shanghai is believed to have first been used.

Paul and Lillian started from the French end of the Bund and walked down Rue Montauban and entered through the North Gate. Passing through the gate into Nantao reminded Paul of the children's Fairy Tale, Alice in Wonderland. They had stepped through the looking glass into a strange and different world. Entering the old Chinese city they passed the temple of Tsung Woo Day. Paul found it of interest that this temple contained a shrine to the Taoist Trinity; he knew the Buddhists venerated Quan yin, the Goddess of Mercy very much as Christians venerate the Virgin Mary. Always curious about the customs of China, Paul had not previously heard of the Taoist Trinity; he made a mental note to someday look into this.

Nantao proved to be a labyrinth of narrow streets. The oppressive summer heat of Shanghai was not quite so noticeable and Paul quickly realized it must be due to the many distractions and a great amount of shade resulting from the height of the buildings and the narrowness of the streets. The welcome shade prevailed with only smatterings of sunlight occasionally reaching the pavement.

Faded layers of worn paper posters and notices were peeling from ancient walls where they had once been posted. The Chinese characters on

them proclaimed everything from miraculous cures for a variety of illnesses to current events, which, in most cases were no longer current. The buildings had been built tightly side by side and most were three and four stories high. Walls were mostly of an adobe-like material and all had obviously been there a very long time. Many of the narrow doors had hanging beaded curtains for privacy that would allow for some air circulation if hoped for breezes should materialize.

Shortly after passing the Tsung Woo Day temple they found themselves on a long, straight street leading to the center of the ancient city. Wind chimes tinkled a dainty welcome and multiple hanging banners bearing large Chinese characters proclaimed the specialties of each of the many business enterprises.

Shops specializing in ivory, sandalwood and fans lined the ancient; narrow street as well as many specializing in brassware, pewter, silks and porcelains. The street had a blue canopy stretched overhead that gave it the effect of a long bazaar. At the north end of this colorful street was the center of the city and their destination, a place that Lillian had read about but had never before seen, the Woo Sing Ding.

The Woo Sing Ding was the famous Willow Pattern Teahouse. This ancient teahouse is supposed to have inspired the original pattern for the blue and white "Willow Pattern" china plates seen throughout the world. The Woo Sing Ding was built on stone pillars in the center of a pond and is approached by zigzag bridges. Paul wondered at the significance of this unique type of bridge but before he could question it Lillian squeezed his arm and exclaimed, "Oh how exciting! Isn't it wonderful Paulchan?" He naively asked, "Isn't what exciting?" "Everything. Oh just everything, look around the pool." Wherever Paul looked there was something going on. There were artisans and craftsmen using old tools that had undoubtedly been passed down to them from bygone generations. It was a truly colorful glimpse of Chinese life. Right out in the open were doctors practicing acupuncture, dentists extracting teeth, toy vendors, cooks and jugglers carrying on their trades with admiring spectators freely offering advice. The people were poor but went about their business industriously in typical Chinese fashion seemingly oblivious to their poverty.

Part III

Near the pool were several bird merchants with gorgeous collections. "Oh Paulchan, we must go over and see the birds after tea." They enjoyed their tea in this ancient setting but Lillian obviously enjoyed the view even more. Once finished, they crossed one of the zigzag bridges and wandered over to the street of the birds.

A wizened old man sat on his haunches with his back against a building. The dust of China clung to his tattered clothing and the long fingers of his bony hands were misshapen and wrinkled with age. A half-dozen small cages of thin bamboo were piled beside him. They contained nervous, shiny black Mynah birds that seemed eager to be released. He croaked in a high-pitched creaky voice, "Talk to the birds. Talk to the birds." Paul had learned never to be surprised at anything he heard or saw in China so it surprised him little that this wrinkled ancient relic of a man was speaking in English.

"Listen to the birds." The old man shook the thin sticks then threw them to the pavement. Only the old man knew the significance of the sticks. Some were long, some short and a few were somewhere in between. Once he had tossed them, the position of the sticks on the ground revealed some deep secret to the old man. He looked up slowly then, with a toothy grin on his weathered face, stretched forth his hand—palm up. Paul dropped a couple of Chinese coppers into the outstretched hand and watched amused as the old man released the catch on one of the bamboo birdcages.

A mynah bird hopped out of his cage and pecked at the thin sticks on the ground. He finally picked up three of them in his beak and deposited them in front of the old man then turned back, picked up two more and returned to the old man with them. After dropping them, the bird returned to his cage and waited patiently for the old man to secure the latch. The old man's eyes looked first at Paul and then turned to Lillian as he mumbled in a low voice,

"Beware, all does not bode well! It is *Li-hsia* and the days are warm and filled with joy. Light from the sun brightens your days but when the time of *Ta-han* is at hand, they will darken and you must guard against the Dragon of Death who lurks in unlikely places." Lillian Kurihara's face paled and showed deep concern. She remembered her amah telling her that a fortune-

teller had told her that *Ta-han* would bring an especially cold and turbulent winter with much sorrow for the Chinese people. Lillian had not confided to her amah or to Paul that she too put much faith in the predictions of fortunetellers. Lillian Kurihara consoled herself that it would still be a few months before the time of *Ta-han*.

Their fortunes having been told Paul and Lillian continued walking through the maze of crowded narrow streets lined with every kind of shop imaginable. She with a frown and a look of great concern on her face and he with no further thought of the fortuneteller. Paul was not a superstitious person.

They entered the City Temple through the Great East Gate. In the center of the temple there was laughter and much glitter and excitement, which provided a needed distraction for Lillian. The large court was bathed in sunlight and contained a fair devoted mostly to amusement. Lillian was watching the tumbling acrobats as she looked at Paul and said, "This has been a wonderful day. It is almost like going to a circus. Do you like the circus Paul?" He looked at her curiously and answered, "Why sure I do, everyone likes the circus. Where did you ever see a circus?" She smiled as she answered, "I saw "The Greatest Show On Earth" the Ringling Brothers Circus when I lived in San Francisco. That was one of the highlights of my years of living in the states. I loved it."

One could discern the pungent aroma of incense and the spicy garlic smells and the sound of soft wind chimes competing with the reedy music of oriental flutes coming from the open upper windows of a building and wafting through the air and Paul thought of a line from Kipling's Road to Mandalay, "*.... you won't heed nothin' else but them spicy garlic smells and the sunshine and the palm trees and the tinkly temple bells.*"

There were refreshment stalls, incense shops, toy salesmen, acrobats and jugglers and there were magicians performing marvelous disappearing acts and sleight-of-hand tricks.

As they left the temple Paul and Lillian passed through a plaza where they beheld: Food vendors balancing small rice bowls and teapots on baskets hung from poles; the hand weavers bent over looms of silk in open-air

factories; the noodle shop workers stretching pasta by hand; the tinsmiths jangling their tin wares through the streets and a cobbler mending shoes for his waiting customers. The cobbler made Paul smile as he remembered the day he had first met Lillian and had sent her shoe out from the Maison Marcel on Rue des Soeurs to be fixed.

There had been much to see and do for the Marine gunnery sergeant and his lady on a bright Sunday afternoon during their visit to Nantao the ancient Chinese city within the modern city of Shanghai at the time of *Li-hsia*.

Nantao was a place that Paul would long remember. He made a mental note that he must return to this exotic and delightful city from the past again when time permitted. Lillian seemed to be reading his mind as she exclaimed, "Oh Paulchan, promise that we can comeback to Nantao again soon." He was smiling as he replied; "Of course we can Lillichan, just as soon as you like."

The Double Seven of 1937

Paul had enjoyed a pleasant and informative trip to Peking and Tientsin where he had been privileged to observe the 4th of July festivities with three of his old friends at the American Legation. Two of them he had served with in Nicaragua and the third Platoon Sergeant John Rose had been a friend while Paul was stationed in San Diego. They were all assigned to the Marine Legation Guard at Peking. Paul reflected on how fortunate he was to be a Marine. Wherever Marines went, they would always have friends. There would invariably be someone they had served with or who knew someone they had served with. In many respects, it was almost like an extended family.

His trip involved more than just a visit to see old friends. He spent two intense days in Tientsin and three in Peking making contacts and exchanging items of information and personal views with other members of the intelligence community and asking and answering questions on subjects of mutual interest. A US Army G-2 agent in Tientsin, who turned out to be Johnny Rose's cousin, was especially helpful. He had successfully cultivated an informant that had provided some startling information, which was probably

false but had to be investigated and considered. Paul's interest peaked when the agent mentioned the name of Colonel Masunobu, something or other, *kempeitai*. Paul wondered if it could possibly be the infamous Colonel Masunobu Tsuji he had been hearing so much about. The agent claimed that he had received good, though not nearly as important, intelligence information from this same informant in the past.

The Incident at the Marco Polo Bridge occurred shortly before Paul's return to Shanghai. It happened on the 7th of July. The Imperial Army of Japan had been poised and ready to invade the China coast as soon as a suitable excuse could be found. The incident at the bridge afforded the Japanese the excuse they needed.

Incident at the Marco Polo Bridge

Having just returned to Shanghai the previous night, Paul entered the office in response to a phone call he had received minutes before. The Fleet Intelligence Officer, Charles Morgan, was sitting behind Major Boone's desk and looked as though he'd been there for some time. The stub of his cigar was down to hardly more than an inch and the two captains had filled the ashtray with cigarette butts. Paul checked the coffee pot and found it nearly empty but with the burner on high.

The R-2 Office was the only place in the building that was restricted. The occupants had to look after themselves, as there were no Chinese houseboys or junior Marines to look after the officers and agents that frequented this particular office. Paul took the coffee pot into the head, cleaned it and refilled it with fresh water. He made a pot of coffee. Morgan looked up and said, "Thanks Pooley, we are going to need more coffee."

Paul reached across the desk to the overflowing ashtray and retrieved and emptied it. Captain Greene looked up and barked at Pooley, "Dammit Gunny, that's not why we sent for you! Now sit down over here and talk to us." Paul replied, "Aye aye Sir" and sat down. The captain looked tired but very concerned. The others also gave the impression that they had been working a long time and were fatigued. Morgan asked, "Just how much can you tell us about what the hell is going on up there?"

Part III

Paul responded, "Well Sir, I don't know how much you already know. From the looks of things you've all been working on this for quite a while. You probably know a lot more than I do about it already." Morgan responded with, "Let us be the judges of that, Pooley, and just assume that we know nothing. Now, start briefing." Paul asked, "Sir, where's the major?" The answer came swiftly from Captain Greene, "Pooley, the major is in Peking or at least he should be in Peking by this time. We are waiting to hear from him but we'd like to hear from you right now. So will you please start talking?"

Paul looked past the captain and staring directly at Mr. Morgan stated, "Sir, the Lu Kou Bridge is at Wan Ping, about 10 miles southwest of Peking. It is an ancient, elaborately constructed, stone bridge. Westerners know it as the "Marco Polo Bridge." It was named that because Marco Polo described it at length after his travels in China during the *Yuan* dynasty, back in1275 to 1295. Marco Polo wrote something to the effect, "It is a very handsome bridge of stone, perhaps unequalled by any other in the world."

Paul looked at Morgan and related, "Mr. Morgan, there is a small *Kuomintang* outpost beside the bridge manned by a handful of Chinese soldiers from the Republic of China's National Revolutionary Army; the post is known as the Wanping Fortress. The Japanese had been conducting maneuvers in the vicinity with a suspiciously large number of troops and when the Japs found that one of their soldiers, a second class private named Shimura, had failed to return to his post and was missing they accused the Chinese of kidnapping him. Chinese soldiers later found *Nitohei* Kikujiro Shimura in a brothel and returned him to his commander, but by then it was too late. The fighting had already started. The Japanese could not afford to have their "incident" spoiled. The way it all happened was when the Chinese refused passage over the bridge to the Japanese who demanded to be allowed over it and into the fortress to search for their "missing" soldier. The Chinese commander stated that they had no Japanese soldier and again refused to let the Japs enter. A firefight ensued and the bridge changed hands three times during the fierce fighting yesterday. When I left, the bridge and compound were still in the hands of the Chinese. I heard that the Chinese were sending General Chang Tze-chung over from Peking to negotiate with the Japs."

Morgan looked at Paul asking, "Is that it? Is that all you've got?" Paul hesitated then replied, "No Sir, I've also got some opinions and some unverified scuttlebutt if you don't mind listening," Morgan answered, "Hell no, if you've got something to say, go ahead and get it off your chest." Paul looked at the two captains then looked straight at Morgan and said, "I'm sorry, but I firmly believe that this time, the Japs really mean to go to war. They've got all the assets they need and there's really very little to stop them unless the western powers get off their collective butts and start doing something about it. If they do, it will have to be right now, before the arrogant Japanese lose all sense of reasoning as a result of their easy victories.

Paul gulped down a swallow of black coffee and went on, "I've picked up a few tidbits of information on the street and up in Peking and Tientsin but until I can confirm what I've heard, I'd rather not pass it along to you as anything but scuttlebutt. The primary source of the most bizarre part of all this I got second-hand from one of Colonel Stillwell's G-2 agents. His informant is a White Russian whore in Tientsin. She apparently was a real beauty at one time but had her face badly disfigured by an over-zealous Japanese *kempeitai* officer by the name of Masunobu something or other who keeps her around to use as a punching bag. She has been with him for years and is reputed to be fluent in Japanese. Personally, I cannot confirm any of what she told the agent but I'll give it to you for what its worth and you can investigate it confirm it or laugh it off whichever suits you.

Paul took a few steps across the room, stopped, turned around and looked down as though in deep thought. Then, looking up, he said, "This guy reportedly keeps her locked up most of the time but he lets her out in the early mornings to go to the market and buy his groceries. That's when Agent Rutledge from G-2 makes periodic contact with her. He claims she has a justifiably passionate hatred for the Japs. She's eager to sell any information, real or imagined, that she can learn from them so that someday she'll have enough money to escape and get plastic surgery. She wants to restore her former beauty and rejoin the human race if her surgery is successful. This woman claims that the Japs have two or three alternate plans to provoke the Chinese into opening fire on Japanese nationals elsewhere in China if their

little fiasco at the Lu Kou Bridge should fail. They've got to start something else right away that will make the Chinese react. They can't wait because as Rutledge's informant claims; they've got thousands of troops embarked aboard ships right off the China coast. They've either got to put them ashore quickly or take them back to Japan."

Paul continued, "Mister Morgan, I know how unbelievable this "fairy tale" sounds to you but if I didn't tell you about it I wouldn't be doing my job. "

A concerned Morgan looked at Paul and flatly stated, "Pooley, it may not be the "fairy tale" you think it is. We have every reason to believe that the Japs are currently landing troops along the china coast or will be in the immediate future and by that I mean in a matter of hours. Banks Holcomb's people at the "On the Roof Gang" have reported considerable radio traffic between several Japanese naval vessels off the China coast. They don't know exactly what is going on yet but it is something big they are certain of that. We don't know their ultimate objectives but it's pretty obvious that they want to occupy at least a major portion of the China coast.

Paul smiled as he thought to himself, so that's what Captain Holcomb is really doing; he's the officer in charge of the radio intercept gang. Paul had always known that Captain Holcomb had to be more than just a language officer. Morgan asked, 'By the way Pooley, that sadistic bastard up in Peking that you mentioned, could his name possibly be Tsuji? Lieutenant Colonel Masunobu Tsuji?"

Pooley reflected a moment before answering then stated, "Sir, I don't honestly know. Of course, I'm familiar with Colonel Masunobu Tsuji's reputation, even the Japs seem to fear and hate him. In this case though, the facts just don't add up. From all I've read and heard about the infamous Tsuji he doesn't like women. So, I don't see how he would have much need of a concubine. If he does feel the need for one I wouldn't think he would keep her up in Peking since his headquarters is right here in Shanghai. He spends much more of his time down here."

Morgan stated, "Well, wherever he spends his time, you can always count on there being trouble. Look what he did to the cathouses in Shanghai frequented by Japanese soldiers. The sonofabitch burned them down."

Morgan speculated, "You say they sent General Chang Tze-chung to negotiate with the Japanese. They must have done it because he is a politician. I've heard that he is little more than an ambitious fool masquerading as a general. The Japanese will laugh at him. The Chinese would have been wiser to send a real soldier, a hardliner like General Sung Che-yuan. Sung would take a firm stand against the Japs. The Japanese respect force but not much else. General Sung would not have taken any crap from them."

The stale odor of cigar and cigarette smoke hung heavily in the room. Both captains and Charlie Morgan were exhausted from lack of sleep. Paul knew it was time to terminate the meeting and wished Morgan would do so; but he had been anxiously awaiting a call from Peking. When the call came through, it confirmed what Pooley had said about the Japanese landings. Thousands of Japs were ashore in China and it looked like they were expecting to stay. The foreign powers would do little more than complain. War clouds continued to gather over Asia as life went on as usual in Shanghai's International Settlement.

War broke out in earnest between the Chinese and Japanese on Saturday the 14th of August 1937. The name of the war was, *Kang Ri Zahn Zheng*, The War of Resistance Against the Japanese. Fighting raged around the concessions, mostly across the river in Pootung. Chinese aircraft, while attempting to destroy the Japanese flagship *Idzumo* that was moored in the Huang Pu River accidentally dropped their bombs on a highly populated area of the International Settlement. After that terrible day in August of 1937, few bombs fell on the central areas of the International Settlement or the French Concession. The 4th Marines manned defensive positions along their sector of the Soochow Creek and waited for the 6th Marines to arrive from the United States to reinforce them.

Paul and Lillian often liked to exchange opinions. He casually asked her when they were discussing the news as they often did what she thought about the incident at the Marco Polo Bridge. She said it was outrageous that the Chinese commander had been so pompous. She went on to explain it as it had been told to her. One of the Japanese soldiers was missing and when his officer sent a body of men to the Chinese outpost to search for him they

were refused entry. The Japanese soldiers dared not return to their officer and report that they had failed to carry out their orders. The Chinese garrison had humiliated them.

Strong words led to physical violence. It became necessary for Japan to land additional troops for the protection of the many Japanese people that were in China. Lillian further reported that, fearing for the lives of their people, Japan had commenced evacuating many of their civilians. Paul neglected to tell Lillian that the Japanese generals had planned the whole incident to use as an excuse for invading the China coast. Lillian's version coincided very closely with that reported in the *Nippon Shimbun* and other Japanese newspapers. No consideration seemed to be given to the fact that the Japanese army just happened to be offshore when the incident occurred and was able to start landing thousands of troops the following day.

Paul knew and was deeply concerned that it had all been pre-arranged. By early August, HIJMS Idzumo had taken on the appearance of a mother duck surrounded by her ducklings. The Japanese naval presence in the Huang-pu now numbered twenty-six warships. On August 13th, sporadic firing began on both sides. Thousands of terrified Chinese had begun fleeing the districts north of the Soochow Creek. The International Settlement became flooded with humanity.

Lillian's explanation of the incident at the Marco Polo Bridge seemed to coincide very closely with what Paul had been reading in the newspapers and was obviously what the Japanese government wanted their own people and the world to believe. There were significant discrepancies between this account and what he knew and had read in the classified intelligence reports. The *Nippon Shimbun* was a daily Japanese newspaper, which major Sullivan had subscribed to and had declared "required reading" as a part of his former protégé's education.

The Brute

Captain Hogaboom's friend, Lieutenant Krulak was a bit different than the other Marine officers. He had been christened "Brute" in his plebe year at the US Naval Academy perhaps because of his size and weight. He was

a mere 5'4" and weighed just 116 pounds. What lieutenant Victor "Brute" Krulak lacked in stature he made up for in enthusiasm and determination. He had only been in Shanghai since April but he was already well known to everyone in the R-2 Office. In addition to his regular duties as a company officer he was assigned as an assistant intelligence officer whose principal duty was to maintain a friendly liaison with the French. He did that and managed to establish liaison with just about everyone else in Shanghai as well. He shared one of the several desks in the R-2 Office with another lieutenant and always seemed to be busily engaged in all manner of activities. Like Captain Greene, Brute was a dynamic workaholic. Where he was concerned, there never seemed to be a dull moment; he always appeared to be juggling several projects at one time. Early on at the urging of his friend and mentor Captain Robert Hogaboom, he acquired a pony, which he named Beauty. The lieutenant became a welcome addition to the 4th Marines Polo Team.

Sitting at his desk doing some rather difficult translations, Paul had not paid much attention to anyone else in the office until he glanced up while taking a sip of coffee and noticed that Captain Hogaboom, who was generally businesslike and took his work seriously, seemed to be having an animated conversation with someone on the telephone; he was beaming with delight. Captain Greene placed a file folder on Paul's desk and commented, "Looks like the cat that ate the canary doesn't he?" Paul answered, "Yes Sir, it is a bit unusual for him." After hanging up the phone, Hogaboom exclaimed, "He did it! Brute did it! He really pulled it off." No one in the office had the vaguest idea what it was that Lieutenant Krulak had done but they would soon learn.

The Second Sino-Japanese War was in full swing. The Imperial Japanese Naval Landing Force, the Rikusentai, had been conducting landing operations along the Yangtze River and thus far they had made several successful amphibious landings against the Chinese.

Lieutenant Commander Ari Nishiyama, Imperial Japanese Navy was an assistant naval attaché who was attached to the Japanese Consulate in Shanghai and often saw Krulak and the other Marine officers at social functions. He was considered a reasonable source of low-level intelligence infor-

mation that was generally gleaned toward the end of an especially successful evening of cocktails. Nishiyama was gregarious by nature and his English was considerably better than his French. Because of his excellent English and his fondness for things American he would often engage Krulak or one of the other junior US Marine officers in conversation at social events. Captain Hogaboom explained,

"It was at a cocktail party at the French Club last week that Brute had gotten word of an impending amphibious landing by the Rikusentai. He asked Nishiyama to try to arrange for him to accompany the landing force as a non-belligerent observer. Meanwhile, Brute got to Colonel Price and convinced him of how important it would be for us to learn how the Japanese conduct their landing operations. He was well aware of the colonel's feelings toward the Japanese so it wasn't too difficult for him to convince the old man that we have a strong need to learn as much as possible about how they operate."

Colonel Price speculated, "It's somewhat irregular to have a mere 2nd lieutenant assigned to observe combat operations between foreign belligerents. Generally it would be a more seasoned and experienced officer" The colonel had a lot of faith in Brute Krulak and after all, it had been his idea. As junior as Krulak is, he wouldn't be as likely to arouse as much suspicion as a more senior and experienced officer. The colonel liked the idea more and more until Brute had to report to him a couple of days later that Ari Nishiyama said he couldn't arrange it after all. His admiral had advised that there weren't any boat spaces left and besides it may be too dangerous to have a foreign observer along.

"It seemed to Brute that the colonel was genuinely disappointed and he felt more convinced than ever that the Japs had something to hide. Brute told the old man that he was going to go through with it anyway but he needed a little assistance from him. He had to have some help in borrowing a gig or a motorboat and a photographer. The colonel looked skeptical so Brute reminded him that he knew that the colonel and Admiral Yarnell were friends and got along well together. Wouldn't he please mention his intentions to the admiral and see if he could spare a small

boat just for this one operation? He really wouldn't need much, just a coxswain to handle the boat and perhaps a photographer. It was to occur at dawn in just two more days and would occur on the Yangtze between Woosung and Liuho.

The admiral had a look of disdain on his face as he addressed the colonel saying, "Charlie, I wouldn't dare condone a screwball scheme like that. I'm responsible for the lives of those men and I'm not going to take any chances by sending them out in the midst of a Japanese task force in a damned gig or a motorboat where their lives wouldn't be worth a plugged nickel." The admiral seemed to be in deep thought as he took a long drag on his cigarette then finally looked up at Colonel Price and said, "I don't have any ships available for such a mission Charlie but I do see the value of learning as much as we can about the way they conduct an amphibious landing. I'll tell you what I can do; tell your "eager beaver" lieutenant that I'll give him a seagoing tug. It's not a very glamorous way to go to war, but it is a Navy ship and she flies a ship's commission pennant. The Japs won't dare fire on it without risking an immediate retaliation from us. In addition to the tug you can have a Navy photographer and I'll send my aide Lieutenant George Phelan along to see that your lieutenant gets all the support he needs."

Colonel Price knew that Admiral Harry Yarnell was not fond of the Japanese in fact it was Admiral Yarnell, a pioneer in carrier tactics, who not only contended that we would inevitably go to war with Japan. He believed the Japs would attack Pearl Harbor in much the same manner as in Fleet Problem 13 back in February 1932. In Fleet Problem 13, Yarnell tried to show that our base at Pearl Harbor was vulnerable to attack from carrier-based aircraft. Apparently the battleship admirals paid little heed to Yarnell's warnings. The admiral still had a serious distrust of the Japanese and was certain the US would soon be at war with them. The colonel stood up looked at the admiral and said, "Thank you Sir, I really appreciate your help." The admiral responded by saying, "Have that lieutenant of yours contact George Phelan to work out the details and be sure I get a full report of this when it's over." Then, standing up with a smile on his face, the admiral

said, "And Charlie, when we get together Thursday night, you're buying the cigars." The beaming colonel replied, "Aye aye Sir!"

It was shortly after dawn when the Japanese landing force went ashore under fire. An American Navy tugboat was in the midst of the Japanese flotilla. The landing party was embarked in landing craft called *Daihatsu*. The boats had large flat bows that opened to disgorge men and vehicles. Lieutenant Victor Krulak was a keen observer and immediately saw the value of the *Daihatsu*. It was an important discovery and Krulak determined that the US should have a similar or better landing craft. Seemingly oblivious to the fire from shore and the fact that Lieutenant Phelan, the admiral's aide was slightly wounded in the shoulder, the Brute went about sketching and photographing as much as he could. From this exciting day forward, the indomitable Lieutenant Krulak was determined and tenacious in his efforts to obtain an effective landing craft for the US. He was also successful.

4th Marines Auxiliary Company, Shanghai Volunteer Corps

Major Boone looked across his desk at Gunnery Sergeant Pooley and asked, "Gunny, you miss being with the troops don't you?" Paul hesitated for a moment wondering what was coming next. He knew he wasn't in trouble of any sort and believed that he had been doing a good job. Was he about to lose his designation as a special agent and be sent to one of the companies as a company gunny? He had no idea what to expect as he answered, "Of course I do Major just as I'm sure you do, after all we're Marines and that's what we signed on to do, but I like my present job too, after all the Marine Corps and Navy spent years preparing me for it."

The major reflected for a moment then asked, "You've spent some time as an instructor haven't you Pooley? You know, basic military subjects like close order drill, the manual of arms, the general orders and marksmanship and the functioning and employment of crew-served weapons. Just the general things most young Marines learn in boot camp?"

Paul wondered if he was about to be asked to assist with the regiment's training program, which was extensive, and, as Paul knew, very

effective. He answered, "Yes Sir, I've had quite a bit of experience teaching general military subjects. First when I was in the 5th Marines in Nicaragua then later at San Diego when I was assigned to the 6th Marines. What makes you ask Sir?"

"Well Gunny, I was just thinking of a way we might increase your value to the regiment and at the same time assist you with building a bit more credibility into your cover as a businessman. It wouldn't hurt you a bit to get to know a few more of the American civilians around Shanghai.

"What I have in mind will help you build credibility but I don't really think we should be discussing it right now, not until I have an opportunity to see what the Fleet Intelligence Officer thinks about it. I'll get back to you in a day or so and let you know what I have in mind." A somewhat confused Paul Pooley answered, "Aye aye Sir, and went on about his business. Wondering, as he did, how much training the troops were getting that would actually help them in a confrontation with the Japanese. He also wondered what the troops were thinking about all the activity between the Chinese and Japanese? It was remarkable that life continued as usual in the International Settlement and the French Concession while the flames of war raged all around them.

Life in Shanghai's International Settlement had a great deal to offer yet he rarely saw Marines on liberty. They seemed to just blend into the great city. He guessed they could be almost anywhere.

Soochow Defense

Privates Brinker and Cosgrove were sitting side by side at the bar in the Shanghai Privates' Club. It was always a treat to be allowed to drink in the club but it only happened for a few days at the beginning of each pay period. Their "chits" were generally used up in two or three days. Staring at his buddy's reflection in the backbar mirror, Private Brinker spoke,

"Ya' know Koz, All that machine gun drill the lieutenant's had us doin' out behind the billet every day may not have been such a waste of time after all." Koz responded by asking, "Oh yeah, what makes you say that Brinx?" Brinker replied, "Well, its about all that's goin' on between the Japs and the

Chinese. You know they're really fightin' now and they've killed a lot of people over in Chapei.

"I heard somethin' back in the company office while I was waitin' to see if the first sergeant was gonna give me my liberty card or not." Cosgrove snapped, "Dammit Brinx, I hate it when you don't just come out and say what you want to say. What the hell did you hear in the company office?" Brinker cast his eyes around the bar to see if anyone was listening and then blurted out, "While the Duty NCO was tryin' to find out if the first sergeant was gonna let me have liberty the door to the company commander's office was open and I heard the captain and lieutenants in there and they were talkin' about a special detail to draw sandbags first thing in the morning and deliver them to our new special posts down by the Soochow Creek. Then I heard the Skipper tell the gunny, "I want a guard roster made up and turned in to the first sergeant in an hour. We'll post it on the bulletin board tonight and most of the men will have seen it by morning. They will be circulating the usual rumors and scuttlebutt but at reveille we'll have a briefing for all hands and let them know just what's really going on."

Brinker had a smug look on his face as he picked up his beer glass and drained it. Cosgrove drained his as well then asked, "How come you waited until now to tell me all this?" "Well when I got out of the office you were already sittin' on your butt in your rickshaw and I wasn't about to carry on a conversation by shoutin' at you between rickshaws going down Bubbling Well Road. That could be a security breach you know."

Koz responded with, "I guess you know what all this means to you and me Pongyo. We're going to be pullin' a lot more guard duty and our social life is gonna' be seriously affected by what the captain intends to do with all those sandbags you heard him talkin' about. This could even be our last liberty for some time." Brinker thought about it for a moment then throwing his chit book up on the bar he shouted, "Boy! Bring us two more." The two immediately began planning the rest of the night's activities as they wondered just how long they could expect to go without liberty.

When they were finally relieved from defense duty on the Soochow Creek and returned to their billets, Privates Brinker and Cosgrove made

a beeline for the First Sergeant's office to respectfully report their presence aboard and draw their liberty cards. Their first objective was a nice quiet little neighborhood bar in Rue Chu Pau-san where there was always bound to be something exciting happening.

The Shanghai Volunteer Corps

Paul was sitting at his desk working on translations and doing the daily clippings for Major Boone when the major spoke up and asked, "Can you spare a few minutes to shoot the breeze about a matter of mutual interest Gunny?" Paul answered, "Sure Major" as he immediately put his work into the desk drawer and locked it.

The major offered Paul a cigarette but he declined, saying, "Thanks Sir, but I've got one right here." Then he added, "What's going on Major? You've really had me curious about what you said the other day. Am I about to be reassigned or what?"

Major Boone answered by asking, a question, "What do you know about the SVC?" Paul replied, "The Shanghai Volunteer Corps? Basically nothing Sir, except that they exist; and each country seems to have their own contingent. I guess they're a sort of quasi-international military outfit of some kind. I know Commissioner Fairbairn has mentioned them a time or two. I suppose they work with the police some of the time and are a paramilitary outfit the rest of the time."

The major explained, " It has been around for quite a while, they were organized back in 1853 during the Taiping Rebellion for the purpose of defending Shanghai against the "Small Swords Society," a radical army that was determined to capture Shanghai and almost did. The Shanghai Volunteer Corps fought alongside the US and British Sailors and Marines and the French and did a commendable job of defending their city. Since then, the SVC has protected the city on many subsequent occasions over the decades

They were mobilized in 1900 during the Boxer Rebellion and again in 1914 for the First World War. Up until 1917, the SVC had a German Company and an Austro-Hungarian Company but these had to be disbanded when China declared war on Germany.

Part III

"In my opinion, its usefulness is questionable. They haven't been called upon to do anything of a serious military nature since they were re-activated by Sterling Fessenden, the Chairman of the Shanghai Municipal Council in 1925. If you want my candid opinion of those guys Gunny, it's this; they are really a good bunch of guys but they have almost become a social club. Most of them are mid-level American employees of the big companies like Shell Oil, the National City Bank, the British-American Tobacco Company or Standard Oil.

"I seriously doubt that they have any intention of risking their lives for the city of Shanghai; they'd rather leave that to the Marines. As I said, it has recently become more of a fraternal or social club. I've talked this over with the Fleet Intelligence Officer, Mr. Morgan and the colonel and they both agree that it could be helpful to us if we could inspire them to have a bit of esprit 'd corps and give them some decent basic military training. God knows, we need all the help we can get right now and we'll continue to need it until reinforcements arrive from the States.

"Major Ralph West over in the R-3 shop has started working with the SVC and here is what he's been authorized to do. He is going to take a part of the American contingent and redesignate it as an infantry company to be known as the Fourth Marines Auxiliary. Then he's going to designate Captain George Cloud over in H Company as the company commander. First Sergeant John McBee will be their "Top" and sergeants Gilb and Beeson will be acting Platoon Leaders. They'll meet in the evenings for training and we'll provide plenty of support from the junior officers of the 1st and 2nd Battalions and a few of our better Staff NCO's. We've got to give them plenty of good leadership from within the regiment so they won't start thinking of appointing their own people as officers or NCO's. It would become too political if they did, since many of these guys work for the same companies and some of them obviously have supervisory positions at work. In order for this organization to succeed, they must all have equal status similar to students in a classroom.

"We want you to become a part of the 4th Marines Auxiliary as a Marine "Reserve" gunnery sergeant. You've been concerned about being seen in uni-

form when you've got the duty; this should resolve the problem. You will be known as a reservist and can just say that you are doing a day of active duty with the regiment whenever you get the duty and have to wear your uniform.

"Since you're a local American businessman and a "reserve" gunny, we can have you assist the 4th Marines Auxiliary as an instructor when you're not out of the city on assignment. If they know you as a bonafide Marine reservist, it won't seem unusual when they see you wearing a Marine uniform. Since these people are all American businessmen, you may be able to cultivate some friendships that could be quite helpful to you."

Paul responded with, "Major, just what kind of a uniform does the Shanghai Volunteer Corps wear anyhow?" Major Boone replied, "Their weapons and commanding officer were previously supplied by the Brits and up until 1914, each of the national contingents wore distinctive parade uniforms copied after those of their respective armies, apparently it was a very colorful outfit. It's interesting to note that they each paid for their own uniforms, except the White Russians. They were in a totally different category from the others. The White Russians are the only element in the SVC that is paid. They're full-time soldiers and are not merely a company; the White Russian element is listed as a regiment." The major continued by saying, "The SVC now has their own distinct uniform and insignia but Major West intends that the members of the 4th Marines Auxiliary Company will purchase Marine Corps uniforms at their own expense, instead of US Marine Corps insignia, they will still wear the insignia of the Shanghai Volunteer Corps."

Paul asked, "Why is all this happening Major?" The major answered, "Because we need all the help we can get. The Japs are getting too ambitious with their takeover of the China coast and their Greater East Asia Co-prosperity Sphere. Pretty soon they're going to decide that we are in their way, and then they may also realize that we've only got a two-battalion regiment and the British have even fewer men than we have. It becomes pretty obvious that we have a great responsibility here and not much chance of successfully fulfilling it if we get into a shooting war.

"CINC Asiatic Fleet has asked for help but the bureaucrats in Washington haven't made a decision yet. There's no telling if, when or how they will

respond to the admiral's request for another regiment. We'd like to see them send the 6th Marines back out from San Diego but the State Department will probably recommend against it. Their opinion still seems to be that all things can be settled through negotiation." Paul Pooley became an instructor in the 4th Marines Auxiliary Company of the Shanghai Volunteer Corps.

The Kit Kat Incident

With the Sino-Japanese War swirling about the boundaries of the International Settlement the 4th Marines had been hard-pressed to carry out their regular assignments of patrolling and guard duty and still man the Soochow Creek Defensive Sector. In the words of Private Brinker and his buddies, it had been, "Day on and stay on" until finally on that happy day in September when Brigadier General John C. Beaumont arrived with the 6th Marines to reform the brigade. Once relieved in their positions by the 6th Marines the men were trucked back to their billets where they were given a Bravo-Zulu for a job well done and told that after they cleaned up and squared their gear away, there would be liberty for those who rated it.

Privates Brinker and Cosgrove were back on the liberty list. They could hardly wait to see the First Sergeant and draw their liberty cards.

Entering the Kit Kat Klub for the first time in weeks Koz exclaimed, "Wow Brinx, Lookit them two white Russian women at the bar will ya? I'm glad we got in here as early as we did. "They gotta be new arrivals from somewhere up north." A startled Brinker exclaimed, "Yeah Koz and mine's really a knockout aint she? Yours isn't so bad either Buddy. Let's go over and buy them a couple of drinks and see what's cookin'."

Small talk at the bar led to a second round of drinks and before long our stalwarts became aware that the place was filling up with the usual Friday night crowd of sailors and merchant seamen and a smattering of soldiers from a score of nations. The "new arrivals from somewhere up north" were attracting the attention of a number of would be Lotharios. Brinx and Koz were soon on their feet doing what they did best and it seemed just like old times.

China

The military police had been rushed to the scene of the riot only to find that the Shanghai Municipal Police had gotten there before them. Paddy wagons were lined up in Rue Chu Pao-san, the street better known by its nickname, "Blood Alley." The main center of attraction seemed to be around the entrance to the Kit Kat Klub. Anxious Gendarmes and Chinese constables were doing their utmost to quell the disturbance inside. There were two American Marines in particular that the police were eager to speak to. Several of the participants and victims had mentioned them but the two were nowhere to be found.

High above the melee in Blood Alley, Privates Cosgrove and Brinker were fascinated as they observed the excitement in the street below. They had a great vantage point from which to observe all the action. Having exited through an upstairs restroom window of the Kit Kat Klub, they had managed to move across two rooftops and were lying down behind some masonry grillwork on the roof of a neutral building where they could finally catch their breaths and casually watch the excitement below.

Fascinated by all the activity Brinker quietly asked his buddy, "Koz, what ever made you throw that whiskey bottle through the backbar mirror?" Cosgrove answered, "Brinx, I really didn't mean to. You know I'd never intentionally do a dumb thing like that. I guess I was just a little confused with so much activity going on at the time. I was only trying to innocently hit that obnoxious Italian sailor in the head. I reached back to throw the bottle but then I got turned around in the scuffle somehow and I thought his reflection in the mirror was actually him."

Brinker stated, "Well old buddy, you sure as hell started a big brawl when you did that. Look at all the cops down there." Cosgrove thought for a moment then reminded Brinx, "Oh it wasn't so big, you seem to be forgettin' what we accomplished in that "plush sewer" that was masqueradin' as a bar when we went down to Tijuana from San Diego while we was stationed aboard that old rust bucket that they called a light cruiser." Brinx responded sorrowfully, "Yeah, and as I remember that was what led to us gettin' off of sea duty too." Cosgrove's immediate response was,

Part III

"Stop yer bitchin' Brinx, we got to Shanghai didn't we?" Private Brinker smiled to himself as he quietly responded, "Yeah Coz, we sure did and it's really been exiting too, except for the times we was in the brig."

The Shanghai Club

It was a Wednesday evening and Paul's third meeting with the 4th Marines Auxiliary had just ended. He was getting to know some of the volunteers and found them a likeable group. Sorensen and Dunn asked Paul if he had his civilian clothes available. He answered affirmatively and was promptly invited to join them for a drink after the training session. They were going down to the Bund to the Shanghai Club. Paul had never been to the Shanghai Club but had often heard it mentioned.

As they were driving down the Bund, Paul noticed the palatial Hong Kong and Shanghai Bank at #12. Ned, nodding toward the bank, asked Paul if he knew why Chinese passersby were burnishing the lion's already glistening paws. Paul thought it odd but admitted that he had no idea why.

Frank spoke up and said, "Legend has it that in ancient times the Great Chinese houses were protected by lions; the symbol of power and prosperity. The Hong Kong and Shanghai Bank is guarded by that huge pair of magnificent bronze lions." The lions were crouching in a position of constant vigilance. Frank continued, "Their paws have been polished by the caresses of millions of Chinese passers-by who believe they derive strength from this contact with the king of beasts." Ned added, "Since there has to be a superstition attached to everything Chinese, the superstition of the lions is that if one rubs their paws it will bring good luck."

Smiling, Bill added, "Word has it that the lions, both males were known to roar whenever a virgin walked by but since Shanghai is not a place known for having many virgins; the lions haven't been heard in quite some time." They all chuckled realizing that there may be more truth than humor in Bill's comment.

Arriving at the imposing stone building, Paul knew from the start it was a bastion of true Victorian male conservatism. They passed through the

heavy wooden doors flanked by Greek pillars and entered the large black and white tiled lobby. There was a caged elevator but his friends weren't interested in going up, instead they turned left and entered the all male long bar. The dark-paneled premises reeked of cigars, leather and fine brandy. Paul had heard about the long bar since first arriving in Shanghai. It was over 110 feet long and was purported to be the longest bar in the world.

Drinks were ordered, cigars lighted and a stimulating and friendly conversation ensued. Paul quickly realized that the 4th Marines Auxiliary was comprised of men whose backgrounds were as divergent as night from day.

The only similarities were that they were all Americans, all upward mobile employees of the more important firms in Shanghai and all seemed to be members of the Shanghai Volunteer Corps because they felt it gave them a certain modicum of security and a feeling that at least they were doing something for the defense of Shanghai. They had seen the carnage and devastation wrought by the heavy fighting between the Chinese and Japanese in Chapei and knew that Shanghai's International Settlement must be protected.

Ned Morris knew nothing about anything military except basic close order drill and the manual of arms, which he had learned as a member of the SVC. He was a valued employee of the Standard Oil Company and had been promoted twice since coming to Shanghai six years before. Ned was dedicated to protecting Standard Oil's assets in Shanghai and thus his own career.

Bill Dunn looked like, and was, a successful American businessman who just happened to have achieved his success in Shanghai. He had a vested interest in keeping the International Settlement free of Japanese control. Bill was convinced the Japs were intent on taking over China and must be stopped. He had been a member of the Army ROTC while in college but declined to accept a commission and went into the corporate world instead. Bill Dunn had no regrets.

Frank Sorensen, a junior executive with the National City Bank said nothing of his background until Paul, who had detected that Frank seemed familiar with everything they were being taught in the Auxiliary, quietly asked him at the bar if he had ever been in the service. The answer did not

surprise Paul. Sorensen had been a first lieutenant in the Marine Corps and had served in Haiti with the Marine brigade in the early 1920's. Paul asked how it felt to be serving as a private in the auxiliary company having been an officer in the Corps. The answer was straightforward. "Pooley, it really doesn't make a damn how I feel. We've all got to assume some responsibility for the defense of Shanghai or the Japs are going to take it away from us. We can't let that happen. We've got a good thing here and we all know it. My real interest is the bank. My job is important to me and I've got to preserve it, even if that means being a part-time private.

Getting off his barstool and standing up, Paul was impressed as he looked around. There was an amazing collection of stuffed animal heads obviously gathered from around the world. Paul wondered if Commissioner Fairbairn's big game hunter friend, Sergeant Eric Sykes, had contributed to the collection. Curious to see the rest of the long bar Paul started walking down its length toward the bay windows at the far end of the huge room when Frank quickly stopped him saying, "No Pooley, that isn't done in here, you've got to stay down here with the Griffins. The far end by the windows is only for Taipans." Bill and Ned went on to instruct Paul that there was a distinct pecking order among the old China hands. One may have to wait years before being welcome at the far end of the bar. He must first attain a high degree of financial success and prominence in Shanghai then be invited.

It was early afternoon and Paul had just returned from his daily "handball" session at the Shanghai Municipal Police armory. Major Boone addressed him asking, "How'd it go last night with the 4th Marines Auxiliary Gunny?" Paul, stepping over toward the major's desk answered, "Pretty good Sir, you should have been there." The major replied, "No thanks, I'll leave that to George Cloud. He seems to think the volunteers are taking their training seriously. He's happy with them so far. What do you think?"

Pooley looked at the major and said, "Sir, I'm with Captain Cloud. Their attitude reminds me of the Minutemen during the American Revolution. They are sure as hell not professionals but they seem willing to fight or do anything we ask of them if it will help protect Shanghai from the Japs. This is their turf

and they mean to guard it. I had a couple of drinks and a cigar with three of them at the Shanghai Club last night and they really impressed me."

The major lifted his eyebrows as he asked, "Do you know what it costs to be a member of the Shanghai Club?" Pooley's answer, "No Sir, but I'm sure it's a lot more than a Marine can afford." The major stated, "Yeah Pooley, It certainly is." He busied himself by returning to the work on his desk as Paul listened to the commands drifting up from outside and assaulting the screened windows.

"On this line action!" or "You, ammo carrier! Get that box up to your gunner then move to the right and take up a firing position! Okay Corporal Rich, roll to the left and get off that gun, your dead now!" then, "Fall out one! Get the hell on that gun Jamieson, your gunner's been shot!" It was the sound of Marines training and the men took it seriously. Paul hoped they would never have to use their combat skills but he knew they would; it was only a matter of time. Everyone he worked with believed war with Japan was inevitable.

Carbide Lamps

Paul was going shopping and told Wu to take him up to Nanking Lu, the Chinese end of Nanking Road, where there were many old Chinese shops and one could find nearly anything. He told Wu to pull over and stop at a busy corner and said he would be a while, as he wanted to look in several of the stores. Pooley knew that normally Wu would follow him and always be close at hand so he told him to wait near a small tea house on the corner. He advised Wu to get a bowl of noodles and be certain there was meat and vegetables in it. Winking, he told Wu he wanted to fatten him up before entering him in a rickshaw race. The smiling Shunsan Wu dutifully answered "Hokay Mastah."

Paul had decided that Shunsan Wu should have a special gift as a reward for his service and loyalty. A pair of carbide lamps was the only thing Paul could think of that would add to Wu's handsome rickshaw and this was the neighborhood in which to find them.

The aroma from a street vendor's cart attracted Wu's attention and stimulated his appetite. The vendor was selling his delicacies right in front

of the place where Pooley had told Wu to wait. He got his noodles with some vegetables and a few thin slivers of meat. When finished, he sat in his rickshaw and rolled a cigarette.

In time, he saw Pooley come out of a shop a few doors away carrying a large package. He quickly stepped out of his rickshaw onto the curb and glanced in both directions. Wu knew he would be needed. He picked up the shafts of his rickshaw and quickly moved to where Pooley was walking.

Directing Wu to take him to his quarters, Paul could hardly wait to arrive there as he intended to present Wu with the lamps before dismissing him for the day. He had thought long and hard about what might please Shunsan Wu and knew it had to be something for his rickshaw. The carbide lamps would be well received.

Shunsan Wu had wanted a pair of carbide lamps for his rickshaw since the first day he had gotten it. The oil lamps that came with it were all right for some rickshaws but not for his. He was overjoyed with his gift but could not understand how a foreigner could possibly know how much the lamps would mean to him but then, he had long ago decided that Pu-lee was no ordinary big nose.

The War Raged On

The Japanese had attacked the North Station and expected to take it in short order but Generalissimo Chiang Kai-shek sent his two best German-trained divisions, the 87th and 88th with orders to defend it which they did with great tenacity.

Generalissimo Chiang Kai-shek launched a counter-attack and ordered Chinese troops to resist what was viewed as a vicious and unwarranted attempt to subjugate China. Two more of his best divisions were called in to help battle the Japanese. The Japanese brought in several more divisions to oppose them. Whole blocks of the city were destroyed by salvos of Japanese naval gunfire. Japanese warships on the Huangpu unleashed salvo after salvo in an attempt to destroy the Chinese defenders.

In November of 1937 the Japanese finally captured the city of Shanghai except for the French Concession and the International Settlement. Thousands of lives were lost and almost a quarter of Shanghai had been de-

stroyed. Japan's growing troop strength in China would number well over 200,000 during the next two months.

The suburban districts of Kiangwan, Hongkew, Chapei and Nantao were engulfed in bloody battles. Incoming refugees flooded the city's population to over 5 million. Many U.S. non-essential personnel and all military dependents were evacuated to safety in Manila.

The commander of Japanese forces in China had assured his Imperial Majesty, Emperor Hirohito that the North Station and Shanghai would be taken in less than one month. Chiang committed his best divisions to counter this effort. They did a commendable job of fighting but ultimately lost through sheer force of numbers. The results were disastrous for these elite divisions of the Chinese army.

The Japanese victory was bittersweet; The Japanese naval forces (*Rikusentai*) entered the North Railway Station area, which had been held by the Chinese for 76 days and which, until the withdrawal of the defenders, had defied aerial and artillery bombardment. The station was thoroughly pockmarked by the shellfire.

The Shanghai *Jinja,* or Shinto Shrine on the Kiangwan Road near the entrance to Hongkew Park, a well-known landmark with its picturesque outlines and gilded roofs was severely damaged by Chinese shells. Rikusentai of the Japanese Naval Landing Party embarked on a major cleaning and restoration operation before fighting on to their next objective.

The victory at the North Station and Chapei, which had taken 76 days, was perceived as a terrible loss of face among the Japanese commanders. In another month, at Nanking, the Chinese would pay dearly for this insult.

On the 2nd of December, Emperor Hirohito promoted General Iwane Matsui and placed him in overall command of the Central China Theater. The Emperor's uncle Lieutenant General Prince Yasuhikoto Asaka assumed responsibility as the new commander-in-chief of the army around Nanking replacing General Matsui who, at the time was feverishly ill with tuberculosis at his field headquarters in Suchow.

For the most part life in Shanghai's International Settlement continued as usual. Foreigners were rarely disturbed by the Japanese troops and the

Part III

4th Marines continued marching down Bubbling Well Road on Saturday mornings. From time to time Japanese officers were seen in and around the International Settlement seeming to enjoy the fruits of their victory. There was a certain arrogance about them that increased as time went by.

The Test

Looking at Paul Wu stated, "The monkey men are very upset with us Mastah, they wished to capture Shanghai in a short time but the war has lasted from August until now. The Generalissimo is still sending very many Chinese soldiers to fight the Japanese but the monkey men have an endless supply of soldiers and they're not just coming from the river. They have been landed somewhere else and they are coming here to put an end to the humiliation inflicted on the Japanese forces at Shanghai by Generalissimo Chiang's army.

Paul decided that this was the time to ask Wu to assist, "I need to learn more about these Japanese troops; how many there are, the landing beaches where they're getting into China and what their ultimate objectives are. No one seems to want to tell me anything about what's going on. You are Chinese, you are their enemy and you are supposed to be my friend, yet even you won't tell me anything. I guess I'll just have to go up the Yangtze to Nanking and go to the liar of the Dragon of Wisdom to get my own answers."

A shocked Shunsan Wu looked at Pooley and stammered, "Mastah Pu Lee, how have you learned this? Very few men know, and no foreigners know, where the Dragon of Wisdom dwells." The scholars have taught that no man comes away from the liar of the Dragon of Wisdom without first being tested.

Pooley looked at Wu seriously as he stated, "I know where the dragon can be found Wu. His dwelling is close to Pootoo Island not far from the shrine of Quan Yin whose birthday is celebrated on the 19th day of the 11th month of the old Chinese calendar. It is on that date that the dragon is most vulnerable and on that date, I will seek him out."

Wu exclaimed, "But Mastah Pu Lee as I have told you, you cannot come away from the dragon's lair without first being tested. On your departure,

he will invite you to go through his beautiful gardens. The garden is laid out so that it gradually becomes a maze. You must pass through the maze. The God of Confusion dwells in the maze. He has many forms; some have seen him as a kindly old Mandarin, stroking his white beard; others have seen him as an innocent maiden gathering herbs. In his natural form Mastah, he is a deadly viper.

"One must be constantly on his guard or the God of Confusion will rob him of his wisdom, part of his memory and all of the knowledge that he has gained from the Dragon of Wisdom. Mastah Pu Lee I Shunsan Wu am but a humble rickshaw puller but I implore you do not go there for the Dragon of Wisdom is jealous. If he shares with you what you wish to know, he will then send you through the maze where the God of Confusion lies in wait to rob you of your treasure. It is not good to tempt the Gods Mastah.

"Please Mastah Pu Lee, tell me what you wish to learn? Perhaps at night I can go to a teahouse and talk with the rickshaw men. They may tell me of a fortuneteller who will be willing to speak to a foreigner. One can learn many things from a good fortune teller Mastah."

Paul fixed his eyes on Shunsan Wu as he stated emphatically, "One can learn much from a good rickshaw man Wu, and I intend to do just that. When the hour is late, go to the little teahouse in the alley beside the theater. I know the rickshaw men frequent that teahouse because I learned it from you. See if Shih Tien-wei is there. If he is, talk with him of the lot of a poor rickshaw man, of the troubles in Shanghai and of his family in Nanking. When his wine glass is empty, fill it.

"Under no circumstances should you ask him about the Japanese until he has drunk well. When finally he speaks of them you may wish to relate what you saw and heard from your rickshaw on the day of the great rain-squall when Yu Shih, the master of rain unleashed his wrath upon the city. When Shih Tien-wei learns that you witnessed his embarrassing mistreatment at the hands of his Japanese master he may lose face and become angry with the Japanese. That is when you must listen carefully to all that he says." Pooley dropped a handful of coppers into the surprised Shunsan Wu's pocket.

Part III

Special Agent Flint

Major Sullivan looked up from the documents he was studying and asked, "Gunny Pooley, are you free tomorrow night?" Paul answered, "I can be Sir, sure, I'm free, what has the Major got in mind?" Sullivan answered, "Well Pooley, I sort of feel responsible for you, so tomorrow night I'd like you to meet someone who may be helpful to you after I'm gone." Paul looked startled as he asked, "After your gone Sir?" The major answered, "Yeah, my orders came in.

"Tomorrow night I'll introduce you to a friend who can sort of fill in for me should you encounter anything unusual that you need help with or would like to discuss privately." Pooley was surprised that the major was being so protective and wondered just what may come up that he couldn't handle himself or by going through normal channels.

The Chez Cannes was a small, intimate restaurant on Rue Consulat in the French Concession that immediately impressed Paul as a place he would like to take Lillian. The booths offered a degree of privacy and the cuisine was superb. The staff was obviously French and all seemed to be related.

The major made the introductions by saying, "Paul Pooley, this is George Flint, Special Agent Flint, George is also a lieutenant in the US Navy but don't hold that against him, he's spent more time actually working as an agent than as a Navy officer." Then, grinning broadly, Sullivan said, "He also happens to be a friend." Paul was more impressed with the statement that Flint was a friend than anything else he'd heard. The major and Mr. Flint each ordered in French. Paul ordered in English; remembering that the major had served in France during the World War and spent two years in Haiti in the nineteen twenties. His French did not appear to be nearly as fluent as his Japanese.

It was an enjoyable evening and Paul found George Flint to be a straightforward, intelligent man with a winning personality. He liked him, but still didn't understand what role Flint was to play in his life. Before going their separate ways, Flint handed Paul his calling card on which he wrote his private phone number. Looking at Paul he said, "Come out to the ship and see

me some time, I'd like to have you aboard for coffee and a chat whenever you'd like. This friendly gesture was greatly appreciated by Paul.

Yuang at the Marketplace

It was very early in the morning when Yuang Siao-sung descended the stairs and opened the back door of the Kurihara's apartment building. She stepped out into the alley considering it a good omen that a cricket was chirping. She had known since she was a small child that a chirping cricket brings good fortune.

Climbing into the waiting rickshaw she placed one wicker basket beside her and held the other on her lap then leaned back and relaxed. If she had walked to the large marketplace near the corner of Boone Road and Woosung Lu she could have saved a few *sen* but she knew the rickshaw would get her to the marketplace faster. Time was important to insure that she would get the best and freshest. To insure this she admonished the rickshaw puller that he should break a sweat if he wanted her as a fare on her return trip from shopping. He knew that Yuang Siao-sung had to be early if she was to get the best and so he increased his gait.

She was proud of the confidence her mistress had placed in her and always endeavored to get the freshest items available. She was a trusted servant and her mistress never questioned how many coppers she spent but often complimented her on finding such fresh and attractive fruits and vegetables.

Yuang, Siao-sung was a quiet woman who was seldom known to raise her voice except at the marketplace; there she drove a hard bargain and was a fierce competitor. Her pride would not permit her to buy anything less than the very best and her style of bargaining assured her of getting a reasonable price. She was known to all the vendors, many of who would keep the best items out of sight until she appeared then they would uncover them and offer them to her so a price could be quickly arrived at and they could get her on her way with a minimum of shouting and haggling. They could then go about their normal business of selling their produce to others.

Part III

The Chinese Lottery

Private Cosgrove had been acting strange lately. He seemed to be in deep thought and was just sitting on the side of his bunk in the billet and watching the houseboys polishing brass and spitshining shoes. He hadn't been himself since last Tuesday's pay call. His buddy Private Brinker sat down beside him and asked, "Hey Pongyo, what the hell's goin' on with you anyhow?" His response, "What do you mean, "What's goin' on with me? Nothin's going on with me; I'm the same as I've always been. Why would you ask a thing like that anyway?"

A concerned Private Brinker answered, "Because you've been acting weird lately, that's why. We had the duty on Tuesday so we couldn't do anything but on Wednesday night when the squad went to the club, you weren't there. Thursday when I was leavin' I asked if you wanted me to hold a rickshaw for you and you said no, you would be along later, but you weren't. Now today is Friday and when little Cooper asked if you was goin' to the club with us you told him no. So that's what I mean by you acting weird You're my drinkin' buddy Koz and you're just not acting like yourself. You haven't even started using your new chit book at the club and normally it would be all used up by this time. What's wrong?" Cosgrove looked at Brinker and said, "Brinx, if I told you what's on my mind you wouldn't understand and you probably wouldn't agree with me anyhow. So what's the use discussing it, we'd just get into an argument?" Brinker snapped back with, "Why don't you try me Pongyo?"

Cosgrove reluctantly responded, "Well Brinx okay, I guess I'd better tell you. Do you remember that civilian I was talkin' to the last time we was in the Majestic Ballroom down on Bubbling Well Road a couple of weeks ago? The guy in the tux with the big diamond rings and flashy studs?" Brinker, shaking his head indicated that he did remember. Cosgrove continued, "Well, he told me some things that really got me to thinkin'. Did you know that the Chinese government has a state lottery? The money they raise goes to building highways and planning airlines. Don't you think those are good causes Brinx?" Brinker answered, "Yeah, sure they are good causes but what's it got to do with us? We don't play the Chinese lottery."

Cosgrove quickly responded, "We've been missing out on something really big old Buddy. The first prize is 500,000 Mex. And the Chinese Ministry of Finance guarantees that all the prizes will be paid. Altogether there are a total of nine prizes that they're givin' away. Do you see what that means to us Brinx? Brinker answered, "Hell no I don't see what it means to us and furthermore, I don't care. Why don't you just put on your green blouse and grab your cover and come along? I'll buy you your first drink at the club."

A concerned Cosgrove answered, "No thanks Brinx, I've got some important thinking to do, maybe I'll see you over there later. Before you shove off though, I want you to know something; there are nine levels of winners going all the way down from 500,000 to 20.00 Mex. The whole thing is run by the Chinese National State Lottery Administration, so you know its gotta be honest.

"I haven't met a Chinaman yet that has enough money to feed his family so they sure as hell don't have anything to spend on lottery tickets; these people are poor as church mice so they won't be any competition for us. Brinx, if we play this lottery, we just can't lose. Don't you see? Hell, after I make a killing in the August lottery, I'm going to request mast with Colonel Price and tell him how the regiment should latch onto this deal. After August's lottery the next one will be on November 2nd. Just in time for all the Marines in the regiment to send home a few hundred bucks just before Christmas before the Chinese government comes to their senses and cancels the whole program."

Cosgrove then blurted out, "The next drawing is gonna be on the 31st of August, that's just two weeks from now. You and me have always been good buddies Brinx, so I don't want you to miss out on a great opportunity like this; I want to share my good fortune with you. Gimme a few bucks to play for you and I'll make you a rich man." Brinker declined this generous offer. During the next few days, the squad, the platoon and to a somewhat lesser extent, the company, were nagged unmercifully to throw in with Private Cosgrove and invest in the Chinese State Lottery. He was having some success with a few of the younger men newly arrived from the States when

suddenly his zealous enthusiasm abruptly ended. The company gunnery sergeant had entered onto the scene. Gunnery Sergeant Palkowski was big and he was powerful; a man who intimidated on sight and was therefore rarely able to actually demonstrate his real physical prowess to the Marines of the company. They respected him and when possible avoided him.

Gunny Palkowski was at his diplomatic best as he reached his huge hand out and grabbed Private Cosgrove by the neck and gently nudged him up against the brick wall outside the company billet then spoke to him softly in his own inimitable way. "Cosgrove, you dumb Pollack! Leave my troops alone. If I hear even the slightest mention of the Chinese lottery again I'll know where it came from and I'll grab you and turn you every way but loose. Then I'll turn you upside down and pound you into the ground like a tent peg. Do you understand me?" A red-faced Private Cosgrove, his eyes bulging out, blurted, "Gunny, I ain't a Pollack!" The gunny seemed to be losing his patience as he advised, "Goddamit Marine, I ought a know a Pollack when I see one! Now, get out of my sight!" Speaking softly in his usual kindly manner the gunny snarled, "If you want to gamble, I'd recommend poker, and then with a greedy gleam in his eyes he added, "I might even be willing to give you a lesson or two some payday evening." Private Cosgrove discreetly stepped into his quarters.

Dancing in the Clouds

Paul and Lillian were meeting for dinner on Wednesday evening. She knew there was a ship arrival Wednesday afternoon so she would be working later than usual. Paul told her that he had a number of things to catch up on at work as well so when she was finished she could stop at his office and they would go right from there. He thought it wise to actually let her see him working at the Victoria Printing and Engraving office to further ensure his cover. Between the sales room and the plant was a modest office with an opaque glass door. When Paul had replaced Oliver Chan, his name was placed where Chan's had been along with the title, Proprietor. Paul encouraged Fang-chu Ah Sam to use the office when he was not in, which was most of the time.

Lillian arrived earlier than expected and Paul was grateful to be in shirtsleeves and sitting at his desk giving the appearance that he really had been working. He promptly got up, put his coat on and escorted Lillian out through the showroom. After bidding the staff good evening. They had a casual American dinner at Jimmy's Place. After dinner it was too early to go home and Lillian had previously told Paul that when she had lived in San Francisco she liked to go dancing. Paul decided to surprise her by taking her to the revolving ballroom atop the Cathay Hotel. He knew this beautiful ballroom would impress her. And he hoped she would be impressed by the music and entertainment. Lillian turned out to be a good dancer and they both enjoyed the music, which Paul knew would be very good.

After Ivan, the announcer signed off radio station RMOK, the band took a break and the sax player strolled over to the grand piano. Paul knew what to expect because he knew Mad Mike Madigan. Mike was a petty officer first class in the US Navy; he played the saxophone in Admiral Harry Yarnall's band and had frequently been a guest at the Regimental Staff NCO Club. He and Paul had gotten to know each other fairly well. Paul wondered what Lillian might think of Mike's humor.

Standing beside the piano, Madigan looked all around cautiously as if to see if anyone was looking, which of course, they all were. Suddenly he plopped down on the piano stool and old-time American rinky-dink music virtually exploded into the ballroom. An unlikely choice for such a dignified place but the guests loved it and so did Lillian. When Mike went into his comedy skits she seemed to understand and laughed merrily.

Mike Madigan either had to take a break or pass out from exhaustion, which was just the way he worked. He always gave his all and the people loved him for it. He took the much-needed break and immediately walked to Paul's table where he sat down reached out and took Paul's drink and downed it. Paul asked, "Mike, aren't you afraid that someone's going to get wise to you and put vinegar or something in their glass?" Mike's immediate reply, "Naw, not a bit, you see I was watching you from the piano, and I saw you take a sip of it yourself, so I knew it was okay." Paul smiled and looking at Lillian he said, " Mike Madigan I'd like you to

meet a very special friend of mine, Lillian Kurihara. Lillian, meet Mike." After a few minutes of friendly, animated conversation, Mike was gone, back to his piano stool where he would lose himself in music and fun and from where he was sure to entertain all comers. Lillian had no more idea that Mike was in the US Navy than she did about Paul's true profession as a Marine or that the musicians in the dance band, except for Mike, were all US Marines.

Death from Natural Causes

During his time in Shanghai, the gregarious Major William Sullivan had made many useful contacts among the diplomatic and foreign military personnel and seemed to know nearly everyone at the US Consulate.

When his time in China was completed he was assigned to the Department of State in Washington, DC, for training and instruction prior to executing his permanent change of station orders to report to the American Embassy in Tokyo, Japan, as an Assistant Naval Attaché a position for which he had long prepared and was eminently qualified. When his time in Washington was completed, he took leave in San Francisco, which was his Port of Embarkation and where he had many friends from a previous assignment with the Department of the Pacific. Sullivan was popular with the Japanese-American community and made it a point to spend much of his time in Japanese restaurants, bars, dojos and playing "go" with the older Japanese men.

During the final days of his time in San Francisco he took a room in the Palace Hotel on Market Street while waiting for his ship's departure. Members of the grateful Japanese community in San Francisco honored the popular Major Sullivan with a banquet on the evening before his ship was to leave for Japan.

On the day of his expected departure Sullivan was found dead in his room at the Palace Hotel. The Police detectives who investigated could only assume that it was a routine case. There was no sign of a struggle. They knew that the deceased was a Marine major and a veteran of the World War,

Haiti and Nicaragua. The police did not know anything else about his background nor could they have known that a packet of personal letters was missing from his effects. The missing letters bore Shanghai postmarks. There was no evidence to implicate the Japanese. After a brief investigation, the case was closed and the death was listed as being from "Natural Causes." Sullivan had seemed to be in the best of health.

When the sad word of Sullivan's death reached Shanghai Paul Pooley was devastated. First Captain Donaldson and now Major Sullivan. Donaldson's death was still under investigation but the major's death was reported as being from natural causes. Paul couldn't see how they could be connected but thought it very strange that they had occurred within just a few months of each other. He thought about Major Boone's words of warning and silently vowed that he must be constantly vigilant and should trust no one.

The Gift

As the spring weather started to improve, the Sunday concerts in Jessfield Park were resumed. Lillian had agreed to accompany Paul to the first concert of the season. As usual, Lillian was dressed in the latest western fashion and was wearing silk hose (stockings). As they were walking down a path together Paul suddenly said to Lillian, "Keep walking, I'll catch up to you in a moment." Then he stopped briefly to pickup a ball beside the path and toss it back to some children. Increasing his pace to catch up with Lillian who was a few yards ahead of him. He noticed her legs and casually said, "Lillichan, forgive me for discussing something so personal with you but, I've never paid attention to your legs before; I just noticed that they are straight, just like western women."

She turned to him with a smile, "Paul, we are friends, you can discuss anything with me that you like. I've told you about my father and his respect for western ways. When I was an infant, we lived in England, remember I told you my father was the military attaché in London. He did not permit my mother to carry us on her back as most Japanese mothers do. He did not want his children to be bow-legged; he wanted our legs to be straight like westerners.

Oh Paul, you should have heard what he had to say about the way Chinese women's feet were bound years ago. He was almost violent in his opposition to that ancient practice. And I agree with him, it was so cruel.

The weeks seemed to fly by and Sundays were never long enough. Paul spent every day and most nights hard at work. He didn't get every Sunday off but was lucky on some Sundays and when he did get off, he and Lillian would be together. On one particular Sunday in May Lillian was carrying a larger than usual purse and it aroused Paul's curiosity. He asked, "Why such a big purse? Did you bring a lunch or something?" Lillian responded with, "Something yes, lunch no. But actually it is still food of a sort. It is food for the mind not for the tummy."

She opened her handbag and withdrew a beautifully wrapped package. "It is a gift for you Paulchan. It is to show you my deep gratitude for our special friendship. We have grown very close and I have shared much with you. Things I do not reveal even to my *amah* or to Iwao I eagerly share with you. Our relationship has taught me to understand the value of true friendship. I had never dreamed I would be so fortunate as to have an American friend as close and as understanding as you." Paul was looking directly at her and he knew in his heart that she meant every word of it.

He felt a pang of guilt as he thought of the information he had gleaned from her. It seemed almost unfair, but it was necessary, after all, he was a Marine and he had a job to do. As he looked at her he was a bit surprised realizing that he felt exactly the same way about her as she did about him. Then, as he looked deeply into her lovely almond eyes he wondered why he had never kissed her.

Deciding he had best change the subject, Paul complimented her on the beautifully wrapped gift. It had been done in classic Japanese style. "I've never received anything so beautifully wrapped. It seems a shame to unwrap it and spoil such beauty." Reaching for the package, Lillian said, "Then I will unwrap it for you and I will place it directly into your hands because it is

an item that is old and it is not beautiful but it has great sentimental value for me and placing it in your hands will mean that the sentiments may pass from me to you.

Lillian unwrapped and presented an old worn volume of *The Complete Works of Rudyard Kipling* to Paul. The book had belonged to her late father. The general had been fond of reading Kipling and thought it helped him to better understand western thinking, especially the British military. "I once told you of my father's fondness for Kipling. He read and understood it. I can read it but I have great difficulty understanding. Perhaps that's because I'm neither British nor a soldier."

Paul reached out and gently took her hand and bowing respectfully, he thanked her for sharing with him something that had belonged to her venerable father. For a few brief moments she permitted him to hold her hand, an act that seemed normal for westerners but was not acceptable conduct for a Japanese lady in a public place. Paul knew that she had developed strong feelings for him and he was glad.

Back in his apartment, Paul removed a thin cigarette case from his inside coat pocket and sat down. He took out a cigarette and tapped one end of it on the case. Lighting the cigarette, he inhaled deeply and opened the cover of the book Lillian had given to him. There was an inscription in Japanese obviously written long ago by Lillian's late father. Below the Japanese inscription, Lillian had written in English, "Shanghai, China May19th 1938. To Paul, with deep affection and respect. Sumiko "Lillian" Kurihara." Paul casually glanced through the book slowly turning pages and reading a line here and there when suddenly his eyes stopped at a passage whose words had a strange effect on him. He silently re-read them.

"At the end of the fight
Lies a tombstone white,
With the name of the late deceased
And the epitaph drear,
A fool lies here who tried to hustle the east."

He briefly wondered at the true meaning of Kipling's verse and then thought of the little tid-bits of information Lillian and Iwao had occasionally mentioned. Could it be possible that she was just setting him up and was not the sweet, naïve person he believed her to be? Did she and Iwao have an agenda of their own? Paul immediately dismissed such thoughts from his mind. He knew they were sincere and he considered his friendship with them, especially Lillian, to be very special.

He showered and turned in for the night. Sleep did not come easily. He kept thinking over and over that if he just knew the right questions to ask the Kurihara's and how to ask them without arousing suspicions he could extract more useful intelligence. This must be the sort of thing Major Sullivan had in mind when he had introduced him to Special Agent George Flint. He would call Flint and make an appointment in the morning.

The Package

It was a typical September afternoon as a nattily dressed American stepped out of the S. J. David Company store. The sign overhead proclaimed, "S. J. David, Ltd. Importers and Exporters of Fine Firearms." A sign in the window indicated that the David Company was the Far East representative of the Remington and Colt Firearms Companies. The wrapped package he carried tucked under his arm, though not a firearm, was a source of great pride to the young man. The tiger heat of July and August was gone and the 70 something degrees of September was not so humid and felt pleasant in comparison. He hailed a cab and was taken to the Bund where he decided to go for a late afternoon stroll through the parkway before finding a bench where he could sit and observe the coming and going of the commerce of many nations.

He got up and walked over to the northeast corner of Nanking Road by #20 the Bund, just across from the Garden Bridge. It was the Cathay Hotel. He had heard that the Cathay was the finest hotel in the Far East and had always been fascinated by it but had only seen it from vehicles while passing by. He had never thought of actually entering it until now. There was an attractive gentlemen's bar on the first floor on the Nanking Road side, which beckoned to him like a magnet. The Horse and Hounds Bar was just about

the finest "watering hole" he had ever seen. He heard one of the gentlemen near him ask for a whisky and soda so he did the same. The Scotch was excellent so he had another.

Listening to the conversations going on around him he decided not to attempt to participate. They were all making business conversation, which was interesting but beyond his comprehension. He knew he was out of his element but was enjoying it immensely. When he asked for his check, the amount was staggering. He paid it without flinching and added a substantial tip. Stepping outside he asked the liveried doorman to hail a cab for him. Tipping the doorman he entered the cab and gave an address on Hart Road near Sinza Lu. He got out of the cab and walked past the Marine sentry on guard then entered a large brick building with his package still tucked securely under his arm.

Conference with Flint

The USS Augusta was riding lazily at her moorings as Paul approached the fleet landing and sought out the officers' motorboat. He was attired in a business suit and wore a snap-brim hat. He looked for all the world like an American businessman and that was just the image he wanted to project. He saw that the motorboat was nearly loaded and would soon be shoving off for the ship so he started to step aboard when the "boathook" exclaimed, "Sir, excuse me Sir, I don't believe I've seen you before. Are you one of Augusta's officers?"

"No sailor I'm a guest of the Asiatic Fleet on my way out to meet with Mr. Flint." With that, Pooley reached into his inside coat pocket and drew out a black leather folder. He flipped it open and reached out so the sailor could see his badge and credentials. The very official looking document bore the logo of the United States Navy and identified the bearer as a Special Agent of the Office of Naval Intelligence, assigned to the Asiatic Fleet. It did not indicate any military rank but bore the signature of Captain William D. Puleston, USN, the Chief of Naval Intelligence. The sailor immediately snapped to attention, saluted and invited Pooley to board the officers' motorboat.

Part III

As the boat skimmed across the river toward the great cruiser Paul smiled and felt very pleased with his lot in life. As an enlisted Marine, he would not normally dare to board the officers' motorboat or to go aboard the flagship via the officers' accommodation ladder. In his present assignment, he enjoyed many privileges not available to most Marines. Mr. Flint had instructed him to come in mufti and to utilize the officers' facilities, which he did with a certain smugness that amused him. He was proud of being a Marine Gunnery Sergeant but it was fun to occasionally masquerade as a civilian gentleman, as long as it was officially sanctioned.

Mr. Flint summoned a steward and had coffee brought to his stateroom, which doubled as an office. Pooley realized that a Navy lieutenant's stateroom aboard the flagship was considerably smaller than his own spacious quarters ashore. Flint was wearing his uniform, which indicated to Paul that Flint, like himself, had certain military duties to perform in addition to what he was doing for ONI. George Flint removed his coat and put it on a hangar then motioned Paul to hand over his coat. As Paul was removing his suit coat, he took note of the four ribbons on Mr. Flint's coat; the first was the Navy Good Conduct Ribbon with a bronze numeral 3 denoting over 12 years enlisted service. The next represented the rainbow colored World War Victory Medal, next was the Haitian Campaign Medal and finally the Yangtze Service Medal. Flint was obviously an experienced Navy man and undoubtedly a good one based on his present assignment and the confidence the late Major Sullivan had placed in him.

George Flint was a good listener. If he had not been, Major Sullivan would certainly not have recommended him so highly. Pooley had to confide in someone and Flint was the only logical person available who would be able to suggest a proper course of action on what to do with his information.

Most of Paul's duties dealt with general military intelligence and translations, which he gleaned from documents and reported through normal channels. He spent a good deal of his time reading Japanese newspaper and magazine articles and clipping them. The information he wished to discuss with Flint was intelligence of a different nature. If he had tried to report this to one of the captains or to the major, they may have laughed at him and they would

surely have questioned his judgment. Extracting intelligence information from individual Japanese was beyond the scope of his responsibilities.

He wanted to be sure Flint understood that the initial contact he had with the Kuriharas had been a purely accidental meeting. His report was speculative to a large extent and it was of a highly sensitive nature.

After first explaining that Iwao Kurihara was an officer in the Imperial Navy and spoke English and a little French and since he had previously been assigned in the United States and then to the Japanese Embassy in Nanking and was now at their Consulate in Shanghai, he could easily be an intelligence specialist of some kind. He had begun to realize that Iwao shared much with his sister and she, not knowing or suspecting what was classified and what was not, innocently mentioned things to him during their discussions. She did not know that Paul was a US Marine or that he was anything more than a Shanghai businessman. He knew that Iwao could be a valuable asset if he could just find a way to get him to reveal what he knows without being aware that he was doing so. Mr. Flint wasn't buying it.

"Remember Paul, if you are ever in a situation where you need to feed the enemy misinformation, you had damn well better have an unblemished record of reliability with them. It is never easy to get an opponent to take the bait when you are trying to set them up. And once you do so, you are not likely to get another shot at them. So, whatever you are trying to do, it had better be important. The same thing goes for Kurihara, if he has any idea of setting you up, he will first provide you with lots of factual tidbits of insignificant, intelligence. He may even employ his sister as a conduit to "innocently" convey this information."

A concerned Pooley replied, "I don't think that's possible Sir. The Kuriharas are just not like that at all." Flint responded by saying, "How about you Paul, would you feed the enemy little tidbits of factual, but classified information in order to plant something you really wanted them to bite on?"

Looking a bit puzzled, Paul answered, "I don't see how I could Sir? If I provided them with any classified reliable intelligence it would make me a damned turncoat wouldn't it?" Flint replied, "It would unless you were required to provide them certain accurate information in the line of duty to build your credibility." Paul responded, "Well Sir, I've been called upon to do a lot of things by ONI and around the regimental intelligence office. It's all been very interesting but I've never had occasion to come into direct contact with the enemy nor do I anticipate doing so anytime soon."

George Flint had a reflective look on his face as he mumbled, "Oh, is that so?" Turning his attention away from Paul, he busied himself loading his pipe with tobacco and then lighting it; wondering as he did so how a trained special agent as intelligent as Paul Pooley could be so naïve?

Paul started at the very beginning. First, was the incident of the runaway horse at the intersection of Avenue Joffre and Rue des Soeurs. In Paul's opinion, it could not have been anything but a perfectly innocent chance meeting. The Kurihara's did not even know that he was an American until they heard him speaking English to the French shopkeeper. He next told of his encounter with Lillian Kurihara at the NYK Steamship Company's passenger office on the Bund. A purely chance meeting. He explained that he was completely convinced the Kurihara's sincerely liked and trusted him based on his invitation to their home and Lillian's subsequent gift to him of one of their late father's treasured books.

Flint wanted to know more of the late General's service and the circumstances surrounding his retirement and death. He informed Paul that he had an associate ashore at the US Consulate that could probably tell them something of the general's background. Paul mentioned that he had planned on asking Lieutenant Bankston Holcomb at the Consulate. Whereupon Flint confessed that Holcomb would have been his source as well.

Flint looked directly at Paul as he stated, "Look Pooley, I promised Bill Sullivan that I'd do whatever I could to help you, and I intend to keep my word. In order for me to do so, I'm going to have to say some things that you are not going to like or agree with, but you are going to hear them anyway. Understood?" Paul returned Flint's look as he stated, "Understood."

Flint continued, "In the first place, your initial meeting with the Kuriharas probably was purely by chance as you suggest. The second meeting

likewise, but let me tell you what a skeptical old intelligence agent thinks.

"When you first met, Lillian told you how to find her again just in case you were interested. She said she worked for the NYK Shipping Company, she also implied that she liked speaking English and enjoyed her years in the United States, that could be construed as a very subtle opening for you to attempt see her again. Paul, in her effort not to seem too eager, she was perhaps a little too subtle, a normal Japanese trait, and subsequently, you did not take the bait.

When you met for the second time, I'm assuming that you had probably forgotten about her and it was really a chance meeting. But consider one important point, you were on her turf. Her casual comment when you bought your ticket, that she hoped you would tell her all about your trip when you returned meant nothing to you, it simply seemed like just a way of being courteous and making casual conversation. But remember, she knew from your round-trip ticket exactly what time and what day you and the Wakasa Maru would be returning to Shanghai and she just happened to make it a point to be working that day and was in a position to offer assistance when you encountered a problem with NYK. I'm not saying that NYK contrived the problem only that it is possible.

"When Morio Saigusa invited you to lunch, supposedly to placate you somewhat for the missing luggage, you accepted. He then did something that should have alerted you to what was going on. He invited a subordinate Japanese female to join the two of you socially. That is not how a Japanese businessman would normally operate especially on the first meeting with a displeased foreign customer.

"You presented them with a golden opportunity when you invited Saigusa and Lillian to lunch in reciprocation for him taking you to lunch. It provided them with the opportunity to get you and Lillian alone together for the first time. Did you really believe he had to drop everything and rush to the Japanese Consulate at the very moment he was supposed to be meeting with you?" Paul had heard enough. He spoke out with, "I disagree completely with your theory Mr. Flint!" Flint answered by saying, "I know you do Paul, remember, before we started I said, I'm going to say some things

that you are not going to like or agree with. I'm simply giving you the opinion of a professional skeptic who doesn't trust the Japs.

"The band concerts in the park seemed so innocent that they were brilliant. Do you see where I'm going with this Paul or should I continue by telling you why it was your luggage that was missing aboard the Wakasa Maru? And incidentally, the luggage caper was strictly a contract job and was done by amateurs. It was most likely employees of the NYK Steamship Company. The *kempeitai* would have been much more professional if they had wanted to go through your luggage and you would probably never have even known about it."

Paul could see that he had not presented a very convincing case to Mr. Flint and hoped that he could terminate this uncomfortable session soon.

Flint looked at Paul and stated, "Look Paul, you don't have to agree with anything I've said so far. Everything I've said here is mere speculation. I just don't want to see you caught up in something you can't handle that's all. You think your friends the Kurihara's are nice people and they probably are. You also probably don't consider them capable of treachery but you overlook the fact that he is an officer in the Imperial Navy, possibly an intelligence specialist and they are members of an old and prestigious family that has been samurai caste for hundreds of years. The Kurihara's love their country as much as you love yours and I'm certain there's nothing they would not do for it."

Paul spoke up, "Mr. Flint, all I wanted to find out from you is how to handle the little tid-bits of intelligence I may pickup from time to time. What should I do with it? And how can I get more out of them?" Flint answered, "Pooley dammit, your job is not to generate the intelligence its simply to translate it, clip it out and occasionally offer an opinion. You're not a super-spy, you're just a Marine who works in the "two" office and does special specific projects for ONI when requested. If I were you, I'd pass that information up the chain of command daily when you turn over your clippings and translations. You might type out whatever you pickup as, "unsubstantiated information learned from confidential informants" and include it at the end of your report. Don't attempt to extract anything further from them; it's not your job. Leave that to the experts.

"If you attempt to get anything from the Kurihara's other than what little Lillian lets slip "accidentally" I promise you'll make them suspicious and they'll never tell you another thing and you'll also almost certainly lose their friendship."

Paul Pooley was sincerely grateful to George Flint for their time spent together. The results were far from what he had hoped for but he did like Flint and respected him for his honest opinions. He was glad to be departing the flagship and going ashore.

Paul was confused and concerned. He knew that any bits of information he learned from Lillian or Iwao could be important when pieced together with other small bits of intelligence. He was reluctant to do as Flint had suggested and add them onto his daily report as he knew the FIO, Mr. Morgan and the regimental intelligence officer, Major Boone, would admonish him for meddling in something that was far beyond his official duties. How was he to deal with the Kuriharas? What techniques could he safely employ in seeking whatever information Iwao might have that would benefit the US? Flint's advise was obviously not what Paul had hoped to hear. He would wait a time with patience and eventually a solution would become clear to him.

Joe Farron's

Paul had been curious about Joe Farron's Night Club for a long time. He'd heard many favorable things about Farron's and even though it was not the sort of place Marines could normally afford to frequent he wanted to satisfy his curiosity and thought he would take Lillian there at least once. It was early December 1937 and Paul decided there would never be a better time than the present.

When they arrived at Joe Farron's they were ushered into the dining room by a dapper *maître'd*, who showed them to their table and seated them. A *sommelier* appeared and presented Paul with the wine list and after a short discussion he stepped back from the table and seemed to vanish into the dimness of the room. The table was small and intimate. Lights were cleverly arranged to bathe each of the white linen-clad tabletops in soft light but left the balance of the room dimly lit. The service by White

Russian waiters was excellent and the food was superb. Dancing was to soft music.

The three floors of gambling rooms above would challenge the best Monte Carlo had to offer. It was very professional with roulette tables, blackjack and all the usual trappings of a high class European casino. Even Monte Carlo did not present a more varied program of gambling. Paul could sense that something unusual was going on. There was more security than a place such as this would normally be expected to have and there was a very strong Japanese presence. Paul guessed that the *Kempeitai* were working overtime on this job.

As Paul and Lillian left the dance floor hand in hand she suddenly let go, stiffened and sucked in her breath audibly in the custom of the Japanese. She quickly stepped behind Paul following him off the dance floor not wishing to walk beside him. For the moment her western ways were forgotten.

She looked stunned. Prince Asaka was present and he was accompanied by one of Japan's most successful business tycoons, Noburo Yoshimura. With the prince and Yoshimura-san was the notorious Colonel Masunobu Tsuji lurking in the background, and standing beside them were General Kenkichi Ueda commander of the Japanese forces in China and his Chief of Staff, General Hideki Tojo. Paul knew that there had just been a major reorganization of the senior Japanese generals in China and they were obviously here to celebrate and to welcome the Emperor's uncle to his new command in China.

Yoshimura-san and Prince Asaka were obviously well acquainted. They were enjoying their conversation and seemed to have had good fortune at the gaming tables upstairs. Yoshimura-san suddenly became disoriented and had difficulty walking. A glance at his face was all that was needed to see that he was seriously ill. Prince Asaka signaled two of his bodyguards to assist the gentleman.

Back at their table Lillian seemed withdrawn, she was obviously uneasy. She was not comfortable in the presence of the Emperor's uncle Prince Asaka or the *Kempeitai* in such large numbers. Paul suggested that it was time to go.

As they left, it was dark outside but not so dark that Paul could not identify two identical black Cadillac limousines. They were parked nearly

in front of Joe Farron's. Walking out of Farron's, Paul noticed men in suits posted every 25 feet or so to the left and right of the canopied entrance. He assumed they too were *Kempeitai.* He listened carefully but heard nothing in Japanese that he thought would be of intelligence interest to the FIO or Major Boone. There was an abundance of security for the Japanese VIP's but no one was saying anything out of the ordinary.

As Paul and Lillian stood under the canopy in front of Joe Farron's waiting for the doorman to hail them a cab, they noticed something highly unusual. The Japanese security people were assisting Yoshimura-san to one of the limos. He was unable to walk without assistance. This was highly irregular for a Japanese gentleman of such stature. Paul felt very uneasy about what was going on around him but couldn't quite put his finger on just what it was.

Yoshimura-san hadn't seemed to him to be excessively intoxicated a few minutes before when they'd seen him inside with the prince. The limo pulled away from the curb with a fury and moved speedily toward Jessfield Road headed back toward the International Settlement.

A cab arrived and the doorman held the door open for Paul and Lillian to enter. Paul gave the driver an address on Rue Cristobal that would put them a few doors away from Lillian's place. The cab pulled cautiously away from the curb; the driver taking heed of the directions given by one of the two Japanese security men who had remained in the street to control traffic.

They had gone hardly more than two blocks when the silence of the night was shattered by automatic gunfire and the squeal of tires then by a loud crashing sound. Paul would read about it in the morning paper and Lillian would learn of it from Iwao. What had started out to be a perfect night was spoiled by the violence and the intrigue that could be so much a part of life in old Shanghai.

The Cause of Death

It was early on a busy Wednesday afternoon and Paul had just placed a stack of newspaper clippings on the major's desk and had included an editorial from the previous day's Evening Post & Mercury by H.G.W. Woodhead. The "Post," an evening paper, was Shanghai's only daily English language newspaper. Woodhead wrote a weekly column titled, "One Man's Comment" covering China and international topics of interest. His humor and knowledge had gained him considerable stature among the foreign journalists in China.

Paul had annotated Woodhead's article to show the major how pronounced the differences were between his translations from the Japanese newspapers about Yoshimura-san's assassination and western views on the same assassination. As he turned to step away from the desk, the major asked.

"Did you read what Woodhead wrote in the Post & Mercury last night? He's beginning to think like you about the Japs." Paul answered, "Yes Sir, I read it. There's a copy of it on your desk with today's clippings. I don't know the man, in fact I've never even met him, but if I did know him, I'd sure suggest that if he's going to keep writing things like that about the Nips he'd better watch his back."

The major looked at Paul and said, "You've really changed your mind about the Japs since you got to Shanghai. When you first reported in, we all thought you were a real Jap-lover." Paul responded with, "That's not it Sir, I was trained in their language and customs and taught all the good things about them. I sincerely liked them and I thought I understood them. Now, I know better. I don't believe any of us really understand them, not even Major Sullivan when he was alive, and he was supposed to be the expert. I'm still not sure he died of "natural causes" as reported. I've got to confess that I've got a gut feeling that somehow, the Japs had something to do with his death. The major responded with, "Well Paul, your judgment is improving and as time goes on you'll come to know that good judgment comes from experience and a lotta that comes from bad judgment. If you know what I mean?" Pooley answered with, "Yes Sir, I get it."

The headlines in the *Nippon Shinbun* had proclaimed, "Prominent industrialist assassinated by Chinese thugs! Driver and bodyguard murdered as well. An unprecedented investigation is underway. Multiple police agencies are clambering to assist in bringing the perpetrators to justice. The French Concession Police are working closely with Japanese police officials

Original ship's bell from the USS Henderson now in its permanent location at Henderson Hall, Arlington, Virginia.

A mixed mounted patrol of Marines and Guardias.

Chevrons of the types worn by:
Staff Sergeant Pooley, Technical Sergeant Sims and
Gunnery Sergeant MacPherson
while saying farewell at the San Diego Staff NCO Club.

View of Shanghai's Bund as it appeared in the mid-1930's.

Various uniforms worn by US Marines in Nicaragua as drawn by the late Marine artist Colonel Donald Dixon.

Thrusting upward through the cloud was the snowcapped tip of Fujiyama, the divine mountain.

Captain Puller and Lieutenant Lee, the C.O. and X.O. of M Company with two of their Guardias armed with Thompson Sub-machine Guns.

Fourth Marines Color Guard flanked by chevrons of a Field Music First Class

"Old Blue", the regimental color of the 4th Marines.

The ancient Kumamoto Castle.

The Suizenji Park.

The Marco Polo Bridge at Lu Kuo

Marine Barracks, Mare Island, California.

The "Hendy Maru", USS Henderson PA-1. Referred to by many old China hands as the "Galloping Ghost of the China Coast".

The Bund in Shanghai.

Marine Corps Base, San Diego home of the recruit depot.

Shanghai Municipal Council Building and SMP Police Headquarters.

PFC Melvin Gunderson, Manager of the Club, poses with his "boys" prior to opening.

The 4th and 6th Marines pass in Brigade Review at the Shanghai Racecourse on December 12th 1937

Private Brinker considered rickshaws to be the most cost-effective means of transportation when on liberty.

Joe E. Brown poses at rickshaw stand with two Marine corporals. The one on the left was practically a boot with only two hashmarks compared to Corporal Nelson's four.

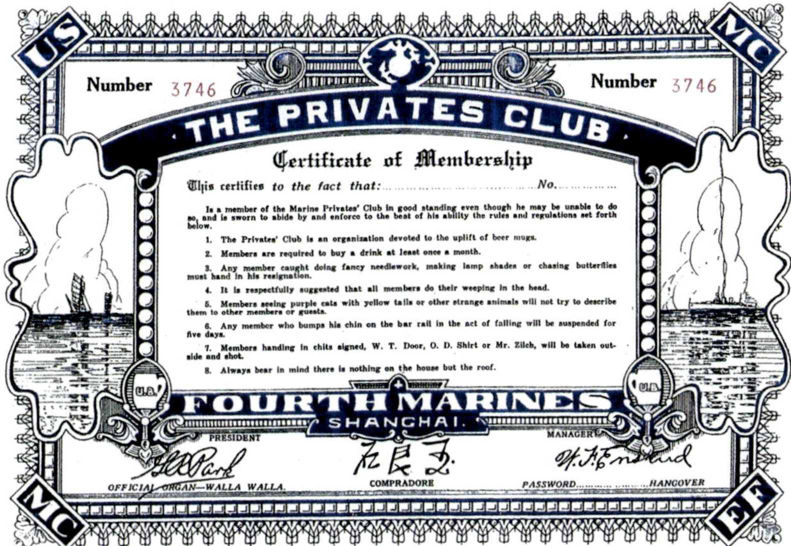

US MC

Number 3746

Number 3746

THE PRIVATES CLUB

Certificate of Membership

This certifies to the fact that:.. No. ....

Is a member of the Marine Privates' Club in good standing even though he may be unable to do so, and is sworn to abide by and enforce to the best of his ability the rules and regulations set forth below.

1. The Privates' Club is an organization devoted to the uplift of beer mugs.

2. Members are required to buy a drink at least once a month.

3. Any member caught doing fancy needlework, making lamp shades or chasing butterflies must hand in his resignation.

4. It is respectfully suggested that all members do their weeping in the head.

5. Members seeing purple cats with yellow tails or other strange animals will not try to describe them to other members or guests.

6. Any member who bumps his chin on the bar rail in the act of falling will be suspended for five days.

7. Members handing in chits signed, W. T. Door, O. D. Shirt or Mr. Zilch, will be taken outside and shot.

8. Always bear in mind there is nothing on the house but the roof.

FOURTH MARINES

SHANGHAI.

PRESIDENT

MANAGER

OFFICIAL ORGAN—WALLA WALLA.

COMPRADORE

PASSWORD........................HANGOVER

MC EF

Privates Brinker and Cosgrove considered it a privilege to be members of this distinguished gentlemen's club in Shanghai

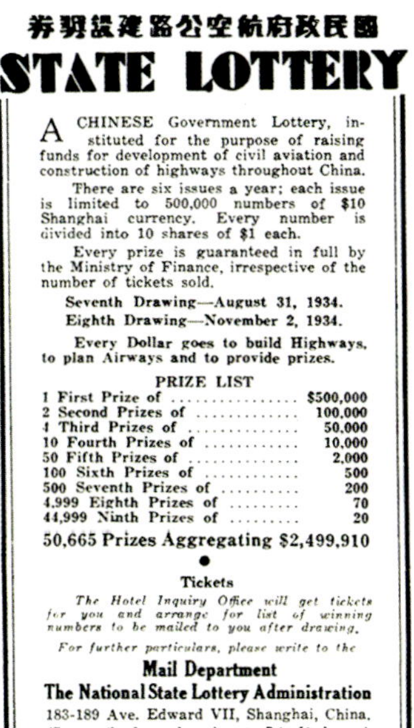

券獎設建路公空航府政民國

STATE LOTTERY

A CHINESE Government Lottery, instituted for the purpose of raising funds for development of civil aviation and construction of highways throughout China.

There are six issues a year; each issue is limited to 500,000 numbers of $10 Shanghai currency. Every number is divided into 10 shares of $1 each.

Every prize is guaranteed in full by the Ministry of Finance, irrespective of the number of tickets sold.

Seventh Drawing—August 31, 1934.
Eighth Drawing—November 2, 1934.

Every Dollar goes to build Highways, to plan Airways and to provide prizes.

PRIZE LIST

1 First Prize of	$500,000
2 Second Prizes of	100,000
4 Third Prizes of	50,000
10 Fourth Prizes of	10,000
50 Fifth Prizes of	2,000
100 Sixth Prizes of	500
500 Seventh Prizes of	200
4,999 Eighth Prizes of	70
44,999 Ninth Prizes of	20

50,665 Prizes Aggregating $2,499,910

•

Tickets

The Hotel Inquiry Office will get tickets for you and arrange for list of winning numbers to be mailed to you after drawing.

For further particulars, please write to the

Mail Department

The National State Lottery Administration

183-189 Ave. Edward VII, Shanghai, China.

(Every mail order purchaser is sent a Prize List by post)

Private Cosgrove was convinced that winning the Chinese lottery was a sure thing.

Captain George Cloud and Staff with members of the 4th Marines Auxiliary Company (the Minute Men).

The Ships Marine Detachment.

ALL THE NEWS ALL THE TIME

Los Angeles Times

IN FOUR PARTS — 40 PAGES

TIMES OFFICE
MAdison 2345

VOL. LX

TUESDAY MORNING, JULY 8, 1941.

DAILY, FIVE CENTS

U.S. MARINES OCCUPY ICELAND

Lieutenant Donovan with his Marines in Iceland.

Sir Winston Churchill troops the line.

TODAY'S WEATHER

The Herald

CITY EDITION

NIPPON PLANES BOMB AND SINK U.S. GUNBOAT PANAY

ALL SET FOR TOMORROW'S P.I. ELECTIONS

JAPANESE STOP U.S. DESTROYER AIDING HOOVER

EVACUEES FROM NANKING ABOARD SHIP WHEN HIT

NEW MERALCO RATES OKAYED

NATIONALISTS ARE EXPECTED TO WIN MANILA

FIND CASHIER SHORT P5,000

MANILA RESIDENT GRANTED DIVORCE

NANKING'S FALL EXPECTED SOON

A war warning that went unheeded.

The China Incident War Medal, July 7, 1937.

Helmet Plate of the Shanghai Volunteer Corps.

Collar Insignia.

Major Harry Nusbaum gives oath to a Samoan recruit. Note emblem and chevrons on sergeant's Lava lava

Second Nicaraguan
Campaign Medal.

Ordwe of Dragon Medal.

Shanghai Municipal Police Helmet Plate (left) and
Long Service Medal of the Shanghai Municipal Police.

Samoan Marines present arms at morning formation.

A general bids farewell to his Marines.

and the Shanghai Municipal Police detectives are assisting and have offered the services of their pathology laboratory and their medical examiner."

Paul Pooley left for the SMP with the intention of discussing the incident with the detectives from the SMP assigned to the case and perhaps pickup a copy of their toxicology report.

He was incredulous as he looked at Commissioner Fairbairn and exclaimed, "No autopsy? Why? How could there possibly not be an autopsy?" Paul expected a logical answer but none was forthcoming. Fairbairn instead, replied with, "It wasn't really necessary Gunn'ry Sergeant, our medical examiner dug three of the bullets out of Yoshimura's cadaver and we've got them recorded and are holding them for evidence. He removed the bullets from the two drivers as well. There really isn't any question about the cause of death. The poor blokes had been riddled by machine gun fire. I am merely telling you that the Japanese authorities picked Yoshimura's body up so it could be shipped back to Japan for proper burial on Japanese soil. Had there been any further questions concerning the cause of death it would have behooved the Japanese to request a more thorough examination, we offered them the facilities of the SMP including the laboratory. As I've told you, they did not."

Pooley looked at Fairbairn and stated flatly, "Commissioner, that sonofabitch was poisoned, I'm certain of it." Fairbairn responded with, Well Gunn'ry Sergeant. Certain or not, our detectives were only assisting on the case. Actually, it did not occur in our jurisdiction. As you know, it occurred outside the Settlement on the Great Western Road Extension. "I'm reasonably sure that they were shot by members of the Green Gang but have no idea what Wang Ching Wei 's motive could have been or who paid for it."

Pride of the Regiment

Saturday morning parades and inspections were very special to Colonel Charles F.B. Price and to his Marines. They were a spectacle to behold marching down Bubbling Well Road and were on display to the citizens of many nations. Everything had to be perfect.

Part III

Private Cosgrove had not been in the best graces of Gunny Palkowski the terrifying company gunnery sergeant lately or of his squad leader Sergeant Briggs or Corporal Nelson. He and his buddy Brinx used to get away with a lot of shenanigans but lately, since Gunnery Sergeant Palkowski had rediscovered him, he seemed to get in trouble all by himself, without any help from Brinx. He hoped to change his image and show them all that he could be a good Marine.

They were in the usual formation with two battalions on line and were at open ranks for inspection. Cosgrove wouldn't dare bat an eye but he knew when the inspecting party was approaching, he had a special feeling for it as all professionals do. Finally he heard them getting closer and sensed from the way the colonel was asking his questions that he was not in a particularly good mood this morning.

Rifles were rippling smartly up to inspection arms as the colonel's party approached. As he came to each individual, he would ask a brief question about military subjects and occasionally snap the rifle out of a man's hands, inspect it, and briskly hand it back. They would then go to order arms. Like all those before him, Koz came to a perfect inspection arms as the colonel faced him. The colonel glanced at him then he looked at his rifle. He stared at Koz and almost as an afterthought snapped the rifle out of his hands and inspected it carefully. Holding the rifle the colonel scrutinized Private Cosgrove from his beautifully spitshined shoes and his perfectly tailored new "China Khaki" uniform to his shiny helmet. The colonel, looking at Captain McClintock finally spoke, "Have you seen this man's rifle Marty?" McClintock, as he stared at Cosgrove's rifle promptly lied with a nod and a smile, "Yes Sir Colonel I have." The colonel looked at Koz and said, "Marine, in all my time in the Corps I've never seen such a beautiful rifle stock or such a squared away Marine. What's your name?" The proud answer came swiftly, "Private Cosgrove Sir, Leonard F. Cosgrove."

The colonel looked at Captain "Merciless Marty" Mc Clintock and said, "Marty, this man should be on a recruiting poster. You must be proud to have him in your company. I wish there were more like him in the regiment.

Corporal Nelson in the next rank heard the colonel's remarks and started to faint. He almost dropped his rifle but caught himself just in time. Captain Mc Clintock's face flushed as he silently anguished, wondering just what the colonel would do if there were others like Cosgrove in the regiment besides enlarging the size of the regimental brig. He hoped the colonel would not question him about this recalcitrant hashmark private that seemed to have suddenly transformed himself into the perfect Marine. The colonel, looking at Cosgrove, said, "Well done Marine!" and passed on down the ranks.

Back at the company billet as they were putting their rifles away and changing out of their inspection uniforms Private Brinker asked Cosgrove, "Koz, old Buddy, what the hell happened to you?" His answer, "Nothing happened to me, nothing at all that couldn't have happened to all of you Doubting Thomas's." Brinker scratched his head wondering just what that meant and then he asked, "It's Saturday, Liberty Call is being sounded early today. Are you goin' ashore? Or are you too good to drink with us peons now that you and Colonel Price are such good buddies?" Cosgrove responded, "Yeah, I thought I might go over to the Privates' Club and have a libation while I decide what I'm going to do later. Want to join me?" Brinx answered, "Sure, why not? C'mon Cooper, were going to have a libation with the pride of the regiment." Then glancing at Koz's rifle he stopped in astonishment as he asked, "Koz, just where in hell did you get that rifle stock?" The answer, "You don't really expect me to tell you that do you? It's a professional secret." Brinker said, "The colonel wasn't kidding, I've never seen a rifle stock that beautiful in my life."

As they left the billet and stepped out onto Hart Road and walked down to the corner of Sinza Lu Brinker started to hail a rickshaw. Cosgrove immediately stopped him, saying, "Oh no, were not riding in those things, let's get a cab."

Seated on their favorite barstools in the Privates' Club, Cosgrove spoke to the bartender, "Ah Sing, let me have a whisky 'n soda and give these Marine friends of mine whatever they'd like.

Brinker couldn't stand it much longer, he waited until Cosgrove had consumed three Scotches and then finally asked, "Dammit Koz, tell me about your rifle stock." Cosgrove casually replied, "Oh that. Well there's

not much to it; I just went down to the S. J. David Company and ordered it. They had it made for me from a really fine piece of walnut stock they imported from the States and then I had them finish and polish it. I figured they'd do a good job on it because the sign in their window said they were the Far East representatives of the Remington and Colt Firearms companies back in the States. The rest of that stuff the colonel seemed so impressed with was not a big deal either, I just found out from the "Field Mouse" where the officers had their uniforms tailored and he got me the address of the Wai Lee Company over at Szechuan Road.

The shoes were easy, I asked a French cab driver if he knew where the best shoemaker in Shanghai was and he took me to Yuyuen Road. There's a place there called The Kiang San Shoe Company. The Chinaman who runs it told me he makes dress shoes and boots for the British officers and I thought I couldn't go wrong there. You know how particular the British officers are. The rest was really easy; I hired the houseboys at our billet to polish and press everything and told them I'd give them double pay if they made it all look better than anyone else in the outfit. I wasn't tryin' to impress the colonel or anyone else except that damned Gunny Palkowski. He's been givin' me a hard time and I just wanted to teach him a lesson, sort of." A bewildered Brinker said, "Damn Koz, that must have cost you a fortune. Where'd you get all that money? Did someone back home die and leave it to you? Koz you aren't in trouble are you?" Cosgrove had a look of disgust on his face as he answered, "Hell no! Easy come, easy go and you guys know where I got the money. I tried to interest you in it but you were too stupid or maybe you just didn't believe me. There's gonna be another lottery on the 2nd of November and you'd better listen to me this time."

The Panay

Paul and Lillian had started going to movies nearly every week. Paul enjoyed the Japanese movies especially because they helped him learn and remember Japanese sayings, mannerisms and colloquialisms that he had not learned in school. Lillian had especially wanted to see American movies so

Paul tried to select films that showcased the United States in a favorable light and that she would especially be interested in.

He had been traveling for the past three days on a reconnaissance mission through a portion of The Yangtze River Valley spotting Japanese Army units and estimating their strengths, capabilities and intentions. A dark shadow was cast over southern China and the Yangtze River Valley like a huge shroud as Japanese forces continued their relentless forward movement. Paul was glad to be back and as he submitted his report he was looking forward to seeing Lillian and taking a night off soon.

He noticed a small sheet of notepaper tacked to the bulletin board in the intelligence office, it read; "Effective 10, December, Captain Wallace M. Greene, Jr. will be on detached service aboard the USS Panay for the purpose of visiting localities of military interest. The anticipated date of his return has not been established. Captain Robert E. Hogaboom will assume his regular military duties and will cover for him on all special assignments until further notice." The Panay had been assigned as station ship to guard the remaining Americans at Nanking and take them aboard at the last moment for evacuation and refuge. They embarked on 10 December and Panay promptly moved about 27 miles downriver past the fishing village of Hohsien on the way to Wu Hu.

Commander James J. Hughes, USN, Captain of the USS Panay, PR-5 an American gunboat assigned to the Yangtze River Patrol, checked with headquarters of the Asiatic Fleet to be certain they had informed the Imperial Japanese Navy of his course and probable locations in the Yangtze River and they confirmed that they had. Paul Pooley wondered if the "localities of military interest" were similar to the ones he had been scouting. If so, Captain Wally Greene was going to see one hell of a lot of Jap soldiers.

The Japanese were moving eastward across southern China and through the Yangtze River Valley. There was activity aplenty in the R-2 Office and at the American Consulate. Everyone found it necessary to work extra hours. The American dependents were being evacuated to the Philippines and China was considered to have become a dangerous place. Paul and several others spent time in the field learning as much as possible about the Japanese forces and their order of battle. The 4th Marines provided troops to the gunboats of the Yangtze Patrol as they assisted in the evacuation of all non-essential personnel from the American Embassy at Nanking. On the surface, life went on as usual in Shanghai's International Settlement.

The 6th Marines arrived in China from San Diego to assist the 4th. in protecting lives and property. They augmented the defensive positions along the Suchow Creek and set up others throughout the American sector in addition to establishing squad-sized mechanized patrols within the International Settlement and supplementing the Yangtze Patrol. With the arrival of the 6th Marines in China, the 4th Marines Auxiliary Company was no longer needed and training sessions were suspended. Many lasting friendships between Marines and these modern day minutemen resulted from their experiences in the auxiliary company.

The Saturday morning parade and inspection on the 12th of December was the largest assembly of US Marines yet seen in Shanghai. Brigadier General Beaumont, the brigade commander reviewed the parade as the 4th and 6th regiments proudly passed before him. Paul Pooley was assigned to ostensibly photograph the parade but paid special attention to the foreign dignitaries in the stands. There was a heavy presence of Japanese generals who he would photograph and later attempt to identify for the R-2 files. As the Marine Brigade departed the racetrack and marched down Bubbling Well Road, Japanese bombers and fighter planes were warming up to take off and attack the USS Panay and other vessels in the Yangtze River off Wuhu.

Shortly after noon on 12 December as the Marine Brigade was marching back to the billets in Shanghai, the Imperial Japanese Army ordered Japanese naval aircraft to, "Attack any and all ships in the Yangtze above Nanking." The senior Japanese naval officer in Shanghai having previously been advised of the USS Panay's location requested a verification of his orders prior to ordering the attack. The verification was promptly received and the attack commenced.

US Navy and Marine Cryptographers of the "On the Roof Gang" were furtively intercepting and decrypting traffic relating to the attacking planes

which clearly indicated that they were under orders during the attack, and that it had not been a mistake.

At 1327 on the 12th, near Wuhu north of Nanking, three Japanese Type 96 Bombers sank the USS Panay. As the crew abandoned ship and struggled towards the shore, nine *Nakajima* fighter planes strafed them repeatedly with machine gun fire inflicting many casualties.

On the evening of the 12th, Major Boone, looking haggard and suffering from loss of sleep sat at his desk anguishing aloud, "Thank God Wally Greene got off that damned ship and went ashore in the valley yesterday. At least he's safe. Now, what the hell can we do to help Asiatic Fleet to assist Jim Hughes? The poor SOB not only lost his ship but he's badly wounded and stuck in the mosquito infested marshes at Wuhu with the bodies of three of his men, forty-three wounded crew members and three wounded passengers. After what he's been through, I'd hate to have to be the one to tell him that we are still not at war with Japan."

Paul Pooley remembered Captain Donaldson and how he believed that the Japanese would rather negotiate than go to war. Paul wondered how the captain would feel now if he were still alive. Sinking the Panay was the most senseless thing Paul could think of. In total frustration he exclaimed, "Well, we're at war now, so we'd better react just as decisively as we can, and do it immediately."

Major Boone's voice rose above the other sounds of the office as he asked, "Who the hell authorized you to declare war Pooley? The last time I checked, you were a gunnery sergeant." Making no attempt to hide his frustration, Pooley barked, "Well Major, if this isn't war just what the hell is?" A frustrated Major Boone replied, "I really don't know what is going on but you people can read the teletypes as well as I can. The Japs have sent an apology to the American Ambassador Nelson Truslow Johnson admitting what they did but they say it was all a mistake. So sorry." The major glared across the room at Paul and said, "You may very well get your war Pooley but your going to have to wait awhile first." The United States had accepted Japan's apology for sinking the Panay.

Paul tried to compose himself and stop showing emotion, it wasn't professional and certainly it wasn't Marine-like. But for the life of him he couldn't understand why important military decisions had to be made by civilians. Once an attack is launched, military commanders on the scene should be allowed to retaliate. He knew that if the Japanese weren't severely punished, they'd consider it a victory and would take it as a significant sign of weakness on the part of the United States.

A Night at the Movies

Paul had been working day and night lately and hadn't had a night off in some time. The captain told him that the major had said that if he didn't call back to the office by 1500 that he was to tell everyone except those with the duty that they could shove off at 1630. They had all been under a great deal of pressure and had been on a brutal schedule. Paul was eager to get away from all the activity in the office and relax for a few hours. At first he was hesitant to call Lillian but then decided that since we were not officially at war with Japan he couldn't be accused of consorting with the enemy. He called and invited her to view a movie with him. He thought she might like a musical comedy so he decided to take her to the Carlton on Park Road. The Warner Brothers big hit Gold Diggers of 1937 was playing at the Carlton. It featured; Dick Powell, Joan Blondell and Victor Moore.

Paul had decided not to mention the Panay incident. He didn't want her to know of his interest in it. If he said nothing, she was more likely to let her guard down and let something slip that she may have heard from Iwao.

Lillian seemed to really enjoy the music and dancing and Paul did as well. But Paul hadn't expected the Universal News to cover the sinking of USS Panay. Somehow the management of the Carlton had gotten a copy of the uncensored, uncut newsreel film shot by Norman Alley the Universal Newsreel man. Lillian was visibly shaken and could hardly believe what she was seeing. American audiences in the United States would not see the uncensored version of this newsreel until after the end of World War II.

President Roosevelt had requested that certain parts be cut (censored) from the original version to preclude an escalation of the growing tension with Japan. After all the Japanese government had apologized for the in-

cident. The censored portion included the strafing of unarmed American sailors as they attempted to reach the shore.

The Panay had been sunk just two days earlier and was now getting newspaper coverage along with considerable activity that was said to be occurring near Nanking. Classified information that Paul was reading indicated that something really big was happening in the capital of Nanking. The nationalist government had rapidly and surreptitiously displaced to Chunking to establish a new wartime capital. The Japanese seemed intent on moving on Nanking expecting to capture or kill the now missing members of the Chinese cabinet. Paul had read the newspaper reports that morning but had no intention of mentioning the incident to Lillian until a few days had gone by and he could learn what she had picked up at work and from her brother. Paul would then compare what she told him with the Japanese newspaper accounts. He needed to make a comparison and hoped there would be some differences in the stories that might be useful to him.

The Philanthropist

In the R-2 Office Paul noted that the major had a large map spread out across his desk and was intently briefing two of his subordinates. Paul could only catch a word now and then but he did distinctly hear the major refer to ". . . a safe primary route to Chunking and at least one and possibly two alternate routes." He also deciphered the fact that the two officers would personally reconnoiter each route and make a report to the major on their return. Paul didn't know for certain what was going on but he surmised this must have something to do with all the Japanese military activity in the Yangtze River Valley and the existing turmoil in the capital at Nanking. Paul knew the officers were taking things very seriously and wondered just how seriously the young Marines in the regiment were reacting to the rapidly expanding war between China and Japan.

At the moment the troops were giving little thought to the Sino-Japanese War; there were more pressing matters to be addressed. In the B Company billet Privates Brinker and Cooper were pooling their money to see if they

could come up with enough for rickshaw fare to the Privates' Club and back and for the price of a couple of beers. Being broke on a Friday night is not a comfortable feeling for a US Marine, especially after Liberty Call has been sounded. Cosgrove was putting on his green blouse and asked, "Brinx, are you guys going to the Club tonight or are you lookin' for something more exciting?" Brinker answered, "We want to go to the Club but we've got to come up with a couple of bucks first. We're both nearly broke." Cosgrove said, "Well I guess it's a good thing I haven't been hangin' out with you guys the last couple of nights. My chit book hasn't even been touched yet. Brinker exclaimed, "That's great! C'mon Coop, Koz is flush." And off they went.

Once at the Club, Cosgrove plopped a big cigar in his mouth and addressing Private Cooper said, "Kid, gimme a light." He threw his chit book on the bar and addressing the bartender said, "Ah Sing, it's Friday night and I've got a full book of chits. Here it is. Let me know when it's all used up." Cosgrove was the hero of the moment. Brinx and Cooper were proud to have such a philanthropic buddy. It turned out to be a pretty good night in spite of the impending war and the dynamic trio managed to make it back to their quarters without incident.

The Rape of Nanking

Paul managed to get off again a few nights later and called Lillian hoping to make up for the disaster of three nights before. He told her that a new feature film was being released for the 1937 Christmas Season. It was really a children's movie based on an old fairy tale and was made by Walt Disney. Paul knew Lillian would like it. The movie was Snow White. She reluctantly agreed to go along but told Paul she could not get the Panay incident out of her mind. He was sure that the full-length animated color feature was just what she needed.

Paul arrived early to pick Lillian up and was invited in for tea before they were to depart. He learned that she had questioned her brother Iwao at great length about the Panay incident. He had somewhat reluctantly told her of his part in the debriefing and of studying the films taken by Imperial Japanese Navy airmen during the attack. He even mentioned to Paul that

an associate of his, Lieutenant Commander Takeshi Aoki who was on the air-operations staff had related that he was embarrassed by the unfortunate incident; explaining that the Imperial Navy had been misled and was much too professional to have done such a thing themselves without senior outside influence. Paul wondered just what that meant. Then as Iwao explained how chagrined he was over the unfortunate incident that had brought their countries closer to a war that they both hoped would never occur. Paul read his expression and believed he meant it.

Paul was surprised that Iwao, an Imperial Navy Officer, would even mention the Panay incident to him. Iwao's face was drawn and grey. He looked much older than he had just a week earlier. Paul readily sensed that something serious had happened to Iwao and tried to persuade him to accompany them to the movie. He looked like he could use a little relaxation. Iwao declined stating that he was very tired and was going to sleep. Paul had no way of knowing that Iwao was fully consumed in what was going on in Nanking. He had read all of the intelligence reports and had been working virtually around the clock. Iwao was to accompany the Japanese Vice-Consul to Nanking for a visit to the embassy and would see the carnage first hand on Wednesday.

Another Sunday and Paul and Lillian were going out to Jessfield Park, as was their custom. They were finally able to convince Iwao to come along. He had been maintaining a brutal schedule at the consulate and had not had any free time since the great Japanese "victory" over the Chinese Capital in Nanking.

Iwao volunteered that he had spoken to a couple of the naval aviators who bombed the USS Panay. He claimed that they had been very remorseful and were deeply sorry for what had occurred. He dared not tell Paul and Lillian that the Japanese aviators who participated had received explicit orders to bomb the Panay and other vessels, orders the aviators carried out reluctantly only after vehement protests and arguments. The day of the bombing was sunny and cloudless as could be clearly seen in the newsreel footage. The official Japanese position was that their airmen were unable to see the huge American Flags painted on the ship's canvass or otherwise identify the ship because of the clouds and generally poor visibility. Paul maintained a poker face while listening to Iwao and wondered just how much of the true story Iwao was really aware of.

Paul was impressed by what Iwao had told him. He knew from the radio intercepts that the Japanese Army and Navy had differences concerning the sinking of the USS Panay. Ultimately, the army gave the order and the navy reluctantly complied while the US and the rest of the western world vacillated.

Paul knew that what Iwao had told him was highly irregular for a Japanese officer. Iwao obviously thought of him simply as a friend and Shanghai businessman who spoke English and just incidentally had been born an American. He seemed to trust him. Paul wondered if this would cause Flint to rethink what he had previously advised. Paul and Lillian were both unaware that Iwao had just returned from another trip to Nanking a few days before and was seriously disturbed by many of the things he'd seen there but was unable to discuss.

Paul felt that the time had come to pay another call on Special Agent George Flint aboard Augusta but she was gone and would be at sea and in the Philippines for the next three weeks.

Snow White lived up to Paul's expectations. It was the first full-length cartoon he had ever seen and was all in color. The musical score was excellent. It was obvious to him that Lillian had liked it very much. As the picture ended, she was glowing with delight.

They were totally unprepared for the graphic newsreel of shame and horror that smashed its way across the silver screen next. It was of the massacre at Nanking—obviously developed right in China and was as close to instant replay as could be accomplished with motion picture film in 1937. The Japanese now occupied Shanghai and an uncensored newsreel could not have been shown in a Chinese theater. The Cathay_was different, it was foreign owned and was in the International Settlement, thus it was not under Japanese control.

Lillian had not gotten over the newsreel of three days earlier, showing the bloodbath at Wuhu where Japanese pilots machine-gunned the American survivors of the Panay as they tried to wade to the shore. The Panay incident was bad but what she was now seeing of Nanking was indescribably worse.

She sobbed uncontrollably and saw nothing further of the movie. When the bright house lights came on at the end of the show, tears were still streaming down her cheeks and she believed she would be an embarrassment to Paul. She vowed to herself that she would never again attend a movie with him and she never did.

The "Rape of Nanking" became an obsession with Lillian Kurihara. She could not hear of it or even think of it without breaking into tears. It was difficult for her to look at Japanese Army officers when she had to speak to them. Every officer she saw was presumed to have been at Nanking; even those who she knew had remained at the consulate in Shanghai at the time were suspect.

Her heart was filled with compassion for the people of Nanking. Previously, she had paid scant attention to the Chinese, they were all around her but, except for her *amah*, Yuang, Siao-sung, she hadn't really seen them. Now, that she did see them, every Chinese face she looked at brought an ache to her heart. How could the soldiers of her own country, her beloved Nippon, perpetrate such uncivilized, brutal atrocities on hundreds of thousands of innocent people?

Answering her own question she thought, "Our generals are drunk with power and there seems to be no one or nothing that is willing to stop them, certainly Tokyo can't. The generals have been blinded by their successes against the poor Chinese. They now believe they can conquer all of Asia and the Pacific and that America and the rest of the world will simply sue for peace. They misjudge the peoples of the western nations. They think Americans and all westerners are weaklings and that their society is decadent. They have no Code of Bushido to give them inner strength and self-discipline and they have no national purpose other than their own creature comforts."

Lillian was beginning to understand now why Prince *Asaka* had replaced General Matsui. Matsui believed as her late father had. He was a compassionate man and preferred diplomacy over brute force. The great Western powers took too little interest in the activities of the Japanese Army in China. There was still time to do something but they all seemed ambivalent. Their lack of action was costly as it would only be a short time before the entire world would be engulfed in the bloodiest war in the history of mankind. The Generals of the *Kwangtung* Army were hopelessly out of control.

Yuang Goes to Nanking

Lillian had serious reservations about letting Yuang Siao-sung go to Nanking especially since she had seen the newsreel film. Speaking to Paul she exclaimed, "Oh Paulchan. What we saw was so horrible I just don't want her to see such things in person. What if she doesn't find her family? She will be so brokenhearted she may never get over it." Paul agreed but reminded Lillian that it was Yuang's right to go if she insisted.

The following week Lillian mentioned to Paul that Yuang, Siao-sung was leaving for Nanking on Tuesday night. He suggested that it would be dangerous and told Lillian to ask Iwao to escort Yuang to the railroad station and put her on the train since the station was in Chapei the main Chinese district of old Shanghai and was now under control of the Japanese Navy's Rikusentai. He recommended strongly that Iwao, a navy lieutenant, wear his uniform.

The train Yuang always took departed the North Station in Chapei at eleven in the evening and arrived in Nanking at seven in the morning. To Yuang, it was always a wonderful adventure. It may have been a time for some to sleep but to Yuang it was much too exciting for sleep. She didn't want to miss one minute of the trip. If she had fallen asleep she felt she would be cheating her master and mistress as the round trip fare they paid for her was nineteen dollars, a handsome sum. Every time she took this remarkable trip she marveled at the great distance the train covered in just eight hours. It was 195 miles from Shanghai to Nanking; they were moving at such great speed that they would cover approximately 25 miles in just one hour; and this included making several stops along the way. Yuang Siao-sung considered, with a shudder, how long it would take someone to walk such a distance.

This time the trip was different. Although it was dark outside during her passage, she could sense that something was terribly wrong. She watched out of the window to see what she could see and whenever there was sufficient moonlight outside she saw destruction. Several buildings she had passed on her previous trips were now mere shells of what they had been. Many had been gutted by fire and artillery. She surmised bombs and hand grenades had destroyed many of the others. Yuang, Siao-sung had heard many times about the war but until now she had not fully understood just how devastating it really was.

The Smell of Death and a Pall of Smoke

When the train pulled into Nanking on this particular trip in mid-December of 1937 her life was changed forever. This ancient city where she had been born and grown to womanhood was so different now. The smell of death was everywhere and a pall of smoke from scores of fires hung heavy over the city. Her family could not be located. The neighborhood where her parents lived and where her ancestors had lived for generations had been completely destroyed by fire. There were no buildings left. None of the Yuang's former neighbors could be found. There was nothing but desolation. Where buildings had formerly stood, there was little more than rubble, smoldering ashes and the stench of death.

The depths of her sorrow and the hollow feeling that all she had known while growing up was completely wiped out. Her family, the neighbors, the buildings and even the once familiar landmarks in her neighborhood had vanished. Her feelings of total helplessness at such a time of tragic loss was indescribable.

Yuang, Siao-sung attempted to enter the Japanese Embassy to seek information and assistance. She was turned away at the point of a soldier's bayonet. Devastated and with tears running down her cheeks she sadly turned and walked away from the embassy where she had previously worked for over ten years.

Part III

Yuang had her railroad ticket for the return trip to Shanghai but when she got to the Shanghai-Nanking Railway Station at Hsiakwan, she could not use it. The Japanese military forces had commandeered all the trains. Yuang, Siao-sung wanted desperately to leave this city of death but could find no way out. Not only were her family and neighbors gone; she had heard that there were more than 300,000 Chinese people dead in and around Nanking. Yuang, Siao-sung was terribly depressed and became violently ill. The overpowering odor of death was everywhere. She dropped to the ground retching as she wondered why the Japanese had massacred her people and devastated this great historic city.

She looked at the waterfront through the smoke and haze and caught glimpses of the Japanese gunboats and the steamships near the dock. If she could find passage by steamer it would cost her $24.00 to get back to Shanghai, far more money than she had. Yuang felt under her clothing for the leather pouch she had suspended from her waist; it was there but held a pitifully small amount of cash.

Refugee

She fell in with a group of displaced persons who had become refugees in their own city hoping that there would be safety in numbers. She soon learned that there was no safety for a Chinese in Japanese occupied Nanking. The soldiers took the men from the group and pressed them into service doing heavy labor. The women and children were terrified, hungry and cold. The men did not return.

They found an abandoned building. The roof and flooring were intact but the walls were gone. The women and children huddled together on the cold, hard floor for comfort and warmth. A little past midnight the rains started and continued on until after daylight. Siao-sung was thankful for the protection of the roof over their heads.

Yuang, Siao-sung's second night in Nanking was dark and frightening. There was little rain but chilly gusts of wind were constantly blowing across the open floor of the abandoned building she shared with the other refugees.

Along with the chill, the gusts also brought the odor of death. It was a dark night except for the reflection of orange flames on the clouds overhead. Much of Nanking was still burning. Siao-sung was tired and wanted to sleep but sleep did not come easily. A younger woman called Mai Ling lay down beside her. They talked for a while but neither really had any interest in conversation. They were too cold, tired and frightened. The sound of gunfire throughout the city did little to help Siao-sung relax. After what seemed an eternity, she dozed off. Awakening with a start, she immediately sensed that something was wrong. Mai Ling had vanished in the night and so had Siao-sung's possessions.

Reaching inside her waist, Siao-sung clutched the small leather pouch in which she kept the coins she still possessed and felt grateful. She realized that she would never see her family again and had to escape this city of horrors. To leave Nanking she would first have to move through the northern harbor to the Yangtze River. To get to the harbor, she would have to move up Chungshan Lu, the main street and then pass through Ichang Men the Watergate; it was the northwestern gate of the city. Then she could enter the northern suburb, Hsiakwan.

She rushed down Chungshan Lu and moved quickly toward the immense stonewall that had surrounded Nanking since the Ming dynasty. As she passed through the ancient gate in the wall, the Ichang Men, she encountered honking busses and automobiles filled with Japanese military officials and bureaucrats winding their way past rickshaw pullers, mule carts and throngs of Chinese pedestrians and even an occasional water buffalo or camel.

She pushed her way through the throngs determined to keep walking until she reached Shanghai. As she walked on, she prayed to *Guan-yin* the goddess of mercy that she would have the strength and good fortune to live to see Shanghai again.

The Endless Walk

A long and dreary day and night of walking passed followed by another and then another. She kept walking. At nightfall, she found a place protected from the wind and rain and fell promptly to sleep.

Part III

Suddenly Siao-sung woke up. It wasn't a natural awakening from a normal night's sleep but a sharp jerk, as if in the time it took her to open her eyes she had been transported from one world to another. She could see only darkness but she could clearly hear the crowing of a cock. Dawn would soon be breaking and somewhere nearby she could hear the sound of men marching, many men. Were they going to Nanking or away from it? She couldn't understand why anyone would wish to go to Nanking, not even the Japanese; they had destroyed it. There was nothing to go back to but sorrow and death. Siao-sung got back on her feet and started walking.

It was another very long, tiring day. Her feet were sore and her muscles ached. Siao-sung was constantly hungry but could find little to eat along the road. As she passed through Chenchiang, Siao-sung came upon a street vendor peddling his wares and the aroma created an irresistible temptation. She told the vendor what she wanted then opened the small leather pouch she carried and removed a couple of coppers. She ate her fill of meat cakes and drank a bowl of millet *congee* (thin rice porridge) cooked with red beans. After paying the vendor she was overwhelmed with gratitude for the few coppers she had managed to save.

Siao-sung walked through the rain and the brisk December wind for days taking shelter where she could find it. She spent frugally as her small supply of coppers dwindled with each bowl of rice or cup of weak broth she consumed. Each day walking became more difficult but she continued plodding on.

At dawn on the fifth day she felt weary and too tired to get up. Her body ached and she didn't want to move, but she didn't dare go back to sleep again. She had to think and think carefully. She needed a plan. How could she get back to Shanghai? How far had she come? Shanghai was nearly 200 miles from Nanking. She wondered how many miles she had walked in the past four days. It did her no good to keep asking herself that question. She must walk and keep walking just as far as she could before her strength was gone. She had to get back to Shanghai—her mistress would need her. If she was away too long, the master may find another *amah* for his sister and there would be no job left for her. Her position with the Kuriharas was all that was left of her life. She must not lose it.

China

Tired, cold and hungry, Siao-sung knew that she must go on but she needed rest from the hours of walking. She found a small teahouse by the railroad tracks near Tan yang and entered hoping to rest for a while out of the harsh winter winds. Clutching her few coppers tightly, she planned on having no more than a pot of tea to warm her but the owner of the teahouse had come from Szechuan and knew well the use of spices and hot peppers. Siao-sung couldn't resist the wonderful aroma and weakening, she ordered a bowl of cooked bean curd.

The vinegar, soy sauce, pepper and tips of leeks with which the hot dish was seasoned gave off a delicious aroma so fragrant that Siao-sung held the bowl cupped in her chilled hands. She drank a mouthful from the bowl and the warmth felt comfortable in her stomach. When she had finished the bowl she was perspiring, and wished she could order another but she knew she must save her coppers. She tarried as long as she dared over her pot of hot tea but finally had to leave the warmth and relative comfort of the teahouse and again brave the cold weather and the long road ahead.

Yuang, Siao-sung continued to distance herself from Nanking, plodding onward, she thought of China and wondered what was to happen to it? People passed her on the road going in both directions. They all seemed intent on getting somewhere but she wondered if any of them really had a destination. Siao-sung had a destination, Shanghai and she worried that she may never reach it. She had been walking for days but she had lost count and could not remember how many days only that there were many. Her cut feet were swollen and bruised. It had been days since her slippers had worn out and had to be cast away. She ached all over but mostly it was her heart that ached. It ached for China, for her family and the *Han* people.

If she made it back to Shanghai how could she serve her mistress? She could not go to the market if she could no longer walk. She was far too tired to carry the baskets of wonderful food. Oh how she wished for some of that food. Even a few scraps from the ground under the stalls in the market would keep her alive.

There was a chill December wind blowing when the rains caught Siao-sung on the road somewhere between Changchow and Wuhsi. There had

been no shelter and she was drenched. As the night came forth to blanket the land in darkness she saw a small fire flickering a few meters off to the side of the road. She left the road and hobbled the few meters over toward the fire. Four beggars in worn, tattered clothing were warming themselves by the small fire. Siao-sung greeted them in a faltering voice and asked if she could come close to their fire and be seated. A voice answered in the affirmative and she sat (hungrily) relishing the warmth of the fire. She promptly fell over in a sound sleep.

Someone was shaking her shoulder as she opened her eyes to see the gray mist of a winter morning. Her benefactors were all staring at her. One toothless beggar handed her a bowl of steaming rice as he said, "Here little sister, you will gain strength from this." She muttered her thanks and took the well-worn chopsticks from his dirty hand and ate the precious rice as slowly as she could, hoping to make it last as long as possible. She savored every grain of the life-giving rice and looking up said, "Thank you second cousin, I have nothing to give you for the rice but I will remain always in your debt for it." Another of the beggars smiled as he remarked, "The fat merchant who lost it will never miss it little sister. We are happy to share with a person who has fallen to a state as lowly as we ourselves." Two of the men had her stretch forth her legs and they applied an ointment then wrapped her swollen feet in strips of ragged cloth. As she watched the men shuffle off, she sat but could not get up. Finally when the noonday sun was overhead and the warmth of its rays eased the aching in her bones she regained her feet and hobbled shakily back to the road. She must go on to Shanghai; her mistress had need of her.

A woman driving an Ox cart filled with straw stopped and motioned Siao-sung to get on board. She climbed laboriously up on the bed of straw mumbling her thanks and was soon fast asleep. When she awakened the woman had unhitched the ox and was shaking her awake. Going into the woman's humble home, Siao-sung learned that her husband had been conscripted to fight the Japanese. She knew that the war was raging all around her and she had seen many refugees who spoke of the utter destruction of Nanking but she had heard nothing of her husband or other details of the war.

Siao-sung told her of her own adventures in Nanking and what she knew of the happenings there. She said the people she had fled with were calling it "The Rape of Nanking." Yuang, Siao-sung could tell the woman nothing of the Chinese soldiers and neglected to say that all she had seen were dead. The only live soldiers she had seen in Nanking and on the roads were the arrogant monkey men, the Japanese. She took from the woman's hands a hot, damp cloth to wipe her face and was surprised to see how much dirt was removed. Siao-sung welcomed a bowl of rice and a cup of piping hot tea. She wanted to remain and rest longer but knew she would only be a burden to her benefactor. The woman told her they were not far from Suchow. Gathering what little strength remained, she shuffled off to the road and again proceeded toward Shanghai.

Evening came and she had not yet found a place to rest where there was protection from the cold wind. Suchow was now well behind her. The more she walked the lighter the skies in the east became. There was no mistake; the glow of light was on the horizon toward which she was walking—she was going east. Even if she was on the wrong road, the direction was right. The reflection of lights far ahead in the distant night sky had to be the halo of Shanghai.

It was the 24th of December 1937, Christmas Eve. Paul and Lillian were returning from a midnight Christmas pageant at church. They stepped out of a taxi on Rue Cristobal and Paul paid the driver then reached out his hand to Lillian as she gave him her key.

Stepping into the vestibule of the apartment building they noticed something crumpled up on the floor in the darkness beside the door. The form whimpered and was trembling. Lillian knew immediately that it was her missing *amah*. She knelt down and cradled the form of the small woman in her arms and sobbed, tears of thanks coursing down her cheeks. Paul carried the feverish body of Yuang Siao-sung up the flight of stairs to the Kurihara's apartment; she was delirious. Lillian opened the door to her *amah*'s room and Paul placed the frail form on the bed. Lillian fed her and bathed her. She refused to leave the side of her loyal servant for three days.

Yuang, Siao-sung deeply loved her mistress and her master. Her newfound abiding hatred for the Japanese soldiers did not extend to the mem-

bers of the Kurihara household. She simply could not understand, and no one could explain to her satisfaction, why the Japanese soldiers wanted to kill her people and burn their cities.

The Ambassador Ballroom

The Ambassador Ballroom was on Avenue Edward VII in the French Concession. Cosgrove had seen their posters and adds but had paid little attention to them until one night when he was at the Brass Rail Bar in Blood Alley and overheard a sailor telling a shipmate that he had heard from a very reliable Chief Petty Officer, who was an old China hand that the Ambassador Ballroom was the best place in Shanghai to meet attractive women.

Koz asked Brinker if he had ever been to the Ambassador, knowing full well that he had not. When Brinker answered in the negative he asked Private Cooper. Cooper was newly arrived in Shanghai and hadn't been anyplace that Brinx and Koz had not taken him to. Koz offered his companions another drink and ordered a Scotch and Soda for himself. He overheard the sailor again; this time he was telling his companion that he would really like to go to the Ambassador sometime but just didn't think he could afford it on seaman's pay.

That was all Cosgrove needed to hear; It was now a challenge. He spoke up saying, "C'mon you guys, drink up. We're getting out of here." Raising his volume he added, " I want to go to the Ambassador in Frenchtown." He glanced slyly at the two sailors, knowing that they had heard him; he felt a certain measure of alcohol-induced satisfaction.

Outside, he spurned the waiting rickshaws and addressing Private Cooper directed, "Kid, find us a cab." Cooper was successful and the three were soon on their way to 745 Avenue Edward VII. A sign in English posted beside the entrance proclaimed, "Experience Shanghai's night life at it's gayest at the Ambassador" On the wall to the right of the door was another sign proclaiming, "100 of the Prettiest Dancing Hostesses in all of Shanghai for your entertainment." Smiling broadly Cosgrove asked, "Okay you guys, read that sign and tell me if I didn't bring you to the right place.

Brinker answered, "The sign reads pretty good Koz but we'd better go in and see what its really like inside." Cooper added, "Yeah Brinx, back home in Indiana I was taught that in a stable full of horses, they're not all gonna be winners." Cosgrove spoke up with, "You guys just haven't got any faith at all. Follow me and you'll both think you've died and gone to heaven when I start introducing you to the 100 angels inside.

Confronted by a tough-looking white Russian bouncer just inside the entrance Cosgrove demanded, "Where's your bar my good man? Take us to your bar." He then slipped 10.00 Mex into the big man's hand and received a smile in return. Cooper quietly addressed Brinx stating, "The sign outside said 100 of the prettiest hostesses in Shanghai Brinx but somebody must have sounded abandon ship just before we arrived 'cause I can't see more than 30 of 'em and they're no better than the women in any of the other places we've been to." Cosgrove, who'd obviously overheard, snapped, "Knock it off Coop and just watch what I do. First, we've got to buy some dance tickets then just look the field over and pick out whatever one you want. When they see you with tickets in your hand, they'll be all over you."

The large chandeliers, bandstand and highly polished dance floor gave an impression of opulence. Sensing that his buddies were still a bit skeptical, Koz noted, "It's better than the Candidrome where you can dance and watch the greyhounds racing at the same time if you want to. I like this place much better than the Candidrome. I've always preferred to look at the girls I dance with rather than running dogs.

The hostesses sat in rows of chairs next to the bandstand acting unconcerned and giving the impression that they were just killing time and chatting and didn't really care whether anyone wanted to dance with them or not. They gave the impression that no amount of dance tickets could tempt them onto the floor. The Chinese hostesses had an advantage the others did not enjoy. Their uniform of the day was a dress that the Marines fully approved of. If the girls were from Shanghai or the South they called it a *cheong-sam* but if they were imports from Peking or Tientsin it was a *chi-pao*, a clinging sheath of silk, slit on both sides nearly to the thighs. It was a dress obviously designed to show off the attractive legs of the Chinese women and the high

collars helped them to hold their heads erect creating an impression of regal sophistication.

Cosgrove had a drink then promptly approached the row of sitting ladies. He stopped short, staring but unable to choose from among them. There were lovely voluptuous blonde white Russians, Eurasians, sleek Chinese in their *cheong-sams* and others he could not readily identify, perhaps Japanese, Korean and Filipino, but all very attractive. At a loss which to select; Koz did something they had not seen before. He handed tickets to the first three girls in a row and invited them not to dance but to join him at a table near the bar. The first, obviously a white Russian, said, "Allo, you nice." Koz smiled. She then asked, "My Prince, please you buy little Sasha one small bottle vine?" He answered, "Why not?" And summoned a waiter letting the three ladies order what they wished; which of course was Champagne (or at least purported to be champagne). Brinx and Cooper chose one girl each and actually danced with them. They returned to the table where Koz was reveling in his newfound best friends and ordered another drink.

The Filipino band was quite satisfactory and Brinx and Cooper got up and danced again. Koz stood up to dance with Soo Lan (one of his three) but felt a bit unsteady on his feet so he sat back down and joined his girls for another drink. Brix and Cooper were becoming quite fond of the cheong-sams, or the girls filling them, and were not ready to leave but Brinker wisely suggested to Koz that it was time to depart. Tomorrow morning was parade and inspection and he knew Koz didn't want to disappoint his new friend Colonel Charlie Price. Koz surrendered to his buddies after proclaiming his eternal love for Sasha and her sisters and vowing to return the following night.

Outside, Brinx and Cooper were eager to look after their buddy and then return to the girls inside. Brinx' main concern was to get Cosgrove back to the billet. He poured him into a waiting rickshaw just as he passed out. The rickshaw coolie understood where *Mei-Kuo Ying P'an* on Sinza Lu and Hart Road was and agreed to deposit the sleeping Marine there and to ask someone to call the corporal of the guard. He felt relieved that one of the Marines had paid him in advance, not being certain of his passenger's ability to do so.

The Sixth Marines Depart

Paul strode across the office to pour himself a cup of coffee. On his return, he stopped at Captain Green's desk and casually mentioned, "Sir, I've been hearing rumors from some of the other Staff NCO's and the scuttlebutt is sure strong that the brigade has served it's purpose and they're going to disband it and send the 6th Marines back to the states. Do you know anything about that?" "Well Gunny, all I can tell you is that, all rumors are false. Only the truth is fact." "Well dammit Skipper, I'm afraid there's a lot of truth in that scuttlebutt about the 6th Marines, yet it just doesn't make any sense after the Panay incident and what's been going on in Nanking." The captain responded, "You're afraid huh? Gunny, I learned a long time ago that if you fear something, it's bound to happen."

Paul went back to his desk and sat down. He could hear the familiar Marine singsong cadence drifting up through the screened windows. A platoon was marching back from somewhere and had entered the compound. He liked the sound of Marines marching and regardless of what he was doing he would always pause and listen for a few seconds whenever men were marching in the compound. It brought back pleasant memories. The 2nd Marine Brigade was disbanded and the 6th Regiment of Marines left China and returned to the United States early in 1938.

Gung Hsi Fa Tsai!

The time of *Ta-han* brought a decided chill to the air but to the celebrants it would hardly be noticeable. This was to be Lillian's second lunar new year in China but her amah, Yuang, Siao-sung, had acted as if it was to be her first. Yuang had been telling her what to expect as though she was a young child. Lillian humored her and was very pleased, as this was the first true sign of a recovery shown by the previously traumatized Yuang.

Lillian's heart was heavy for Yuang and tears coursed down her cheeks as she thought of the horrors of Nanking and silently cursed Lieutenant General (Prince) Yasuhiko Asaka, the emperor's uncle who was the Commander-in-Chief of the Imperial Army in the Shanghai-Nanking Area.

Part III

Lillian believed him to be the person most responsible for the Rape of Nanking. Yuang, for the first time in her life had no home or family to go to. Nanking was in ruins, her people massacred. She became closer to the Kuriharas and their strange American friend with the unlikely Chinese name of Pu-Lee.

It was a time of great anticipation among not only the children but also for all the Chinese people. Much activity could be seen in the Chinese neighborhoods. The people were frantically cleaning and scrubbing to wash away the evil spirits and bad luck of the past year. Those who could afford to do so acquired new items of clothing. It was 1938 and January 31st was rapidly approaching. That is the day that would usher in The Year of the Tiger.

The Chinese New Years celebrations officially began with the rattle and bang of firecrackers. The firecrackers were everywhere; hundreds, no thousands of them, and the people seemed to be as excited as the children. It is believed that the noise of the firecrackers, the loud beating of the drums and the deafening sounds of the cymbals together with the face of the lion or dragon dancing aggressively can evict the bad or evil spirits.

It was a time to forget one's cares and join in the great celebration. Lion dancers filled the street winding their way through the crowds in a long colorful silk and paper mâché dragon with the fierce head of a lion. The loud beating of drums and the crashing of cymbals and tambourines was deafening as Chinese flutes played their mystical tunes intended to drive away the evil spirits. As evening approached, lanterns appeared, hundreds of lanterns carried by the children.

It was a time of great happiness for a people who could forget, only briefly, the war that surrounded them. Paul was glad for the many distractions as he hoped it would help to take Lillian's mind off of the previous month's horrors that included the sinking of the Panay and the devastation that occurred at Nanking. He wondered if Yuang, Siao-sung would ever recover from the trauma she had experienced while escaping from Nanking.

Red envelopes were passed out during the Chinese New Year's celebrations, from elders to the children and from employers to subordinates. The tradition of red packets containing coins evolved from suppressing or put-

ting down evil spirits. Red symbolizes joy, truth and sincerity and so the envelopes that were passed out were always red.

Above the din of the firecrackers the clouds of war floated ominously over the Shanghai night and the tiger stealthily crept in almost unnoticed amongst the noise and merriment.

A night like this called for celebrating with Chinese food and Paul had previously consulted with his gourmand friend Detective Sergeant Cahill, who suggested a four story building at 719 Nanking Road that housed an upscale restaurant, the Sun Ya known to serve extravagant western and Cantonese dinners. That is where he would be taking special friends for a Chinese New Years feast.

Iwao had consented to come along and surprisingly; Lillian had insisted that Yuang, Siao-sung accompany them. Paul was genuinely surprised. Normally, an Asian lady did not invite her *amah* to be a guest at dinner. It reminded Paul of something an American woman might do on a special occasion but was very unlike a Japanese lady. Paul was pleased and his already significant respect for Lillian was further enhanced. Yuang should not be left at home alone or otherwise neglected until her memories of Nanking became a distant memory.

The Chinese banquet, which consumed the entire evening, was superb, and the unique, friendly conversation, sparkled along in three languages; Japanese, Chinese and English. Paul, Iwao and Lillian enjoyed every bit of the dinner as it arrived course after course in true Chinese style. Yuang studied every dish with the practiced eye of a lifelong critic. Yuang, Siao-sung had never dined in such an exquisite setting or been waited on by perfect strangers. She savored every moment of this dream-like experience. Happy New Year. Gung Hsi Fa Tsai!

The Private First Class

The Field Music stuck his head through the door and proclaimed, "Brinker, get your butt down to the office, the company clown wants to see you right away." Private Brinker looked up from his footlocker that was serving as a card table and asked, "What does he want to see me for Mouse

I aint done nothin' to him?" Brinker then directed his attention back to the top of his footlocker and the playing cards laid out thereon as the Field Music answered, "How the hell should I know what he wants to see you for, he's the company clown and I'm just a poor field music. Now get down to the office and report to him!"

Brinker casually replied, "Okay Field Mouse just as soon as I finish this game of solitaire." As he departed the Music replied, "Okay, I'll give him your message and tell him to expect you sometime after you finish playing an important game of solitaire."

The company clerk was a corporal and a man of great power and authority. Corporals, especially the company clerk, were not to be taken lightly. It was he, who controlled the duty roster and influenced special assignments like mess duty, and it was obvious that he had the ear of the first sergeant. He even had a certain amount of control over the liberty card box.

Private Brinker moved rapidly, even taking two steps at a time as he passed the Field Music going down the billet stairway. On the first deck he turned right and approached the First Sergeant's office with some trepidation. What could they possibly want with him this time? Stepping into the office, Private Brinker spoke.

"Hi Corporal Donnelly, the Field Mouse said you wanted to see me." The corporal glanced over to his right where the Company First Sergeant sat intently digesting a new Marine Corps order just in from the States; prior to placing it in the company commander's in-box. Corporal Donnelly then turned and looked directly at Brinker stating, "It's Field Music Brinker, Field Music, not Field Mouse." Brinker shuffled uneasily as he said, "Oh yeah, sure, the guys are only kiddin' him when we say that corporal, we don't mean anything by it." Donnelly looked across his desk at Brinker, pausing just long enough to be certain he had Brinker's complete and undivided attention then he spoke.

"Brinker, Corporal Nelson and your platoon sergeant have informed the "Top" that you intend to reenlist when your time is up and that you hope to remain on station. Is that correct?" Brinker's immediate response was, "You bet it is Corporal, I want to stay right here in Shanghai with my buddy Cosgrove and all the guys in my squad." Donnelly leaned back in his

chair, frowned, and then mustering up all the power and authority vested in him by his important position as the company clerk and a corporal of Marines, he stated,

"I believe you are about to undergo a rather drastic change in your lifestyle Private and I don't really know if you are up to it. In fact I'm damn near certain that you are not up to it." Raising his voice Donnelly bellowed, "You are on the wagon Brinker! Do you hear me? On the wagon! You will not touch a drop of anything stronger than coffee during the next sixty-three days. Your liberty card is here in the first sergeant's office and to get your hands on it you must first go through the "Top" or me.

"You will be permitted to have your liberty card on Sundays to attend divine services if you desire but you must return directly to the billet after church. Everything you do for the next sixty-three days will be done in a highly efficient manner with skill and enthusiasm. You will not step out of line, not even one inch out of line. Do you understand everything I am saying to you Private Brinker? Everything?"

A shocked Private Brinker looked over at the silent first sergeant then back to the waiting company clerk as he timidly stated, "No, I don't. What the hell is going on here? I'm not even in trouble. I haven't done anything really bad in weeks. I haven't even been in a good fight lately. What the hell is this all about Corporal?"

The corporal answered, "The way things stand right now Brinker; you are not eligible for re-enlistment and if you can't reenlist you sure as hell are not going to be allowed to stay in Shanghai. The next time the USS Henderson gets in, which will be in just two months, you will go aboard as a time expired man, be transported to the west coast of the United States and be discharged. The Marine Corps and this regiment will finally be rid of you." Corporal Donnelly relaxed slightly as he glanced over at First Sergeant Charles H. Jackson whose turn it was to speak.

"Brinker, listen to me and listen very closely. You and your buddy Cosgrove are a couple of drunks. You are considered by most of the officers and NCO's as "liberty risks." Major Puller, the XO, is an exception. He likes you

because he thinks you saved his ass during that incident with the Japs at the Garden Bridge awhile back. You've been in and out of just about every kind of trouble there is and it's about time you came to your senses and grew up. I've been looking over your SRB (service record book) and it reads like a dime novel. Your platoon sergeant and your squad leader believe you are capable of being a good Marine, they tell me you are always dependable when on duty and they've seen you really perform well when under great stress. Of course, they didn't mention anything about your activities when you were on liberty with that maniac buddy of yours, Private Cosgrove." The First Sergeant continued,

"To reenlist in this regiment you'd have to be qualified for a Good Conduct Medal and if you were, with all of your seniority, you'd be eligible to make PFC. Our battalion has been authorized to promote three Marines to PFC on the next regimental promotion list.

"Looking over your Service Record Book Brinker, I find something very strange indeed. It would appear that a certain amount of administrative sleight-of-hand has occurred here. I used to think these conduct marks were 1's but they seem to have magically become 4's. Now I may be mistaken Brinker but it certainly looks suspicious to me. However, you can rest assured that there will be a thorough investigation into this matter. Falsifying government documents is a pretty serious offense and if one is found guilty under the Articles for the Government of the Navy (Rocks and Shoals) he can be put away for a long time.

Private Brinker's eyes were open wide and they had a look of terror in them as he blurted out, "Dammit First Sergeant, I didn't have anything to do with this! I know my conduct marks were bad but I had no reason to want to change them. Hell "Top" I've never even touched that book except when one of you called me in to the office to sign new entries that were put in it." The First Sergeant replied, "Alright Brinker, I didn't accuse you of anything, I simply said an investigation was going to be conducted. I didn't even say you are a suspect. But I will say one thing, if those really turn out to be 4's, you are more than qualified for a Good Conduct Medal. And your conduct marks would be high enough to qualify you for reenlist-

ment. This company rates another PFC. As a PFC you could reenlist, get a pay raise and stay in China."

The first sergeant continued, "Now I know Corporal Donnelly is right in doubting that you are up to this and I also know that you would have been in a hell of a lot more trouble if some of the officers and NCO's hadn't given you numerous breaks. You should have been written up more often. I've seen you on duty and I've seen you operate under pressure and I know you'd be a damn good Marine if you'd just start taking things seriously. You'll rate your second service stripe at the end of your enlistment in just sixty-three more days and then you'll be discharged. I'm offering you a chance to stay in the Corps. You can go ahead and become a two-hashmark private if that's what you want, but you'll have to put the hashmarks on your civilian clothes because you won't be wearing a Marine uniform. Or," the First Sergeant paused staring right at Brinker and then continued, "You can straighten your life out starting right here, right now and we'll get you reenlisted, make you a PFC and keep you in China for another year. We might even overlook the possible alterations to your conduct marks. It's all up to you now Brinker. We're asking a lot of you but if you are a real man you should be able to do it. And if you want to stay in the Marine Corps you'll have to do it."

The shocked Brinker responded, "Top, what the hell are you asking of me? You want me to completely change my life for the next 63 days so I can re-enlist? And if I do it you're gonna let my record book stay falsified so I can qualify for a Good Conduct Medal? Wow! You know there's no way I can be a party to a scheme like that. It's an affront to my personal sense of integrity and a violation of the "Rocks and Shoals." Brinker hesitated for a moment then continued, "Besides, if I had a Good Conduct Medal, all the guys would make fun of me. It would destroy my reputation! What about my buddy Cosgrove? He would be embarrassed even going on liberty with me if I was wearin' a Good Conduct Medal. No "Top" I just can't get involved in a scheme like that, I don't have much, but I do have my reputation and my dignity and I've got to protect them. No dice Top." The First Sergeant stared at Brinker in stunned silence, amazed.

Part III

It was Saturday night in Shanghai. The morning parade and inspection had gone well and Private First Class Brinker was wearing his full greens (Winter Service A) and sporting the two hashmarks of an old salt. He was also wearing the red and blue ribbon of the Marine Corps Good Conduct Medal. His cordovan leather (Peter Bain) belt glistened as though it was patent leather and it matched the shine of his highly polished shoes. His brass belt buckle sparkled. Brinker reached into his pocket as he strode up to the bar and withdrawing his freshly issued chit book, placed it on the bar. He smiled at Cosgrove and the other regulars as he hailed a mess boy and signing the chits directed that a round be provided for the bar and that thereafter his friends should drink until all the chits were gone. He ordered a beer for himself.

PFC Brinker pushed his empty glass toward the back of the bar and stated, "Well, that's it for me, I've got things to do." As he started to depart a confused Private Cosgrove asked, "Brinx, you've only had one beer. Where the hell are you going? We always go places together. Besides, You've still got plenty of chits left, have another beer with us while we plan some exciting things to do later." PFC Brinker answered, "No thanks Koz, I've got a lot to do. I want to get back to the billet and start studying for the corporals' exam." A surprised Private Cosgrove started to speak when Brinker cut him off with, "What the hell's the matter with you men? You don't expect me to stay a goddam PFC forever do you?" With that, PFC Brinker strode out of the Privates' Club to the astonishment of all his buddies at the bar. He hailed a rickshaw and promptly returned to his quarters.

The Letter

Yuang Siao-sung was on a personal mission for her mistress. She was very proud to be trusted on such an important mission but was greatly concerned for her mistress. She had been acting different lately; the smile that normally graced her face had disappeared and had been replaced by a look of great concern. Siao-sung asked the rickshaw puller to wait for her then went into the building, found the door she was looking for and slipped a letter under it. She then scurried back to the waiting rickshaw and was on her way.

Lillian had been acting strange; she often seemed to be depressed and confided to Paul of her concern for Iwao. She knew the *Kempeitai* had been watching him and she suspected that they had even questioned him. She wondered aloud if it could be because of her friendship with Paul and then felt embarrassed for mentioning it. He was deeply concerned but dared show no emotion. Waiting for the appropriate time he excused himself and departed. Paul couldn't believe the Japs were on to him but he could take no chances, he would have to report his activities in great detail to the FIO and the major; and he would have to include some very graphic details of his personal life. He returned to his apartment to do some serious thinking. When he arrived back at his apartment he found that a letter had been slipped under his door. When he opened the letter, he read,

> "*Dear Paul,*" not Paul-chan, as she nearly always referred to him but simply, Dear Paul. He read on, "*Sometimes I dream that I am an American lady living in the U.S. I'm married to an American man who works during the day and when he comes home at night I will have a delicious meal prepared and waiting for him. I will sit at the table with him and we will discuss all of the things that interest him. I will tell him of the things that happened during the day and I will always agree with what he says. I will be a good American wife and I will do all I can to make my husband love me but Paul, when I look in the mirror, I see an Asian face and I know it is all just a cruel dream. Paul, I want to be an American but I cannot stop being Japanese. I've told you before that I had never dreamed I would be so fortunate as to have an American friend as close and as understanding as you.*
>
> "*I would like to embrace Christianity but should I do so, it will never be understood nor accepted by our family members in Japan or even by Iwao. I am certain it would impact unfavorably on his service as an officer in the Imperial Navy. Perhaps I can be a follower of Christ without announcing it publicly. My employer, Saigusa-san, has strong feelings about Christianity as well, and we have often discussed it.*

Part III

"Perhaps, I have put myself into the jaws of the dragon by revealing so many things to you. I pray that you understand my motives. What I do, I do for Japan and for your great country and yes, even for China. We must do everything possible to insure peace. If our countries go to war against one another, the Japan I know and love will cease to exist. America is too big for Japan to fight and it would be a formidable enemy.

With deepest affection,

Sumiko Kurihara"

Paul was confused, she had always called herself 'Lillian' but this time she had used her Japanese name. Was this an indication that she was reverting completely to her Japanese self? Was it an indication that she no longer wished to have an American friend? What could she mean by, "*What I do, I do for Japan . . . etc.*"? He had to see her, and soon!

Paul knew that her roots were Japanese and that she was from a venerable old samurai family. Her upbringing was steeped in the culture and traditions of the East. To Paul, she was a paradox. He knew she wanted to be an American yet she had certain traits that were hopelessly and irrevocably Japanese. He felt that he must get to her very soon and have a serious talk. There was no longer any doubt in his mind, he knew now that he was in love with her.

Death on Rue Cristobal

It was already dark and there was no time to look for Shunsan Wu. Paul hailed the nearest rickshaw he could find and gave the puller an address on Rue Cristobal. The smoky rickshaw lantern gave off a heavy scent of burning oil that mingled with the viral tinge of garlic from the coolie's humble supper, as with labored breath he drew his rickshaw past quaint shops and cafes along a boulevard that could have been on the outskirts of Paris. He turned onto Avenue Roi Albert and then turned into Rue Cristobal. Leaning

forward in the seat, Paul addressed the rickshaw puller directing him to pull over to the side. He wished to walk the rest of the way.

Paul needed to spend some time in the cool damp air to collect his thoughts and decide just what he would say to Lillichan. He could think more clearly when he walked. Speaking in pidgin He told the rickshaw puller to stop. "My wantchee walkee," and the coolie padded to a stop. Paul alighted and expressed his thanks in the local jargon, "*M'Goi*" and reached his hand out and said, "*Cumshaw*" as he paid the coolie a slightly more than expected fare. The coolie responded with a rapid bow uttering, "*Do jay Mastah Mei-Kua.*" Turning his empty rickshaw around the puller padded back down the Rue Cristobal into the foggy darkness. Paul listened to the clip-clop of the rickshaw puller's sandals as he passed into the murky shadows of the French concession.

There were halos around the dim streetlights as they bravely but vainly attempted to penetrate the fog and illuminate the street below. Visibility was limited and Paul's footsteps on the damp pavement were amplified. Suddenly he turned into a dark entranceway and stopped. He looked both ways but saw no one.

Paul lit a cigarette and listened but could hear no other footsteps; the sound of his rickshaw coolie's padding on the pavement had disappeared. He was alone on Rue Cristobal. He stepped out of the entranceway and quickly covered the next half block, listening to his own footsteps on the pavement in the dampness of the night. He finished his cigarette and "field stripped" it in the proper Marine Corps manner simply out of habit. His shadowy figure turned into a familiar doorway and stopped. He rang the bell but to no avail. He knew she was there, she had to be and he had to see her. He rang again but without success.

Rummaging through the inside lining of his suit coat he quickly produced a strip of thin flexible metal which he proceeded to use as a "shove knife" to jimmy the latch and overcome the western-style lock on the door. He smiled to himself as he remembered his classes on surreptitious entry and the man who had taught them. Willis deVern George was the undisputed master of surreptitious entry. He had been on loan from the US Customs

Service while teaching a small group of detectives from the New York City Police Department and ONI special agents at the "USS Concrete" at 90 Church Street in New York. Paul was thankful for the special training he had received. Returning the strip to the lining of his coat he quickly stepped through the unlocked door into the vestibule and started up the familiar stairs to the Kuriharas' flat.

He knocked gently on the door but there was no acknowledgement. He rapped louder and called her name. When there was still no response he called Iwao's name but again, no answer. He could feel his pulse throbbing in his temples and his mouth was dry. Paul knew that something was seriously amiss; he also knew that someone was inside that flat. There was a crack of light under the door and he sensed movement inside. He silently cursed their Japanese way of thinking and hoped that if she wouldn't open the door and let him in, at least Iwao would. He felt a great sense of urgency, getting in quickly was important—he did not want her to do something foolish. The "shove knife" was not going to work on this door as an extra molding strip prevented it. There was no time to remove the strip and pick the lock. He contemplated the door and frame and decided that it's most vulnerable point would be where the doorknob and lock were. If he could kick the door near the frame right at that point, and do it with sufficient force, he may be able to break the frame and gain entrance. As he prepared to make his move, the door quietly opened and Iwao Kurihara stood there facing him. He seemed different; his eyes reflecting both fear and sadness

Paul's eyes fixed on Iwao's face, as he demanded, "Where's Lillian What's happened to her?" Iwao looked like he'd aged ten years. His face was grey and his brow furrowed as he answered, "Lillian is not with us." Paul snapped, "What the hell do you mean she's not with us? What's happened to her dammit? Answer me man, where is she?" It was only then that Paul realized that they were not alone. There were two Japanese men in the living room. In typical Japanese fashion, they had removed their shoes but both were still wearing their overcoats. "Who are these guys Iwao?" Paul asked, knowing full well that they were *Kempeitai* and they were not here on a social call.

Iwao had spoken to him only in English and Paul, sensing his concern had answered in English. Speaking in Japanese one of the officers told Iwao to get rid of Paul quickly. He must have assumed that Paul did not understand Japanese and Iwao did nothing to dispel this assumption. Paul grabbed Iwao's arm and again demanded, "Where is she? Where's Lillian? I'm not leaving here until I see her." Iwao answered, "You must go now Paul." "Dammit, I'm not leaving until I see her. Just who the hell are these guys anyway?" One looked at Iwao and again told him to get rid of Paul.

Iwao was visibly shaken as he asked Paul to leave the apartment immediately. The older of the two men took a swipe at Paul's arm to brush it away from the grip he had on Iwao. Paul instantly let go of Iwao and turned on the little man. He grabbed him by the lapels of his greatcoat and falling backwards, propelled him over his head then quickly straightening his legs, gave a mighty shove; then watched as the little man flew across the room smashed into the wall and crumpled onto the floor where he decided to remain for the time being. Paul noticed that when he grabbed the man's lapels, one of them concealed a small brass pin, the chrysanthemum! He had always been amused by the fact that the *kempeitai* officers proudly wore their small chrysanthemum badges but wore them concealed behind lapels. Paul turned on the younger officer who was about to engage him.

The younger of the *Kempeitai* officers had a bit of difficulty getting back on his feet. He stood looking at Paul, his back pressed against the wall. A cunning and slippery suggestion of a smile crossed his face and his narrowed eyes had a glint in them that was ugly to behold. It was a look of pure hatred and Paul Pooley knew that somehow, somewhere, he would see this nasty little man again.

He strode across the room to Lillian's door and opened it. The light was on and everything seemed to be neatly in place as always, there was no obvious sign of violence or a struggle. Lillian was formally attired in her best ceremonial *kimono* and *Obi*. She was lying face up on the western-style bed. Paul noted that she was very still and very pale. He grasped her wrist and felt for a pulse but found none. The body was cold.

Part III

Lillian's amah, Yuang, Siao-sung, sensing that with Paul there it would now be safe to enter the room; raced past Iwao and the two *Kempeitai* officers and rushed into the room to offer help. She stopped short, aghast when she saw Lillian's still body. Her eyes filled with tears and she dropped to the floor sobbing.

Paul knew the Japanese police had no jurisdiction over him. He was an American and they were in the French Concession but Shanghai was an unusual place with confusing laws, treaties and customs. The two French gendarmes who promptly arrived with two uniformed Japanese police officers took him into custody.

The paddy wagon halted and the back door opened. The handcuffed Paul Pooley was helped out of the vehicle by the two gendarmes. He was relieved to see that they were back in the International Settlement and had arrived at the headquarters of the Shanghai Municipal Police.

Paul had been relieved of all duties and was beside himself with concern over the length of the investigation. He continually searched his mind for a motive that Lillian may have had for her tragic suicide but found no sound reasoning for it. He often thought about the things Mister Flint had mentioned but always dismissed them as being out of the question. Paul knew Lillian could not have been a Japanese agent. He also knew her love for him was sincere.

Usually confident and self-assured, Paul Pooley was lost. He had always been in control of things but now he suddenly found himself in such an unusual and depressing situation that it seemed more like a bad dream than reality.

He had been temporarily relieved of all duties pending the outcome of an investigation and to make matters worse he could think of nothing he might do to help speed up the investigation. He could only wait. The Japanese police wanted him taken into custody on trumped up charges which he knew would never stand up in a court of law in the United States but this was Shanghai.

Lillian was dead and he had not even been permitted to attend her funeral. There were rumors reaching him that his Marine Corps career may be on shaky ground. He wanted nothing more than to get this all over with and go back to work, he couldn't stand the loneliness and inactivity.

China

Except for the International Settlement and the French Concession the Japs had taken Shanghai. They were furious that it had taken them so long. The Japanese had underestimated the Chinese will to fight and Chiang Kai-shek had sent his best troops to confront them. With the Japanese it was a matter of pride and loss of face. They had expected to effortlessly push the Chinese army aside as they advanced on Shanghai but the fight had lasted for over 3 months.

The Japs were vindictive and they showed their wrath when they stormed through the ancient cities of Hongkew, Kiangwan, Chapei and Nantao surrounding modern Shanghai. The cities sustained considerable damage.

Paul sat in his room trying to piece together the events that had so disrupted his life. He looked at the worn copy of Kipling lying on his nightstand. It had belonged to Lillian's father and she had given it to him beautifully gift-wrapped. He knew it held great sentimental value for her. Once again, he turned to the passage in which Rudyard Kipling had cautioned, "At the end of the fight, lies a tombstone white, with the name of the late deceased, and the epitaph drear, "A fool lies here who tried to hustle the east."

Kipling knew what he was writing about. In a way, Paul Pooley had ". . . tried to hustle the east." He believed it had been his responsibility to learn about and report on Japanese affairs. Lillian was Asian and he occidental and they had tried to believe it made no difference. Paul had believed it, she, obviously, had not. Paul had been confident that he and Lillian had understood one another perfectly and that the bond they shared was strong enough to last forever. He would never have believed that she was capable of taking her life and shattering his.

As he mourned Lillian, Paul thought of Nantao, the place she had liked so much, he had promised to take her back there but now things had changed, it was under Japanese control and she was dead. Memories were all that remained.

Chang Wu and the Dragon of Destiny

Paul went to great lengths to find the ancient fortuneteller in Nantao and was pleased that he had been successful. Following a session of complex but necessary negotiations steeped in the ancient customs

of China they finally settled on a meeting place and a price for the old man's time.

With a package cradled in his left arm Paul walked behind the old man down an unfamiliar alley and followed him as he disappeared through a beaded doorway into the recesses of a dimly lit room.

Handmade wooden birdcages lined one wall and the odor of bird droppings convinced Paul that sanitation was of little importance to the old man. The opposite wall was home to a small *Ti Ju Chia* with its little *Shen Tai*. The ancient Buddhist shrine had an odor of it's own from burned joss sticks. A cot with an old blanket was along the third wall and the fourth was bare except for the door and a small window that permitted the only light in the room. A table with two rickety wooden chairs sat in the middle of the modest room.

Paul unwrapped the package he had been carrying and placed a clay bottle in the center of the table. He tossed the crumpled paper onto the table. The old man quickly reached for the paper. Opening the crumpled paper he smoothed it out on the tabletop then neatly folded it. Everything in China was of value to the poor, even a piece of paper. The old man produced two teacups and put one in front of Paul. He held the other in his shaky hand in anticipation. Paul filled their cups and they drank what Paul considered the worst liquor he had ever consumed.

He and the old man, Chang Wu, discussed their earlier meeting when Lillian was still alive and Paul reminded him of how their fortunes had been told and what had transpired since. The old man spoke:

"Everyone on this earth is here by plan—everyone is fulfilling his destiny. Each of us has his karma. Your Missy Lillian is on her journey; that is what she had to do. Life was not easy for her. Her birthright was to be what she was. She was never the enemy; she was merely fulfilling her destiny. You were her friend and more." The old man rambled on, sometimes knowing, sometimes guessing. His were words of wisdom to which Paul thoughtfully listened.

"Death does not diminish her. What she was to you, she will always be. She left her gifts behind for you to have. There are few gifts more precious than pleasant memories of a loved one. So many questions in life go unan-

swered. So many puzzles remain unsolved—and that is the will of the creator. Chang Wu's voice was a soothing balm to Paul's' wounded spirit. "Of course you feel cheated. Your pain of losing Missy Lillian is a part of your karma but always remember no one is really dead until they are forgotten.

"When all this is over, when you once again live in normal circumstances Chang Wu advised, "You will be able to recapture your true self from within, and you will be enriched by the wisdom that comes with time. As time passes we are everything we have ever been, only more. Life is not only about events, what has happened or what is happening, it is about people. It revolves around understanding who we are, what we came here to do, and about becoming our own selves."

"My dear Master Pu-Lee, always remember, we don't come here to stay, we come here to go. Missy Lillian has gone; you are here. Do what it is that the Dragon of Destiny has sent you here to do, fulfill your karma. Then perhaps someday, somewhere, you will rejoin her."

Draining his cup of the powerful *Ng Ah Pei*, Paul thought to himself, I'll be with her in the old teahouse right here in Nantao, she loved Nantao and wanted to come back here and I couldn't bring her back, the Japs changed things too much. When I join her again, I'll bring her back to Nantao. It will be just like it was when we came here together. Everything will be the same and we will be together again in Nantao. He picked up the clay flask, reached across the table and filled the old man's cup with *'Ng Ah Pei* and then, draining the flask, he refilled his own.

The time to depart had come all too soon. Paul returned to his quarters with Chang Wu's soothing words fresh in his mind. He was not a superstitious man and certainly he had never believed in fortunetellers or the Dragon of Destiny but what the old man had said pleased him. He would get a good night's sleep and see what the next morning had in store for him. Perhaps the whole thing would go away like a bad dream. Before he could get undressed for bed, there was a gentle rapping on his door.

Paul opened the door in response to the knocking and found Captain Piper standing there. "Good evening Skipper come in. What's going on? How come you're wearing your uniform?" The captain responded, "I'm

wearing it because I'm on duty Gunny and it's my sad duty to inform you that your freedom is about to come to an end. You are to pack your things and come with me, I've been requested to take you into custody."

"What! What the hell is this all about Skipper? You know as well as I do that I didn't do a damned thing that any other Marine wouldn't have done under the same circumstances. "Captain Piper responded with, "Yes Gunny, I know it and so does everyone else on the regimental staff but this is a very sensitive case. We've got to be extremely careful not to do anything to further provoke the Japanese at this time. Com Asiatic Fleet and the US State Department have a lot of interest in your case and the word came down to regiment to take you into custody pending the outcome of the investigation."

Command Decision

In the admiral's in-port cabin aboard the flagship Augusta, the Commander in Chief, U. S. Naval Forces, Asiatic Fleet was steaming mad. His Chief of Staff nodded to a frightened steward to bring coffee. The admiral looked at the Marine colonel, who had just arrived and barked, "Sit down dammit and tell me what you know about this incident! The colonel promptly sat but before he could respond the admiral barked at the Fleet Intelligence Officer, Charles Morgan, asking, "What are you doing here Charlie?" Morgan answered, "I was summoned Sir, the accused is one of ours Admiral, he is a special agent of the Office of Naval Intelligence. He is also a Marine gunnery sergeant on the muster roll of the Intelligence Section, Headquarters Company, 4th Marines, so he belongs to both Colonel Price and to me." Admiral Yarnell retorted, "All right, what you two are confirming for me is that this man is a Marine on active duty and he is member of my command. He has allegedly committed an offense against the Japs and the State Department has an interest in having it adjudicated expeditiously in order to keep the Japanese happy. Is that correct?" The colonel answered, "That's basically correct Admiral."

The admiral said, "From what I understand about the case, this incident occurred in a Japanese home, is that correct?" The colonel answered, "Yes Admiral, that's right." Grimacing, the admiral said, "Well as you must know,

I don't have a lot of sympathy for one of our people who is so palsy-walsy with the Japs as to be in one of their homes. Those bastards sank one of my ships last December, killed three of my sailors and wounded fifty-three others including three civilians. I think our people should be more discreet in whom they are friendly with and who they trust.

"I'd like to get to the bottom of this expeditiously myself and I don't give a damn what the Japs or the State Department think about it." The admiral paused briefly as though in deep thought then looking up he said, "I'm going to order that a general court martial try this damn case. Let's get all the facts out in the open and settle this mess once and for all.

If either one of you have anything further to say about the matter, speak up now, otherwise, you're dismissed," The colonel and the Fleet Intelligence Officer looked at one another knowing that they each had further things to say about the matter but neither thought it prudent, or career enhancing, to say anything at this time. They promptly departed.

The Court-Martial

The Court-Martial was convened at Headquarters, Fourth Marine Regiment, Asiatic Fleet, Shanghai, China, by virtue of a precept signed by the Commander in Chief, U.S. Naval Forces, Asiatic Fleet on 10 March 1938.

The court met pursuant to the above-mentioned order on Friday the 13th of March 1938 at the Headquarters of the 4th Marine Regiment.

Present were: President, Lieutenant Colonel Arnold L. Hansen, U.S. Marine Corps, members: Lieutenant Commander Thomas S. Kelleher, U.S. Navy, Captain Leonard Piper, U.S. Marine Corps, Captain Leslie R. McKenna, U.S. Marine Corps,

Captain Richard G. Brown, U. S. Marine Corps,

Lieutenant David N. Jones, U.S. Navy, First Lieutenant Victor H. Krulak, U.S. Marine Corps and Judge Advocate, Lieutenant Colonel Clarence P. Mason, U.S. Marine Corps.

The clerk and interpreter were admitted to the court. The accused, Gunnery Sergeant Paul Pooley, U.S. Marine Corps, appeared before the court,

and in reply to a question by the judge advocate asked permission to have Major George L. Hollett, U.S. Marine Corps, act as his counsel. At the request of a member the court was cleared until Major Hollett could be informed and his answer returned.

It was Monday when the court reopened, the Judge Advocate and the accused entered and the Judge Advocate announced that Major Hollett was serving on Guam and was not available to act as counsel because of pressing duties, both military and legal, on Guam.

The president reminded the court that it was the expressed desire of the convening authority that this court be convened as expeditiously as practicable. Paul Pooley understood this and heartily agreed with the convening authority. He considered it fortunate that the admiral had referred his case to trial by court martial. He wanted to be tried before the admiral changed his mind. At least being tried by court martial gave him the possibility of remaining in the Marine Corps.

The judge advocate advised that the accused could select some other person as his defense counsel. Pooley answered that he would accept whatever counsel the court deemed appropriate. Lieutenant Junior Grade Maxwell Shapiro, U.S. Navy Reserve, was appointed as defense counsel.

The accused was asked if he objected to any member present, and Pooley submitted the following objection. Captain Leonard Piper, USMC. Paul had always respected Captain Piper but he couldn't forget that it was Piper that had taken him into custody and who had commented on the sensibilities of the Japanese. The challenged member, Captain Piper, did not desire to make a reply. The court was cleared. The challenged Captain Piper also retired.

The doors being opened, the judge advocate, the accused, his counsel and the challenged Captain Piper entered. It was announced that the objection of the accused was not sustained. The accused having requested that the challenged member be examined on his voir dire, he was duly sworn by the judge advocate, in the presence of the accused: You, Captain Leonard Piper, do swear or affirm that you will true answer make to questions put to you, touching your competency to serve as a member in this case: So help you God? His answer was, "I do," whereupon Lieutenant (jg) Shapiro conducted his examina-

tion. Does the accused wish to introduce testimony in support of his challenge? Paul's answer was, "No" The accused did not object to any other member.

The Judge Advocate was duly sworn by the president, and the members were duly sworn by the judge advocate; all of which oaths were administered according to law, and in the presence of the accused.

The judge advocate read aloud a letter from the convening authority authorizing him to employ a stenographer and an interpreter and asked permission of the court to introduce Yeoman's Mate 1st Class Edward Johnston as stenographer and Mr. Wayne Akiro Watanabe as interpreter, which being granted, Johnston and Watanabe were duly sworn by the judge advocate, in accordance with U.S. Navy Regulations

In reply to an inquiry by the judge advocate, the accused stated that he had received a copy of the charges and specifications preferred against him.

The court was cleared to examine the charges and specifications and to consider all matters preliminary to the trial.

The doors being opened, the judge advocate, the stenographer and interpreter, Paul Pooley and his counsel Maxwell Shapiro, entered, and it was announced by the president that the court found the specifications in due form and technically correct.

In reply to an inquiry by the judge advocate the accused stated that he was ready for trial.

All witnesses were directed to withdraw. The judge advocate read aloud in the presence of the accused the charges and specifications of charges preferred against him, and arraigned the accused as follows;

"Gunnery Sergeant Paul Pooley, you have heard the charges and specifications of charges preferred against you, how say you, to the specification of the first charge, guilty or not guilty? Paul Pooley stood mute. "To the first charge, guilty or not guilty?" Pooley again stood mute.

"To the specification of the second charge, guilty or not guilty? To the second charge, guilty or not guilty?" Paul again stood mute. The president directed the judge advocate to proceed as though the accused had pleaded "not guilty."

The prosecution began here. Major Charles D. Boone, U.S. Marine Corps, appeared as the first witness for the prosecution, and was duly sworn

by the president in the presence of the accused. The oath was administered to the witness.

You, Major Charles D. Boone, do solemnly swear that the evidence you shall give in the case now before this court shall be the truth, the whole truth, and nothing but the truth, and that you will state everything within your knowledge in relation to the charges: So help you God." The major answered, "I do" The Judge Advocate continued his examination. "What is your name, rank, and present station?" The major answered, "Charles D. Boone, Major, US Marine Corps, Headquarters, 4th Marines." "Do you recognize the accused, if so, as whom?" The major again answered in the affirmative and gave Paul's name and rank. He then proceeded to answer all questions put to him by the Judge Advocate.

On Paul's behalf, Shapiro when afforded the opportunity to cross-examine Major Boone declined to do so. The prosecution continued calling it's witnesses and as they were examined and cross-examined the case against Paul Pooley was being built.

Paul wanted to seem as inconspicuous as possible leisurely glancing around the courtroom trying to identify the faces of all those who had come to witness his "crucifixion." Among the spectators there was a well-dressed Japanese gentleman who sat alone along the north wall. Paul could not place him but thought he must be a representative of the Japanese government. The two Japanese *Kempeita*i officers that he had fought were there, dressed in western style business suits and sitting side by side they would each appear as witnesses against him. They showed no emotion. The inscrutable little bastards; he could surmise absolutely nothing from the complacent looks on their faces. Iwao Kurihara was there, also dressed in a civilian business suit and Yuang, Siao-sung was seated beside him. She looked frail and smaller than Paul had remembered and appeared to be terrified. Iwao would be a witness testifying against him and apparently Yuang Siao-sung would be a witness as well. He could read Iwao's face like a book. Iwao was uneasy, he would not look at Paul and he obviously did not want to be there.

Paul Pooley looked at the younger of his two accusers and wished he had hit him harder. He couldn't help himself there was just something evil

about the man. His name was Takahashi and he was obviously a junior officer in the *Kempeitai*. He was still in his twenties and Paul knew he'd seen him before that awful night in the Kuriharas' apartment. It had to have been at Joe Farron's when there were so many *Kempeitai* security people in attendance; he had to have been one of them. That was the night that Yoshimura-san had been murdered.

It had been a very long and depressing morning when the President finally called for a recess for lunch. All present were admonished by the President not to discuss matters pertaining to the trial and then were permitted to withdraw.

During the lunch recess Paul was smoking a cigarette and talking with Lieutenant Flint and his counsel. Flint was speaking. "Dammit Pooley, the Navy Department has made a major investment in you. A great deal of time and money has been spent on your training and education and now it all has come down to this.

"If you are found not guilty, the United States Government will be placed in a very embarrassing position with the Japanese government. Relations between Washington and Tokyo are strained nearly to the breaking point as it is. The slightest provocation could send the diplomats on both sides into orbit. If you are convicted, we will lose your services permanently. Do you realize that your security clearance has been suspended? If you are convicted, it will be permanently revoked and you will not even be able to get cleared for scuttlebutt."

Paul gave Mr. Flint a confused look as he asked, "What the hell do you mean, if convicted? They'll never convict me. I only did what any Marine would do under similar circumstances." Flint turned and looked straight at Shanghai as he stated, "You beat the hell out of two Japanese police officers that were on their own turf conducting an official investigation. You had no right to be there and in fact, you had been asked to leave the premises. It doesn't sound to me like you have much of a case. Just what the hell do you intend to say in your own defense?" A remorseful Paul Pooley looked at him and then at Shapiro, he shrugged his shoulders as he said, "I don't know, I honestly don't know."

Part III

Max Shapiro was bewildered as he confided, "We really don't have much of a case Gunny unless there's something you haven't told me. All I can do is enter a plea of temporary insanity for you as a result of Lillian's death. If you will show some remorse, we can appeal to the court for leniency."

Paul was incensed as he retorted, "Don't you dare enter a plea of insanity on my behalf! If you did that and you were successful, my Marine Corps career would be finished forever. I'd never get reinstated with insanity on my record. I didn't think I'd have to bring this up Lieutenant but you need to know that the Marine Corps is my life, it's not a job or a career, it's my life. I don't have anything else and now with Lillian gone I don't even want anything else." The lieutenant sighed as he stated, "My job is to defend you to the very best of my ability. You sure aren't making it easy."

Back in the courtroom the trial dragged on and Paul Pooley could guess at the final outcome. He was going to lose this one; there was no doubt in his military mind. Mr. Shapiro was doing a very professional job, he was a fine lawyer; but the deck was stacked against him. Paul must accept whatever the Dragon of Destiny had in store for him.

Over the strong objection of Shapiro, Paul insisted on taking the stand in his own defense and was duly sworn; "You, Gunnery Sergeant Paul Pooley, do solemnly swear that the evidence you shall give in the case now before this court shall be the truth, the whole truth, and nothing but the truth, and that you will state everything within your knowledge in relation to the charges: So help you God." Paul responded," I do." He was then examined by the judge advocate: At the conclusion of the JAG's examination Paul Pooley made one of the most dramatic and important decisions of his life.

He knew it was all over for him; he was about to be convicted. He had to do something for himself and for his Marine Corps while he still had the opportunity to speak. He wanted them to know that he was still a Marine. When he had answered all of the questions asked of him, he suddenly turned to face his accusers, then, completely ignoring Watanabe, the interpreter, he spoke loudly and clearly in his best Japanese as he related exactly what had happened at the Kurihara's apartment. He placed special emphasis on the

fact that he was alone, there were two *Kempeitai* officers and the sequence of events occurred just as they themselves had testified. They were beaten up by him, a lone American emphasizing that he used no weapons but his hands to subdue the two, Paul hoped this would be sufficient to embarrass them and make them lose considerable face.

Pooley's testimony was strongly objected to by the Judge Advocate. Disregarding the Judge Advocate's objection for the moment the President of the Court demanded that Paul repeat his statement in English. Paul was glad to repeat it in English. He had accomplished what he had set out to do; he had embarrassed his accusers. Paul was pleased that an English translation of his statement was called for. Now everyone in the court would hear it and know that the mighty *Kempeitai* were not infallible.

Curse of the Enchanted City

The Fourth Marines Brig was situated in an unfriendly building in the Motor Transport Compound. The Marine Corps seemed to take a special delight in seeing that all of its Brigs were tough. Paul's erstwhile friend Gunnery Sergeant "Slug" Marvin was the Brig warden. The reputation of the old Shanghai Brig was known throughout the world as one of the toughest in the Corps.

Paul was relieved when the time finally came for him to leave the 4th Marines' Brig. He was transported in a US Navy grey Plymouth sedan with an MP driver and two military policemen. They drove slowly out of the compound and along Ferry Road, down Bubbling Well bound for Nanking Road and the Bund. As they turned into Bubbling Well one of the MPs said, "Corporal Andersen, look in your side-view mirror and tell me if it's my imagination or if that black car is following us." Andersen looked, then after a few moments answered, "Yeah Reed, it sure seems to be trying to stick close to us; turn left at the corner and drive around the block that will let us know for sure. Did you notice that the vehicle just happens to have Jap diplomatic plates?"

The MP corporal turned around to look at the prisoner in the back seat and exclaimed, "Wow Pooley, you sure must have done something

big to piss the Japs off this much. They must be following to be sure we really put you aboard ship and get you out of China." Pooley knew that the sedan was tailing them but was curious as to why they would use an official car. The *kempeitai* were usually very discreet in such matters. He could only surmise that it was intentional. They wanted to be sure he would see them. It would give that little SOB Takahashi an opportunity to gloat. Paul had somehow known that they would be there when he was deported. They wanted to be certain that his court martial was real, not a sham just for their benefit.

When the car stopped Reed got out first then opened the back door and beckoned to Pooley who promptly followed. Andersen slid out of the right rear seat and walked around the car to where Reed was detaining Pooley. Andersen quietly asked, "Let me have your right hand." He placed a handcuff on Pooley's right wrist and double locked it then he placed the other cuff on his own left wrist. Anderson asked, "Is it too tight Gunny?" Pooley answered, "Naw, its okay, but forget the gunny stuff, its private from now on."

The black sedan stopped a discrete distance away and two well-dressed Japanese men got out and walked to within a few yards of the landing. Pooley immediately recognized them and as he made eye contact with the grinning Takahashi, the elf-like Japanese *kempeitai* officer bowed mockingly. Pooley could not say or do anything. He was beaten and disgraced and Takahashi was the winner. As he boarded the lighter that was to take him out to the USS Chaumont, Paul thought to himself, "I really should have killed that little son-of a bitch when I had the chance."

The lighter plied through junks and sampans on the teeming river and came alongside the Chaumont's accommodation ladder. As they stepped onto the ship's deck Corporal Andersen addressed the OOD. "Sir! Permission to come aboard?" He and Private Reed saluted aft then inboard as the OOD returned their salutes and answered, "Permission granted." Pooley looked down in disgrace, he had never before boarded an American naval vessel without rendering the proper double salute but as a prisoner, he had lost the privilege of saluting.

Reed handed Corporal Andersen a manila envelope which he promptly gave to the Officer Of the Deck and remarked, “Sir, I was instructed to request that you read this as soon as we’ve turned the prisoner over to you.” The OOD signed a receipt for the prisoner and handed it to Corporal Andersen then the two MPs departed.

The O.D. instructed a boatswain’s mate 2nd class to take the prisoner across the quarterdeck and stand by with him for a few minutes until he could read the prisoner’s orders and decide what had to be done with him. When he finished reading, the OOD approached Pooley and stated, “You must have friends in high places.” An astonished Paul Pooley asked, “What do you mean Sir?” The OOD answered in an almost friendly manner, “Your period of confinement and the fine have both been suspended effective immediately but your reduction to private stands. While aboard you’ve got the run of the ship Marine.”

He was glad for the chance to be up on deck when the ship slipped her moorings and headed down river. He wanted to get a last long look at Shanghai before it was too late.

It was almost twilight when they passed His Imperial Japanese Majesty’s Ship Idzumo; flagship for the Imperial fleet in China. She mounted powerful guns and was the symbol of Japanese might in Shanghai. Paul watched the sailors moving about on deck making ready to fall-in for evening colors. He could hear the band playing as the sailors formed up smartly. Looking at the old ship and her crew and then at the Japanese naval Ensign he felt disgust. Paul Pooley had developed a great disdain for everything Japanese.

He didn’t know or care if he would ever see Shanghai again. So much was changing; Lillian was gone, war was inevitable and he was now a private. Even Shanghai had changed and it would never be the same. The Japanese were everywhere and he believed they would soon control the International Settlement. He would always cherish his memories of the old Shanghai that once had been.

The sky was darkening and he could see twinkling lights starting to come on all along the waterfront. More and more lights were added until all the buildings of the bund were aglow. This was Shanghai, it was the way

he would always remember it. They called it the "Pearl of the Orient" and it truly was a pearl; it was one of the world's great cities.

He watched the gentle wake trailing the ship as he contemplated Shanghai—the city that had broken his heart. His eyes were misty as he quietly muttered, "Sayonara Lillichan."

The dragon of destiny was waiting patiently as the great ship slowly wound its way through the Huangpu, entered the great Yangtze River and steamed out into the vast Yellow Sea bound for the United States and unknown adventures.

Soldiers of the Sea, Mare Island, California.

Part IV

Mare Island to Saipan

Crossing the Pacific Ocean was a long, slow voyage with port-calls in the Philippines, Guam and Pearl Harbor until finally the Navy transport steamed through the Golden Gate; entrance to the beautiful San Francisco Bay then turned northeast into the San Pablo Bay and cruised the twenty-two and a half miles up to Mare Island, Paul marveled at the unique twist of fate that had brought him here.

His conviction and sentencing had called for 6 months confinement in the US Naval Prison at Mare Island. The Commander in Chief, Asiatic Fleet had suspended his confinement but here he was aboard ship about to tie up at Mare Island where he was now to be stationed for duty as a Marine rather than to be confined as a prisoner.

Part IV

Paul Pooley was introduced to Sergeant Barstow, one of the squad leaders in the 2nd Guard Platoon, who showed him up to the squadbay that was to be his home.

Mare Island's famous old Marine Barracks was designed by a corporal in 1862 and built by the Marines who would be stationed there throughout the War Between the States as well as by future generations of Marines for nearly a century and a half thereafter.

Paul stowed his gear, drew his sheets and blankets and his 782 gear (field equipment) from the police sergeant, made up his bunk and made all necessary preparations to embark on his tour as a private in a traditional Marine barracks.

He, like all the new arrivals, was granted a three-day indoctrination period before standing his first watch. He learned the chain of command, every nook and cranny in the old barracks and as much as he could absorb of the US Naval Shipyard, Mare Island; the oldest US Navy base on the west coast. His indoctrination included a tour of the US Naval Prison, which Paul had a special interest in. He found it quite enlightening but depressing.

He took note of the shops and warehouses and the docking facilities and even the dry-docks and ammunition bunkers and the old-fashioned octagonal wood-frame bandstand located in the north end of Alden Park. The flagpole where Paul would stand many morning and evening color details is only a few yards north of the bandstand. Built in 1895, this structure was and is a prominent feature at Mare Island. Paul absorbed as much of the layout and geography of the Naval Shipyard and the Marine Barracks as time would permit and he felt fully capable of standing any of the posts.

Standing his first Guard Mount at the barracks was a new and interesting experience for Paul; he had often stood Commander of the Guard in Shanghai, but since leaving boot camp, years before, had rarely stood the duty as a sentry.

When falling out for Guard Mount, Paul could feel a certain amount of pride surging through him. He knew his appearance was up to and perhaps even surpassed Marine Corps standards. He had spitshined his cordovan

leather shoes and holster and his barracks cap visor to perfection. His flat-bottomed cotton khaki field scarf was properly tied and both ends matched perfectly. He had made certain that his winter service green trouser legs were wrapped tightly into his tan, canvass leggings and were neat and uniform. His M1911A1 Pistol was immaculate. He had studied the Special Orders for every post on the station and could recite the General Orders as though he had written them himself. He was ready.

As Paul fell-in he considered that this might be one of the very few places in the Marine Corps where formations of this type could be held inside. The huge enclosed barracks porch on the first deck was of sufficient size to hold a full company formation indoors.

Getting into formation, Paul briefly buffed the already mirror-like visor of his barracks cap. He marveled at the appearance of the other Marines. Knowing how much effort he had put into his own appearance when he considered it, he hadn't done much better than the others. They were all as close to perfection as any commander could wish.

This was the era of the professional private and the time of spit 'n polish. Marines were single and lived in barracks. The barracks were immaculate. All duties were performed in a professional manner and discipline was firm but fair. Paul Pooley considered that this was soldiering at its best. He could sense the pride and knew that all hands made a determined effort to meet the high standards expected of them.

Light marching packs were made up ready for inspection at all times and were affixed to the foot of each man's bunk. Marine green woolen blankets, which matched the men's' green uniforms were stretched tightly over each bunk and secured at the foot with hospital corners.

Later, on post, Paul had lots of time to reflect on his past. Walking a remote post around an old warehouse and rattling doors and checking locks did not present much of a challenge but Paul had been given another chance to be a Marine and he was determined to make the best of it. He would walk his post in a military manner and would perform all of his duties to the very best of his ability. His free time would be spent studying military subjects that would increase his value to the Corps.

Part IV

Thus far, Paul's Marine Corps career had been unusual. After completing boot camp he had been assigned to the brigade in Nicaragua where he spent his first two years as a Marine in the field.

He had done well in Nicaragua; having been slightly wounded, decorated and he had received accelerated promotion. Returning to the US as a corporal he was assigned to the Office of Naval Intelligence where he spent much of the next 5 Years in civilian clothes.

Now, with nearly 9 Years service, he was finally getting a chance to experience what most Marines do during their first couple of years in the Corps. The barracks routine was basically the same as it had been throughout the Corps down through many decades.

The Marines at Mare Island were generally assigned to the Marine Barracks or the U.S. Naval Prison. There was plenty of guard duty, military and field training and a reasonable amount of time off for study and for liberty.

The city of San Francisco was an ideal place for Marines to go on liberty but was nearly twenty-five miles away. Access from Vallejo was by bus to Oakland and then by ferryboat from Oakland to San Francisco. The trip was too time-consuming for a regular liberty so they spent their six-hour regular liberties in and around Vallejo and went to the city of San Francisco on weekends when liberty was from noon on Saturday until midnight on Sunday.

Vallejo, California was an old town on San Pablo Bay that had always been home to men who go down to the sea in ships. Georgia Street was unique indeed. Nowhere was it more evident that this town owed its livelihood to the US Navy than Georgia Street where many of the bars were named for battleships. One after another you could see bars sporting the name of a battleship like: California, Arizona, Utah, Oklahoma and most of the battlewagons of the Pacific Fleet. There may have been other towns like Vallejo somewhere, but Paul had not heard of them.

On a bleak Monday morning the Marines of the 2nd Guard Platoon were assembled in classroom number 3. Sergeant Barstow, the acting platoon sergeant, had designated Corporal Sweeney to give a class on the nomenclature and functioning of the M1917A1 water-cooled machinegun.

Sweeney was less than ten minutes into the class when he developed a serious nosebleed and had to leave the room.

Sergeant Barstow, noting that Sweeney's fieldscarf and khaki shirt were quickly saturated with blood, determined that Sweeney's nosebleed could be serious so he decided to accompany him to sickbay. Prior to leaving the classroom he directed, "Corporal Mulligan, get off your butt and take over for Sweeney and it better be a good class." It was obvious that from the way he spoke, Sergeant Barstow placed only a limited amount of confidence in Mulligan.

Paul had seen Mulligan in the squadbay and knew that he was an "old Corps Marine." He noticed at guard mount when Mulligan was wearing his green blouse that he had three service stripes. A corporal with over twelve years service was an indication that he'd had problems sometime in his career. Previously, Paul had little sympathy for such men, considering them a liability to the Corps. Until what had happened to him recently in Shanghai. His unfortunate court-martial and conviction changed his mind about such men. He felt certain empathy for and an attachment to them, knowing that any of them could truly be a victim of circumstances, as he believed himself to be.

Corporal Mulligan stood up and walked to the table on which sat a Water-cooled Browning machinegun. He looked at the men with an expression that could only have been embarrassment; as he asked, "Have any of you guys ever taught a class on this machinegun before? I think all of you know as much about it as I do." Then he glanced through the room at the Marines looking at him, one stood up and said, "I know some things about it Corporal maybe I can help" It was Private Pooley.

Paul walked to the front of the room and with complete confidence, repeated a class that he had given in Nicaragua, San Diego and China. He held the men's attention and was pleased at the quality of the questions they were asking. When Paul was ending the class and reminding the men of the salient points he had shown them and explaining the important things he wanted them to remember he noticed Sergeant Barstow sitting in the back of the class and not having seen him re-enter he wondered just how long the sergeant had been there listening.

Part IV

At 0145 on a rainy night Pooley was on Post #4. The rain had been intermittent with heavy clouds overhead. He had to be especially alert because of the darkness. Glad that the uniform of the day for the guard included the long woolen overcoat. He wished that the Marine Corps issued a better quality glove.

The leather of the gloves was satisfactory but the lining was of a poor quality cotton material. They should have been fleece-lined for warmth. His hands felt cold. Cold hands could be a serious impediment to accurate and effective marksmanship. Paul thought to himself, "Who am I kidding? I'll never have a need to fire my pistol on this post." Then he wondered, why are we even armed in a safe area like this?" He answered his own question when reality set in and he remembered that the United States would be at war with Japan in the near future. The American public may not have believed it but Paul and every Sailor and Marine that had served on the Asiatic Station recently was convinced. War with Japan was inevitable. The Japanese would prove to be a cunning and treacherous enemy.

At approximately 0200 Paul sensed, then heard, someone approaching. He took cover in a shadowy doorway until his visitor had passed. Now, behind his visitor and with his drawn pistol at the ready, he challenged, "Halt, who is there?" The dark form of a man immediately stopped, then he turned and answered in a loud voice, "Sergeant of the Guard, how the hell did you get behind me?" Paul answered, "Its my job to challenge all persons on or near my post. I didn't want to step out in front of you like a target. Just in case you were unfriendly, I wanted to be in a position to disarm or kill you." Sergeant Barstow replied, "You take your job pretty serious don't you Pooley?" You bet sergeant, that's what I get paid for."

Barstow said, "I heard what you did to the corporal of the guard a couple of hours ago, everybody back at the guardhouse is talking about it." Paul responded with, "Why didn't he keep his mouth shut, I would never have told on him? I just wanted to teach him a lesson that he wouldn't forget and that might save his life someday." Barstow answered, "Mulligan could never keep his mouth shut about anything."

At about 0030 when the Corporal of the Guard had checked posts he did so in a staff car. Pooley heard the car coming and stepped into the shad-

ows. When the staff car got to post #4 it stopped and the corporal got out to check the post and question the sentry. Paul stepped out of the shadows and surreptitiously removed the key from the ignition. The Corporal of the Guard was looking between two buildings for the sentry just as Paul called out, "Halt! Who is there?" The answer, "Corporal of the Guard!" Paul was standing behind the corporal as he said, "Turn around Corporal of the Guard and identify yourself." Corporal Mulligan questioned Pooley about his special orders and then began asking about his general orders. Finally, when Mulligan considered that he had sufficiently impressed Private Pooley with his thorough line of questioning, he turned and reentered the vehicle only to discover the key missing. He furtively searched the floorboards then his pockets and finally the muddy ground under and around the vehicle. When he thought enough time had elapsed, Private Pooley handed the key to the greatly relieved corporal with an explanation of what he had done and why.

Gunnery Sergeant O'Rourke was not an easy man to approach but Sergeant Barstow felt that this time it was important. He had a recommendation. "Gunny, you should sit in on some of the classes that new guy Pooley has been giving. He's really good." The gunny responded, "Yeah, so what? What do you want me to do take lessons from him?" Barstow replied, "No, I just think we ought to transfer him into training or someplace where he can do the most good." The gunny retorted, 'Yeah, transfer him into training, that would get him off the guard roster and he wouldn't have to stand the duty anymore. Don't let that goldbrick con you Barstow anyone can give a class. I've seen lots of phonies like him. He used to be a gunnery sergeant, he had it made, and then he showed his true colors, he couldn't handle success. He didn't just get busted all the way down to private, he had a general court martial and was convicted; he's had his chance and its not up to us to give him another. I'm warning you Barstow keep an eye on that guy and remember that I warned you he's bad news.

Sergeant Barstow took heed of the gunny's admonition but still considered Private Pooley an excellent instructor on military subjects and continued to make use of his expertise and even shared him with Platoon Sergeant Mc Graw of the 1st Guard Platoon.

Part IV

Gunnery Sergeant Robert O'Rourke was beside himself; he didn't like Private Pooley giving classes to a platoon he didn't even belong to. He sent word for Sergeant Barstow and Platoon Sergeant Mc Graw to meet with him in the Guard Company office, where he addressed them in no uncertain terms. "Look you two I don't know what this "brig rat" Pooley has got on you guys but I'm going to make certain he gets what's coming to him. You guys are trying to make some sort of a hero out of him, and as I told you before Barstow" The gunny looked directly at Barstow sticking out his index finger and shaking it in Sergeant Barstow's face, "He's nothin' but bad news!"

Platoon Sergeant Mc Graw spoke up, "Gunny, I don't know what you've got against Pooley, but he impresses me as one of the most professional Marines I've run into in a long time." The gunny shot back, "Okay Mc Graw, just ask Barstow about him, I told him what I thought of this guy a few days ago. In the meantime, you'd both better start having your NCO's conduct their own training classes because your "fair haired" boy Pooley may be off the skyline for a while. The Top has asked me to recommend four men from the company for mess duty next month and you can bet your bottom dollar that Pooley's name will be at the head of the list. That's the worst job I can think of for him right now but I'll think of something worse before his month of mess duty is up. Now you guys get back to work and don't let me hear anything else about how great your pet brig rat is."

First Sergeant Gregory Miller didn't miss much that went on in his company. While the company gunnery sergeant was counseling the two platoon sergeants, Miller seemed to be busily engaged in reading through the mounds of papers on his desk. He was actually listening and wondering what the real rational was behind the gunnery sergeant's serious dislike for Private Pooley. He was also very curious why the two NCO's thought Pooley was so competent.

PFC Milliken entered the squadbay and walked up to Pooley's bunk. Paul stopped spitshining his shoes long enough to look up and ask, "What's up Milliken, what can I do for you?" The PFC answered, "Pooley, I understand the gunny's really pissed at you, what did you ever do to him?" Paul

replied, “I really wish I could tell you Milliken but I can’t. I’ve never even had a real conversation with him. He just doesn’t like me. It’s my looks I guess. Why do you ask?” Milliken answered, “I was just down in the Guard Company office and the First Sergeant asked me to come up and tell you he wants to see you. I hope he’s not out to get you too.” Paul answered, well we’ll soon find out I guess. He promptly stood up and started for the office.

Paul reported to the first sergeant and immediately noticed an open Service Record Book on his desk. The first sergeant looked up and asked, “Pooley, I’ve sent for you because I don’t want any problems in the company. What’s up between you and Gunnery Sergeant O’Rourke?” Paul responded, “I wish I could tell you Top but honestly I don’t know. The man just doesn’t like me that’s all. To find out why, you’ll have to ask him.”

Miller said, “I’ve been looking through your service records Pooley and I find what I see here very interesting. How did a man with a record like yours wind up with a general court martial?” Looking directly at him, Paul said, “I screwed up big-time Top. I kicked the crap out of a couple of Jap secret police officers and I guess it was an embarrassment to the State Department. They had to court-martial me. I was guilty. “Basically, that’s all there is to it. The Marine Corps did all they could to help me; you may notice that they vacated the 6 months confinement and the loss of pay for 6 months. The only thing they let stand was the reduction to private. I couldn’t ask for a better break than that.” Miller looked at Paul and said, “Pooley, I don’t trust the Japs. I’m sorry you got busted but if you had to fight someone, I’m glad they were Japs. I really think we are going to have to go to war against Japan.” Paul responded, “Yeah Top, from all I’ve seen, I’d bet a year’s pay we’ll be at war with them before long.”

Miller asked Pooley, “How long has it been since you had mess duty? Paul responded, “I’ve never been on mess duty Top, why do you ask?” Miller answered, “Well, your name has been submitted as someone eligible and recommended for mess duty starting next month. How do you feel about it?” Paul answered, “Top, “I’m a Marine, I’ll serve wherever I’m needed. I’ve never had mess duty so I guess it’s about time. I have no objections.” Miller grinned and said, “Okay, not many people volunteer for mess duty but somebody has to do it. In your case, I think it may actually be a good thing. It would get you off the skyline for thirty days and that means Gunny O'Rourke will have to find someone else to kick around for a while. What do you think of that?"

"I sure as hell wouldn't want to create the impression that I'm going on mess duty just to get away from him! That would make me look like a coward. It would be better to stay right where I am and prove myself." First Sergeant Gregory Miller looked at Paul and said, "You already have proven yourself Pooley. I believe in you. I'm going to assign you to mess duty because I don't want anything to happen to you. If O'Rourke pushes you too far, I don't want you to retaliate by kicking the crap out of him. Even if you should be not guilty, it would be hard to defend you with a general court on your record."

Reveille for cooks and Messmen was at 0400. They started work early and generally worked until late. On Pooley's second day of mess duty, the chief messman pulled him aside and asked if he'd ever worked in a mess hall before. Answering in the negative, he was asked if he could type and if he was a high school graduate. Surprised, Paul said he could and he was. The chief messman said to come along; he was taking Pooley to see the mess sergeant.

The crusty old mess sergeant, a veteran of the World War, was a product of the old school. He ran a good mess as far as the men were concerned but left much to be desired when it came to the new administrative system that the Navy had forced on him. During the past three months, he had tried various young cooks in the office, but none seemed to like it or want to understand it. They all wanted to do their jobs as cooks and bakers, not work in an office. Mess Sergeant Emil Rasmussen was reaching the point of desperation. He knew that the big Inspector General's inspection was only a little more than two months away and that his records were in a shambles. He needed help.

Paul Pooley attacked the mounds of paper with a vengeance. He set up the records in accordance with the Navy Mess Management System and studying all documents for the past year, he purged those that were not needed and filed all others where they could be rapidly accessed. He was

able to streamline the system of orders and inventories and teach the new system to all who had a need to know. Even though officially on mess duty, after the first week, he worked normal hours in the mess office. Starting at 0600 Paul was told by a grateful Mess Sergeant to secure early whenever he wished, as long as he was on top of the paperwork.

First Sergeant Gregory Miller encountered Emil Rasmussen, the barracks mess sergeant at the mailroom and after casually passing the time of day the Top asked how the new crop of messmen from his company was doing. Rasmussen assured the Top that they were all good workers and were doing just fine. The Top was mildly curious so he thought he would ask specifically about Private Pooley. Rasmussen recoiled with obvious concern, "Pooley! Is he one of yours Greg? I didn't realize he was from the Guard Company. I'm glad you brought him up, we're going to have to get together soon and talk about how I can get him transferred into the mess field." Miller queried, "Is that what he wants Emil?" Rasmussen responded, "I Don't know Greg, honestly I've never asked him about it, but we sure need him and I hope we can get you to leave him on mess duty for an extra thirty days. That will bring us almost up to the I.G. inspection He's really been a big help to us."

This was just the opening First Sergeant Miller had been waiting for. He responded, "Oh I don't know about that Emil, I don't recommend anyone for mess duty, that's the company gunnery sergeant's job, he and the platoon sergeants make those recommendations, I just write the orders. You had better talk to Gunny O'Rourke about Pooley." Rasmussen quickly responded, "Okay Greg, I sure will, I'll see O'Rourke as soon as I can and let him know how bad we need Pooley." First Sergeant Gregory Miller could hardly contain himself. Inwardly smiling, he was pleased and decided that he should come to the mailroom himself on a more regular basis instead of sending the company clerk or a runner. O'Rourke was going to have a blue fit over this. O'Rourke's idea of punishing Pooley by putting him on mess duty was not working out quite the way he had expected.

While assigned to the mess hall, Paul found himself with Saturdays and Sundays off, compliments of a grateful, Mess Sergeant Emil Rasmussen. It

was an ideal opportunity to visit the city of San Francisco. From Mare Island, Paul walked into Vallejo to the bus station where he caught a bus to Oakland. From Oakland he caught a ferryboat across the bay to the city. The ferry moved across the bay slowly but Paul didn't mind as there was much to see and the whole trip was a pleasant interlude. The alternative was much faster but considerably more expensive.

Paul actually enjoyed the boat trip. He was impressed by all the activity going on in the bay. Yerba Buena Island was ablaze with activity; as was the flat island being dredged up and created from the bay that was to be the location of the 1939 San Francisco World's Fair. It was to be called Treasure Island.

The new San Francisco Oakland Bay Bridge had been open since November of 1936 and would have been many times faster for anyone having a car. The price had been reduced from the original sixty-five cents to fifty cents each way, still a bit pricey for a private making less than twenty-one dollars per month. Pooley determined that he would go across the bridge sooner or later. It was the longest bridge in the world and Paul thought it was a beautiful sight to behold. Nine million people are said to have crossed the bridge during the first twelve months it was open. If this trend continued, the bridge would be fully paid for in just a few years and the government could fulfill its promise to the people to eliminate the fare entirely.

Paul noticed from the ferry that there was an active causeway going from the Bay Bridge to Yerba Buena Island and another from Yerba Buena to the new flat island they were dredging up from the bay. He thought this was perhaps the most remarkable thing he'd ever seen. The huge new island was entirely man-made. Trucks were moving everywhere and construction for the World's Fair was well underway. When the boat got to the Ferry Building at San Francisco, it moved slowly into the slip to tie up, the wooden pilings creaked and groaned until finally all forward movement stopped with a thud. Heavy lines were thrown onto the dock and made fast and the passengers stepped off into the Ferry Building, a bustling and exciting place with much activity and throngs of people, especially sailors. Paul stepped out of the Ferry Building into the sunlight of downtown San Francisco, he

was faced with a choice of getting on any number of trolley cars each of which he could ride to the end of the line for a nickel or he could start walking up Market Street. It wasn't Nanking Road, but it was a big and very interesting street. He opted to walk and as he did so memories of that other great city far across the sea came flooding back to him. Paul walked a few blocks up Market Street then turned to his right. As he looked northwest, he noted what appeared to be a pagoda style building. Chinatown! Fate had directed him to Chinatown.

He had heard about San Francisco's Chinatown for years but had never actually been there before. It was world famous. Now that he was approaching it he was exhilarated and looked forward to comparing it with the cities of China. He entered several shops and found much of the same merchandise that he had seen in Shanghai but at greatly inflated prices. He enjoyed chatting with the shopkeepers and noted that Cantonese was the dialect of choice here. Before leaving Chinatown he wound up having a sumptuous Chinese dinner that he would have enjoyed far more if he'd had someone to share it with and had not been dining alone.

Paul walked back down Market Street to catch a ferryboat back to Oakland. Stopping along the way for a couple of drinks he attempted to make small talk with the locals. Paul got the impression that other than the San Francisco Seals baseball season, all the people wanted to talk about was the upcoming World's Fair. He mentioned his feelings about the inevitability of the United States going to war with Japan and found the people to be ambivalent. They simply had no interest in war or what Japan may be planning. One bartender did mention that he thought it incredible that Paul should think that a little backward country like Japan would ever consider going to war with a world leader like the United States. The subject was promptly changed.

Back at the Marine Barracks on Mare Island, Paul looked forward to the next weekend when he planned to again visit San Francisco. In the meantime, he applied himself diligently to training the cooks and bakers in the effective use of the new Navy Mess Management system. He found that as daunting as the job had seemed at first, once the files were purged of

years of unnecessary papers and the ones that were current and important were properly filed for ready access, the system was fairly simple for nearly anyone to use and helped in facilitating inventories and requisitions. In the eyes of the old mess sergeant and his senior mess personnel, Private Pooley was a hero.

The weekend was rapidly approaching and Paul was planning his return trip to San Francisco. Technical Sergeant Manning had just placed a stack of receipts for rations on the desk in front of him and commented that the Marine Corps was rapidly going to hell. "In the old Corps we requisitioned the rations we needed to prepare the meals for the monthly menus the Navy published. Once we received the chow, we stored it. On the appropriate days, we prepared and served it. That was it, a minimum of paperwork and good chow properly prepared to keep the troops happy. Now, they want us to do all this paperwork and there doesn't seem to be any real need for it. It sure wasn't like this in, "the old Corps."

Paul responded, "Sergeant Manning, I hope you'll share your thoughts with the inspection team when they get here. The new system does allow them to look back at any previous month or week within that month select a specific day, find out how much food was consumed on that day for each meal and checking with the Navy master menu for that date ascertain that the correct meals were prepared and precisely what the cost was per man depending on exactly how many men were aboard for chow during each of those meals. Of course, to be sure your figures are accurate, you've got to check the muster role for that date, the sick list and the liberty list and deduct any missing men from the total number fed before you can come up with a really accurate cost per man, per meal. A breakfast that costs the messall forty-two cents one day may only cost thirty-nine cents the next day. Then to really complicate things we'll have to keep up with the cost to the Navy Supply Department of each product. As you know, the cost of various foods is in a continuous state of flux. It can, and often does, go up or down overnight.

"It's a wonderful thing to be able to come up with such accurate figures whenever they're called for. I'm just wondering how we can sustain this new system. It will take at least one man in every mess in the Marine Corps and

the Navy and that man will have to do his job full-time, if he should be on the rifle range for two weeks or on leave or gone for any other reason for more than just a few days the whole system could fall apart. I'm sure as hell glad that I'm not in the mess field. I hate to say this Sergeant but I have a feeling that if someone doesn't make some serious changes right away there is going to be an epidemic of courts-martial among mess sergeants."

While Pooley and Manning were talking, Mess Sergeant Emil Rasmussen entered the office. He leaned against the doorjamb and looked pale and drawn. It was obvious that Rasmussen was ill. Manning asked, "What's the matter Emil? You look like hell." Rasmussen answered, "I may only look like hell Manning but let me tell you, I feel a lot worse than that. How'd you like to be in my shoes? I've been cooking in this Marine Corps since 1918 and I've had a good reputation. The men have always liked my food but now, I can't do my job. They don't give a damn about my food, only the paper work. It sure as hell wasn't like this back in, "the old Corps."

Pooley reassured the old man that the system and all the files would be up to date and correct and that he would teach it all to anyone willing to learn before his thirty days of mess duty was up. Rasmussen said," "Damn! I like the Marine Corps, it was always my intention to stay in for thirty years but now that feeling is gone I'm glad I've got my twenty in."

Paul said, "Look dammit, we're all acting like fools about this. You're going to be in great shape for the inspection and when it is over, just continue doing your jobs as you've always done them in the past. Sergeant Rasmussen, you've got a reputation for being one of the best mess sergeants in the Corps. Don't give up!" Pooley knew that all they would need is someone to keep the files up to date; a simple task. The other complexities of the system would not present a problem since no one would be following them. They served no useful purpose other than creating more paperwork.

Rasmussen sat down at his desk, wiping his brow and said, "I'll sure be glad when this damned inspection is over." Manning looked at the mess sergeant and, changing the subject, asked, "You going into the city this weekend Emil?" Rasmussen answered, "Hell no, I'm staying right here, I'll go to the Chiefs' Club or find a nice quiet little neighborhood bar in Vallejo and

forget all about messhalls and inspections. Why'd you ask?" Manning answered, "Well three of us are going in and we still need one more man to fill Dutch's Pontiac. How about you Pooley, do you want a ride into Frisco on Saturday? It'll only cost you a buck." Paul's response was immediate, "Sure Sergeant, I'll be glad to help you out."

Paul was delighted. He had been looking forward to riding across the Bay Bridge and now, here was his opportunity. Riding with other Marines for just a dollar was even cheaper than taking the bus and the ferry. He would try to negotiate a return trip with Dutch, whoever he turned out to be.

Paul met Technical Sergeant Manning at the time and place prescribed on Saturday. Dutch, the owner of the car, turned out to be a gunnery sergeant assigned to the Naval prison. The other passenger was a boatswain's mate first class called "Sails," who apparently worked with Dutch at the Naval prison, which they kept referring to as "old 84."

Paul, self conscious at first about being a private in the company of three seniors, was soon relaxed and enjoying the company of Manning, Dutch and Sails who all turned out to be friendly and had either forgotten about, or didn't care about, his lack of rank. Dutch dropped Paul off at a location on Market Street convenient for him to catch a streetcar to wherever he wished to go after admonishing him to be at the same location Sunday evening at exactly eight o'clock in order to ride back with them. Giving Paul a friendly reminder that the return trip would cost him another buck. After all, as Dutch explained, the toll on the bridge was fifty cents and gasoline was twenty-three cents a gallon. It was expensive to drive a car these days. Paul agreed to meet them at the time and place prescribed.

He stood for a moment, a complete stranger in a big, wonderful city filled with strangers. He knew he could walk in any direction and find things to interest him but he opted to go to the local Japanese community. He remembered Lillian talking about her Nisei friends in San Francisco and how she had attended the Pine Methodist Church with them.

San Francisco's Japanese community was certainly not as large as the Little Tokyo area he remembered in Los Angeles. He entered several modest shops and stores many of them selling similar inexpensive souvenirs and

toys all made in Japan. But he could sense them staring when they thought he would not notice

He went into a little Japanese restaurant and immediately realized that he was the central attraction. The patrons and workers tried to seem unconcerned as they looked at him curiously whenever they thought he was not looking. A couple of young girls were giggling and hiding their faces behind their hands in typical Japanese style. He felt like the main attraction in a sideshow. It was obvious to Paul that very few customers patronized this place that were not Japanese. He had a choice; he could opt to get up and leave, he could remain and dine like a curious tourist or he could really give the people something to talk about. He decided on the latter.

He asked for a menu. It was crudely typed in English on one side and written in *kanji* on the other. The Isei man who handed the menu to him did so with the Japanese side up, as though by accident, then quickly retrieved it and handed it back with a smile, English side up. Paul promptly turned it back over and read from the Japanese side. He was amused as he glanced out of the corner of his eye and noted that some very curious people were watching him. He made a point of using expressions and movements that were typically Japanese.

Having finished his meal, Paul ordered a bottle of beer and was told that they had no alcoholic beverages. He asked if there was a place nearby where he could get a cold beer. A Nisei man about Paul's age introduced himself as Hiro Yamaguchi and said there was a typical Japanese bar right around the corner and in a friendly manner offered to walk there with Paul. They entered the Fuji Cafe, which only had four tables beside the six seats at the bar. It reminded Paul very much of some of the little bars he'd seen in Japan and in the Japanese neighborhood in Shanghai. Hiro sat down with him and they ordered a couple of bottles of beer; Golden Glow Beer, which was a local San Francisco brew. Imported Japanese beer was not available and would have been too expensive if it had been available.

Paul told Hiro and a group of other Nisei's who had drifted in and joined them about the "Worlds Fair" in Nagoya that he had visited. That started them all talking about the upcoming World's Fair in San Francisco.

Part IV

None of them had ever been to a World's Fair before and they were really looking forward to having one right here in their hometown. They mentioned that they, and especially their parents, were very proud that one of the features of the Fair was to be the Japanese Pavilion. All the materials used in constructing it were being brought over from Japan.

Paul noticed a strange phenomenon. The Nisei that sat with him and Hiro all spoke English to one another. At the next table were four Isei who frequently joined in the conversation, but always in Japanese. As the evening progressed, he learned that nearly all the local families were originally from Kumamoto or Fukuoka Ken. The conversation became much more animated and certainly the Isei seemed more interested and pleased after learning that Paul had been to Kumamoto; had visited the ancient Kumamoto Castle and the famous Suizenji Park and Mount Aso Yama.

As time passed, Paul understood clearly that the Isei had all come to the United States for the same reason. Their objectives were to make a better life for their families and they were willing to sacrifice and work endless hours to do so. One truth Paul could not overlook was that the Isei loved their new country but they were proud of the land of their birth and of their ancestry. They were hopelessly and irrevocably Japanese. The Nisei, on the other hand, were Americans of Japanese decent. They tolerated and respected the Isei but seemed to embrace all things American. Paul thought of his Lillian, she was a paradox, she wanted to be American and said so but she too had been hopelessly and irrevocably Japanese.

Paul wondered with some concern what was going to happen to these two generations and what their relationships would become when the great war that he felt was inevitable finally descended upon them? During their conversation, the prospect of the impending war was never mentioned.

Paul asked about the Pine Methodist Church and the Japanese Tea Garden in Golden Gate Park and learned that the church was only two blocks from where they were, on Pine Street. He would attend services there in the morning before going out to the Golden Gate Park.

It was a beautiful Sunday morning and Paul had no trouble finding the church. He was greeted in a courteous and hospitable manner and noticed

that most of the attendees were in family groups and were there to worship not to engage in conversation with the *hakujin* stranger in their midst. There were two services, the early one in Japanese for the Isei and the later service in English for the Nisei. As he looked at the congregation, he wondered who among them had known and befriended his Lillian.

It was early in the afternoon when he entered Golden Gate Park near the panhandle at Stanyan and Fell Streets and walked westward. It was a perfect day for a walk lots of clean air and sunshine. Paul enjoyed walking in the park. The Japanese Tea Garden wasn't too far by Marine Corps standards, not much over a couple of miles.

Once there, Paul was impressed, he could see why Lillian loved this place so much. He believed it to be even more beautiful and picturesque than the tea garden in Jessfield Park in Shanghai. It certainly brought back memories of his trips to Japan. Strolling through the grounds of the tea garden, he was in a world all to himself and was oblivious to the other visitors.

Paul stopped half way over an arched bridge and leaning on the railing at the top and looking out at the beautiful scene around him, Paul remembered the words of the old fortuneteller in Nantao, Chang Wu, just as clearly as though Wu was right here beside him. "My dear Master Poo-Lee, always remember, we don't come here to stay, we come here to go. Missy Lillian has gone; you are here. Do what it is that you were sent here to do, fulfill your karma. Then perhaps someday, somewhere you will rejoin her. There are few gifts more precious than pleasant memories of a loved one,"

Paul wondered to himself, as he had done many times since Lillian's death and his court-martial, what the hell was his karma? What is it that he was sent here to do?

Walking back toward the panhandle, Paul felt as though he had turned another page in the book of life. He had seen Chinatown and had been to Lillian's church. He had visited with and spoken to the local Japanese people he had gone to the tea garden in the park and he had been haunted by the words of Chang Wu. Now, it was over, no more memories, he was through torturing himself. Lillian was dead and so was his past. He was still a Marine, which is what he wanted; he had started his life over and could not

allow memories of the past to interfere. He would meet with Dutch at 2000 for transportation back to the barracks and he would concentrate all of his future efforts on being a good Marine.

He felt almost apologetic reminding the mess sergeant that his time on mess duty would be up in just one more week. It was not what Master Sergeant Rasmussen wanted to hear. Rasmussen would see the Guard Company gunnery sergeant and attempt to negotiate an additional thirty days for Pooley. Gunnery Sergeant Robert O'Rourke listened to the mess sergeant in disbelief. How could this fine old staff NCO be taken in so completely by a bum like Pooley? He tried to explain to Rasmussen that Pooley was just a brig rat and that he had been tried by a general court-martial and convicted.

Master Sergeant Rasmussen didn't give a damn what Pooley had done before, he knew what he was doing now and that he was saving him and his mess hall from a very embarrassing situation. O'Rourke would have nothing to do with Rasmussen's plan. Every Marine private and private first class was eligible for thirty days of mess duty per year that was all. Pooley would have served his thirty days and needed to be back to his regular duties as a member of Guard Company. O'Rourke promised Rasmussen that his new messmen for the following month would all be good Marines and he could select one of them to be Pooley's replacement.

Paul felt that his thirty days on mess duty had been a vacation. He could not have had a luckier assignment, but now it was over and he would be returning to his regular duties and once again would be in the clutches of Gunny O'Rourke.

He went to the first sergeant's office to check back in from mess duty. First Sergeant Miller sent the company clerk out to the mailroom leaving him alone with Pooley. "Pooley, I understand from Master Sergeant Rasmussen that you did a really good job for him. In fact, he even tried to get you extended for an additional thirty days." Paul answered, "Thanks First Sergeant, I'm glad to be back and I look forward to getting to work here in the company."

Miller responded, "Pooley, I hate to see you thrown to the wolves. The gunny can hardly wait to get you back and you know how he feels about

you. I've been waiting to talk to you about the prison it may be your way out. I've got a requisition here to detach two of our Marines from Guard Company for duty with the Naval Prison Detachment. He couldn't touch you if you were over there."

Paul looked at the first sergeant with great concern as he said, "Top, I really appreciate what you are trying to do for me but there is something I absolutely have to say to you. I screwed up once and got court-martialed, you've seen my records, you know all about it. I did something that was legally wrong so I got convicted. The Marine Corps did me a big favor and suspended as much of my sentence as they could. I know that if I make one mistake, if I break the rules just one time, the suspension will automatically be vacated and I will be sent to prison for six months and I will sustain a loss of pay for six months. That is not what I'd like to see happen

"I've been walking on egg shells, I'm damned near afraid to spit on the sidewalk. They can lock me up for almost anything; so running into a character like Gunny O'Rourke that is senior to me and doesn't like me is like playing Russian roulette. The way I look at it, every move I make is a big gamble. I need to get away from this guy because he is very dangerous but, and this is the part I hope you will understand, of all the assignments I could be given there is only one that scares the hell out of me." Paul looked into the first sergeant's eyes as though pleading as he said, "I'm scared to death of the Naval Prison. You have to understand that, for the grace of God, I'd be a prisoner in there right now. If I were stationed there as a guard, I couldn't handle it. Every prisoner I met would remind me of myself and of how unfair life can be sometimes. I appreciate your help, but please Top, don't send me there." First Sergeant Miller looked at Private Pooley and felt a surge of compassion, he understood. "Okay Pooley, I'll do what I can for you but right now, you'll really have to watch out. You're on your own. Report to your platoon sergeant for duty." Paul drew his 782 gear and linen and made up his bunk in the squadbay

Sergeant Barstow the platoon sergeant, and Sergeant Lloyd, Pooley's squad leader said they wanted to talk to him outside. Leaving the barracks they walked over to the octagonal bandstand behind the flagpole in Alden

Park. Sergeant Lloyd told Pooley that he was glad to have him back in the squad. Barstow wanted to warn Paul to be careful of everything he did. He had heard that the mess sergeant had talked to O'Rourke about Pooley and told O'Rourke that Pooley was a good man and had done an exceptional job for him. That was not what O'Rourke had wanted to hear.

Barstow reminded Paul that O'Rourke was a vindictive SOB and he had no idea why O'Rourke wanted to take out all of his hatred on Paul. Paul looked at the sergeants and said, "Look, you two are sergeants and I'm just a private but I've been in the Corps quite a while now and I've seen characters like O'Rourke before. Usually, they are on the other side of the law, apparently he is not. He is really looking out for the good of the Corps and he thinks that anyone convicted by a general court-martial has got to be bad. He can't trust me and he probably never will. It's really frustrating because he probably has no idea what I was even charged with. You two have to be careful, if you show me any friendship or favoritism, he may turn on you and you don't need that. Remember, he may be nuts but he means well. I'll just keep doing my job to the very best of my ability and you two need to treat me just like you would any other private."

Sergeant Lloyd offered Pooley a cigarette then sat back and briefed him on the squad's activities during the last thirty days. He also reminded him that their squad had the duty the following night. Paul said he was ready for it. The two sergeants started walking back to the barracks and Paul went to the Navy Exchange before returning.

It took no time for Paul to get back into the barracks routine. After the second day it was as though he'd never been gone. The duty and military training classes went on as usual interspersed with parades, reviews and ceremonies. Liberties were spent in Vallejo and were of brief duration; Paul found no reason to return to San Francisco.

First Sergeant Miller noted with some concern that Private Pooley's name appeared with some frequency on working parties and special details. O'Rourke continued as the company gunnery sergeant and managed to sustain his reputation as a strict disciplinarian. The first sergeant looked forward to the gunny receiving orders before any serious problems devel-

oped but knew the gunny was not due for orders for nearly a year. Miller considered Private Pooley to be a good Marine; one of his best in fact and he wasn't eager to lose him but he knew Pooley was making a supreme effort to do his job and have minimum contact with Gunnery Sergeant O'Rourke but sooner or later they would clash and the end result was obvious, O'Rourke was senior.

First Sergeant Miller had arrived at a decision, which was not what he wanted for Guard Company, but he believed it would be good for the Marine Corps. He had found a way to salvage Private Paul Pooley. He saw Sergeant Lloyd in the passageway and asked him to send Pooley to the company office when he got off post.

"Private Pooley reporting as ordered First Sergeant." Miller looked up from the papers in front of him and acknowledged him by saying, "Oh Pooley, come in and sit down." Paul wondered what was going on, the first sergeant had never invited him to sit down before. Miller spoke up with, "I've got a little problem on my hands and I just wanted to know if you might know someone who can help me?" Skeptical, Pooley answered, "What is it Top, How can I help you?" Miller said, "Well, as you know, the Sea School Company is right here at Mare Island and from time to time when they have new classes starting up, the barracks is tasked with providing men to fill them out. They've got a class starting up next week, but still need four men. They've asked the barracks to provide one of the four. Do you know of anyone who would like to go through Sea School and then pick up a ship? It's a two-year tour of duty." Paul responded with a positive, "I sure do Top, I'd be glad to volunteer for sea duty myself."

"Well, okay Pooley I had hoped you would. Now I won't have to draft up a notice to put on the bulletin board asking for a volunteer. I'll have your orders ready for you anytime Thursday. You can checkout Friday morning and you'll have to move into the transient squadbay for a couple of days until the next class is ready to convene and then they'll have you move into the Sea School barracks."

Paul spoke up, "Thank you Top, I know you've done everything you could to help me and I really appreciate it. I'm looking forward to Sea School

and I guarantee I won't let you down." Paul stood up and turned to leave just as Gunnery Sergeant Robert O'Rourke entered the office. Paul heard the company clerk say, "Morning Gunny," and the answer "Hi Ya Pinky," then, as O'Rourke noticed Pooley he asked, "What's he doin' in here? Is Pooley in trouble again?" It was the first sergeant's turn to speak up as he said, "No Gunny, he's not in trouble but we do have good news for you, Pooley has been transferred, and you're finally getting rid of him." "I'm sure glad to hear that Top. I've always known that brig rat was a trouble maker and I was afraid he was gonna cause problems in Guard Company."

Checking out of Guard Company and into the transient squadbay was accomplished with little effort and Paul found that he was free to go on liberty or do as he wished until the following Monday. He decided to stay close by so he went into Vallejo for a few hours.

On Monday morning Paul presented his orders to a corporal at the Sea School Company Office and was processed aboard and given the opportunity to move into the Sea School Barracks, which he did. The corporal, whose name was "Zeke" Zimmerman, was a gregarious character who seemed eager to have someone to talk to. Zeke explained that the captain who ran the school and most of the NCO's were off on leave.

Paul was curious and asked Zeke if there weren't any Marines from the Sea School staff aboard besides him. He replied, "Yeah, old Wilson is here, he's acting police sergeant. Right now he's out in the Navy yard scrounging some stuff. The rest of the guys are taking advantage of the slack time. In one more week, this place will be busy as a beehive. The staff will get very little time off once we start the next class, your class." Paul looked surprised as he asked, "Wow, is the school that intense?"

Zeke answered, "Naw its not a bad school it's just that there's a lot going on all the time. You'll be firing on the range part of the time and you'll have a lot of classroom work on shipboard subjects and you'll be out at sea for gunnery practice then you'll probably get more close order drill than you got in boot camp. It's really a good school, you'll like it but once it starts you're on the go all the time." Paul responded with, "It sounds pretty intense to me Zeke." Zeke asked, "What are you doing tonight? Maybe we could

go out for a couple of beers and I could tell you all about it. Wilson will be back soon and I can take off anytime after 1630."

Paul thought it might be worthwhile but mentioned that now that he was aboard but not fully checked in; he did not have a liberty card. Zeke promptly took a blank liberty card from the desk, placed it in the typewriter and proceeded to fill it out. He reached into a desk drawer and took out a rubber facsimile stamp bearing Captain Nelson D. Jones's signature. When he handed the card to Paul he said, "Here, I handle the liberty cards for the whole school."

The fleet was out at sea and it was a reasonably quiet weeknight. There was little activity in the Oklahoma Bar or anywhere on Georgia Street; the two Marines had been sitting in a small booth for the last couple of hours and Zeke had given Paul a fairly thorough description of the curriculum of the Sea School and he had promised to give him a copy of the latest Bluejackets' Manual the following morning; it was used extensively in the school.

During the past few minutes they had become aware of a four-way heated discussion going on at the far end of the bar. The other patrons had been trying to ignore it but it started becoming quite animated and was annoying. Zeke and Paul heard the Marines mentioned repeatedly in disparaging terms. Obviously this disagreement had the potential to explode into a full-blown barroom brawl.

Paul Pooley suddenly reached across the table and grasped Zimmerman's arm. Looking him squarely in the eye he said, "Look Zeke, I don't know you very well and you don't know me either but we're both Marines and I know that means something to you. I'm a two-hashmark private so you know I've screwed up. If I get into any kind of trouble I'm going to be sent to prison to serve out a suspended sentence, so I've really got to be careful. Do what I tell you now and do it fast! If that damned fool Marine starts swinging the other three guys will beat the hell out of him and he'll either wake up in the hospital or the brig.

"That opening just beyond the end of the bar goes to a little dark hallway where there are three doors, the men's' head, the women's' head and the alley, that's where I'll be headed for. I want you to quietly go out the front

door and get a cab. Do it quickly, as though your life depended on it. Open the cab door and hold it open 'till we get there. Tell the cabbie that we're going to the Marine Barracks on Mare Island and there will be a good tip in it for him.

"I'm going to make my move in just about a minute and you be sure and do what I've told you. When I move toward the back, you go out the front." The worst thing Paul could think of was just about to happen and it did. The drunk Marine started to swing. The bartender was dialing the phone; there was little question who he was calling, it had to be the police, the Shore Patrol or both.

Paul Pooley ran the length of the bar, picking up speed as he moved. By the time he reached the four troublemakers, they were all swinging. Two of the customers from the bar were now involved and were trying vainly to separate the combatants. Paul grabbed the Marine and shoved him toward the door and then, helped by considerable momentum, nearly carried him out the alley door. Grabbing him by the arm Paul pulled and dragged him through the little alley beside the Oklahoma Bar 'till they reached the sidewalk on Georgia Street where he threw him into the waiting cab.

Paul directed the cab driver to take them to the Marine Barracks and handing him a wad of bills said, "This should be enough to help you forget where you dropped us." The driver stopped briefly at the main gate where ID and Liberty Cards were shown, he then proceeded to the Marine Barracks. When they had gotten out of the cab, Paul turned the Marine around to face him and said, "Get up to your quarters and clean yourself up so you resemble a Marine. If I ever catch you in any of the bars on Georgia Street again I'll personally whip your ass. Do you understand me?" The answer was a weak "Yes. Thanks for what you did, I guess you saved my stripes." Turning away, Paul said, "C'mon Zeke let's go back and turn in for the night."

Next morning in the Guard Company office, First Sergeant Gregory Miller was sitting at his desk sipping a cup of coffee and looking through Marine Corps directives when Platoon Sergeant McGraw stepped into the office. Miller asked, "Well, how'd the duty go last night McGraw?" The platoon sergeant answered, "It was pretty much a routine night Top, noth-

ing in the log to talk about but I personally got a hell of a shock when I was checking posts." Miller asked, "Yeah, what happened to shock a tough guy like you?" "Well Top I was checking the main gate at about 2100 last night when a taxi came through the gate with three Marines in it." The First Sergeant said, "Nothing unusual about that. You see cabs going through the gate all the time." McGraw looked at the first sergeant and smiled. I've never seen a cab come through that gate with Private Pooley and Gunnery Sergeant O'Rourke sitting side by side in the back seat." The First Sergeant exclaimed, "McGraw, you gotta be kidding!"

True to his word, Zeke handed Paul a copy of the Bluejacket's Manual, which he would have been issued the first day of school anyway but Paul wanted to get an early start studying. Looking at Pooley a serious Corporal Zimmerman said, "Pooley what you did last night was really gutsy. That gunnery sergeant must be a really good friend for you to risk so much to save his butt." Paul answered, "On the contrary Zeke, I hardly know the guy and what's more, I really don't like him but he is a Marine. Now, unless you need me to do something, I'll be in the squadbay for the next couple of hours studying this Bluejackets Manual. I want to look over some of the things you mentioned last night."

During the day, four more Marines checked in early for Sea School and one of the sergeants from the school staff came back from leave. This would continue throughout the week with a larger number reporting in each day.

Zeke Zimmerman stuck his head in the squadbay door and shouted to Paul that it was time for noon chow. Paul answered that he was on the way. As he stepped out of the squadbay Paul noted that Zeke had the four new men in tow. Zeke sat next to Paul in the mess hall and while eating, casually asked, "You goin' into Vallejo tonight?" Paul answered, "Naw Zeke, I think last night was enough to last me for awhile, I'm gonna stay aboard." Zeke responded, "Okay, you can join us at the White Hat's Club then, I'll buy you a beer. I want to show you guys our section over at the White Hats' Club. We've got a corner of the club that's reserved for Sea School Marines." Paul agreed and looking at the four new men he could sense that they were eager to be included.

Part IV

Paul considered that it had been a productive day. He'd spent the morning studying parts of the Bluejackets' Manual and had a good workout in the gym for two hours of the afternoon.

The White Hats' Club wasn't new to Paul; he'd been here a number of times while stationed at the Marine Barracks. The new men all seemed eager to ask many of the same questions he had asked the previous night and Corporal Zimmerman enthusiastically answered. He obviously enjoyed letting the new men see how much he knew of what they would soon be experiencing. It turned out that Zimmerman had graduated from the school himself just two years before, and then had gone to sea aboard the battleship Nevada.

When the pitchers of beer they had initially ordered were gone, they decided to have another round. One of the new men called Luke was designated to go get this round. When he returned, not being sure of Paul's name, he remembered Paul mentioning that he had served in Shanghai. Luke handed him a beer and said, "Here Shanghai." Throughout the rest of the night the new men kept referring to him as "Shanghai." As the conversation progressed Paul was asked about his background. They were curious how he could be wearing the ribbons he had and still be a two-hashmark private. Paul knew that this would continue to haunt him wherever he went in the Corps. He determined not to let it bother him but always answered as briefly as he could. He told them that he had been court-martialed, found guilty and had been convicted. He then went right into his service in Nicaragua, he decided to pass over his ONI time but mentioned that he was with the Sixth Marines in San Diego and finally the Fourth Marines in Shanghai.

They all questioned him about Shanghai and Paul did his best to answer them. Without describing what his duties actually entailed, he described the city itself and how much the Marines liked it. He gave them a word picture of the Saturday morning parades down Bubbling Well Road.

The inevitable question that always came up among Marines and Sailors was, "How did you get along with the Japs?" Paul told them honestly that he believed we would soon be at war with Japan. All had heard this before but none wanted to really believe it. They returned to the Sea School

Barracks slightly before taps, each with his own thoughts about what the future held.

The next morning, Corporal Zimmerman rounded up the future seagoing Marines and informed them that they would be pulling targets on the rifle range on Thursday and Friday. They were to report to a sergeant at the Marine Barracks who would take charge of them and march them with the rest of the detail out to the range. Paul noted that when Zimmerman spoke to him he now referred to him as "Shanghai."

The Sea School finally convened and on the first day the captain himself spoke to them. Captain Nelson D. Jones was a no-nonsense Marine officer who had undoubtedly been carefully selected for his assignment. He spoke of the importance of sea duty; the first mission of the Corps, and let them all know of his high expectations for them. The sea school staff reflected the attitude and professionalism of their captain. Paul thought the school was off to a good start.

The first day consisted mostly of orientation and drawing uniforms and equipment. Each man was issued an extra set of blues, which were tailored at the Marine Barracks Tailor Shop. Training was taken seriously and was intense. Even going to and from meals was done in formation. By the end of the first week the men's close order drill had improved and a steadily increasing esprit 'd corps was apparent.

Marines were accustomed to bugle calls and bell time and all had heard the high pitched boatswain's pipes when at sea as passengers but now they were embarking on a tour of sea duty and entering a new world where men lived by the bugle and the bell. The ever-present shrill whistle of the boatswain's pipe had finally started to make sense.

They became familiar with the colorful International Code Flags and learned basic semaphore signaling. The geography of the ship took on great importance as the sea soldiers learned the location of every passageway and compartment on the ship. The men new to the Corps who considered themselves to be "salty" and were inclined to call every door a "hatch" soon learned that in addition to hatches, there really were doors on a fighting ship and the "real salts" would never refer to some of the watertight doors as hatches.

Part IV

They learned that in addition to the many "lines" on a ship, there was in fact, a "rope." It was attached to the clapper on the ship's bell, which was traditionally polished by the ship's cook. They became as adept at running up and down ladders as walking down a flight of stairs at home. They learned that it was prudent to be below decks if possible when the ship blew stacks; especially when wearing white cap covers.

They all became familiar with the early morning procedure of holystoning the ship's wooden decks and with the art of chipping paint, even though the Marines were exempt from such duties on most of the ships.

Gun drill was serious business and if they wanted the "Gun Boss" and the ship's captain to look with favor on the Marines, they must excel at gunnery.

Liberty was not intended to be a contact sport although some individuals had their own bizarre interpretations of it. It was really a team sport where Marines looked out for one another. The object was to have a good time ashore and still get all hands back aboard in a timely fashion, checked in C&S (clean and sober).

The Ship's Landing Party took on great significance. The officers and non-commissioned officers of the Marine Detachment trained it in infantry tactics and weaponry and took considerable pride in "their" sailors' accomplishments.

All in all, the school was good and Paul looked forward to his tour of sea duty. Two days prior to graduation they were told the names of the ships to which they were being assigned. The names of five great battleships and seven sleek cruisers were read off, followed by the names of the Marines being assigned to them. The men scrambled to learn as much as possible about "their" ships. They questioned the staff and made a concerted effort to meet sailors or Marines that may have served aboard. Some were being shipped to San Pedro to meet their ships, others to San Diego and the balance would be held at the transient barracks at Mare Island to await their ships coming into port in the San Francisco Bay Area.

Paul Pooley listened intently as the sergeant read off the assignments. He had high hopes of getting assigned to one of the huge battleships. He heard the ship's names and then the men being assigned to them, the Califor-

nia, Idaho, Texas, Maryland and the Virginia were the battleships to which some of his classmates were being assigned. Sergeant Pope directed the men whose names he had called to fall out and report to Corporal Zimmerman in the Sea School office to pick up their orders. Sergeant Pope then started calling off the Cruisers and who was being assigned to them. He named the heavy cruisers; Indianapolis, Houston, Northampton, Petaluma, Pensacola, Salt Lake City and two light cruisers, the Cincinnati and the Milwaukee and then he asked, "Is there anyone whose name I haven't called?" Private Pooley spoke up, "You didn't call my name sergeant, Pooley, Private Paul Pooley" "Oh yeah, Pooley. Okay, go into the office, they've got a special assignment for you Pooley."

Wondering what the Dragon of Destiny had in store for him this time, a very skeptical Paul Pooley stepped into the Sea School office to ask Zeke what was going on. He was confronted by Captain Nelson, who shook his hand, congratulated him and told him that he had the highest academic and leadership grades and was number two in marksmanship. The captain said, "Pooley, if we had an award for Honor Graduate, you'd have taken it, nice work," Paul looked at the captain, thanked him and asked, "What about my orders Sir? What ship did I draw?" The captain answered, "We're sending your record book up to the Flag Secretary of Cruiser Division Seven. They've got one opening in the flag allowance of CruDiv7. The admiral is transferring his flag to the Petaluma while she is here in port.

As soon as the Flag Secretary gets your records he'll give them to the admiral's Chief of Staff for his approval and then we'll give you your orders. Mare Island just happens to be Petaluma's home port and she's in all this week, so we'll have your orders later today." Corporal Zimmerman looked up from his desk and said, "Congratulations Shanghai, you really did well in the school. Check back with me right after noon chow and I'll try and have your orders ready by then."

Paul thought it might be a good idea to pay a visit to Guard Company over at the barracks and see First Sergeant Gregory Miller. He entered the barracks, went to the company office and saw that the first sergeant was having a discussion with two of the platoon sergeants. He stepped into the

office and was speaking to the company clerk when Miller noticed him and said, "Hi Pooley, what's up?" Paul paid his respects to the first sergeant and reminded him that he was especially grateful for what he had done for him. The first sergeant asked, "How'd you do over there?" Paul answered, "Number one in the class, First Sergeant." Miller replied, "Good, that's just what I expected to hear from you. Good luck."

Paul made his visit a brief one; he was concerned about packing his gear and getting ready to go aboard ship. Stepping out into the passageway to leave, Paul encountered his former nemesis, Gunnery Sergeant Robert O'Rourke. Looking at Paul, O'Rourke exclaimed, "Pooley, damn, it's good to see you. We've missed you around here. Things just don't seem the same without our Private Pooley." Paul looked at O'Rourke, trying to maintain a straight face, while secretly harboring strong feelings of contempt. He uttered, "Thank you Gunny." And moved on knowing in his heart that Gunnery Sergeant O'Rourke would never again be a person to be feared.

Back at the Sea School Office, Paul spoke to Corporal Zimmerman, "Hi Zeke, I'm back. Have you got those orders yet?" Zeke answered, "Hi Shanghai, yeah, I've got your orders but they're not what you expected. There's been a change since this morning when the captain talked to you." Paul responded, "Oh Yeah, where am I going now?" Zeke answered, "Well, you're still going to the USS Petaluma but not to the CruDiv flag allowance, after the admiral's chief of staff saw your record they wouldn't accept you. You'll be in the regular Marine Detachment. They're transferring one of their Marines to the flag allowance so that leaves a billet in the detachment for you to fill." Pooley said, "Okay Zeke, it's all the same to me, at least it's on the same ship." But it wasn't all the same to him it was a serious blow. Once again the terrible stigma of the court-martial had arisen to haunt him. He had graduated at the top of his class but was still a private. The admiral's chief of staff had seen his record book and undoubtedly noticed the court-martial conviction. He silently cursed Takahashi, his nemesis and the circumstances that had brought him to his present station in life.

Mare Island to Saipan

No Marine who had been convicted by a general court-martial could expect to serve in a flag allowance. He had to get used to it. No matter how hard he tried or how well he did, that stigma was sure to be there it was part of his karma. As he thought about it, he knew he had to find an acceptable way to live with this awful problem that would undoubtedly keep coming back to haunt him.

Psychologically crushed and depressed, Paul once again remembered the words of Chang Wu, the old fortuneteller in Nantao. "My dear Master Poo-Lee, always remember, we don't come here to stay, we come here to go. Do what it is that you were sent here to do, fulfill your karma. Paul wondered to himself, as he had done many times since Lillian's death and his court-martial, what the hell was his karma? What is it that he was sent here to do? He only knew that it had to do with his being a Marine. He must dedicate himself to being the best Marine possible. He had to somehow force himself to ignore the terrible reoccurring stigma of the court-martial that he should never have had.

Sea Duty

The word was passed throughout the ship that CruDiv-7 was transferring his flag to the Petaluma and the captain was fit to be tied. That damned admiral had badgered him about one thing or another ever since they first met. It had all started at the Naval Academy during his plebe year back in 1912. The admiral had been an upper classman and seemed to take great delight in reminding Midshipman J.C. "Bill" Willis that he was a mere plebe and plebes were the lowest things in the Navy.

Captain J.C. Willis ran a tight ship; he had a well-disciplined crew and didn't need Admiral L.P. Rampage looking over his shoulder. The admiral sometimes had a twinkle in his eye and had even been known to smile on occasion. He and the captain were very different.

Paul had a feeling of anticipation as he went aboard the USS Petaluma. He felt a surge of pride when rendering the double salute for the first time as he went aboard this great ship that was to be his home for the next two years. She was one of the new heavy cruisers, and was to be the flagship of her Cruiser Division.

Part IV

The ship was beautiful. The muzzles of the 8" naval rifles that were the ship's main battery had polished mahogany plugs with shiny five pointed stars of brass centered on them. The white teakwood decks were holystoned daily when she was underway and the haze-gray paint had a clean military look about it that impressed Paul. He also noticed, with some concern, the amount of highly polished brass brightwork on the ship and wondered how much of this was the responsibility of the Marines and how much of it was taken care of by the sailors of the deck force.

When he went below to the Marine compartment everything was exactly as it should be. He could smell the ever present, aroma of Kiwi Shoe Polish, Hoppes' Gun Oil and Brasso; the place was immaculate. Gone were the hammocks of old and every Marine had a designated bunk in which to sleep and the bunks were only two high. The rifle racks had heavy springs to hold each rifle firmly in place until needed and the steel deck was covered with tile. After his weeks at sea school there were no surprises everything was as he had expected. He was pleased to have been assigned to a new, modern man-o-war. What a departure from the first ship he had embarked on years ago when he had gone to Nicaragua. He was especially glad that these new ships had bunks. No longer would the Marines and Sailors have to sling their hammocks every day.

Getting underway for the first time, Paul could feel the ship come to life as the crew scurried to set the special sea and anchor detail and all hands manned their appointed stations. The steady throbbing of the engines always imparted a feeling of confidence. Paul Pooley knew he was going to like sea duty. The Marine Detachment had fallen-in at their regular quarters for muster station forward on the starboard side of the main deck up near the forecastle. The detachment gunnery sergeant supervised the formation. Following muster he had the men fall-out and man the rail along with the bluejackets not actually on watch. Sailors and Marines manning the rail aboard a fighting ship putting out to sea or returning to port was a custom as old as the Navy itself.

Gunnery practice at sea was given high importance. The target ship was the old battleship Utah and she was steaming a few thousand yards off

the starboard beam towing barges that held huge vertical targets when the captain decided to exercise the main battery. The roar of the ship's 8" rifles was deafening. A stupendous sound of such magnitude that it is difficult to describe to someone who has not personally experienced it. A sufficient number of hits were on the targets to satisfy the captain; who was not easily satisfied. The following day navy aircraft pulled target sleeves on long cables for the anti-aircraft batteries. Paul looked upon the pilots who pulled the target sleeves with admiration and respect. A slight error in judgment could cause them to be shot out of the sky. Paul needed no convincing; those pilots really earned their flight pay.

Night firing was done using the ship's bright searchlights beaming across the ocean's surface to illuminate the Utah's pulled targets. Again the eight-inchers gave a good account of themselves and the captain was pleased. Paul Pooley was standing orderly watch assigned to the ship's executive officer who was all over the ship. Paul was as impressed by the main battery's success as his shipmates but he had serious reservations about surface combat at sea.

Searchlights at night may have been the way to seek out enemy ships years ago during the Spanish-American War and the World War but to Paul, it was unthinkable in modern warfare. Turning the searchlights on was a dead giveaway as to the ship's location, turning it into a bright target for the enemy. He loved sea duty but wanted no part of surface warfare during actual combat conditions.

A few weeks later In the vicinity of the Hawaiian Islands one of the ship's floatplanes took off on spotting missions for gunnery practice and actually adjusted the main battery's fire on a target that was twenty miles distant. A feat that Paul thought was remarkable. He also reasoned that if the floatplanes could effectively adjust fire so could carrier-based planes, and they could do it at sea. Thus eliminating the old fashioned dueling between ships within sight of one another and use of the antiquated searchlights at night.

Once underway, drills were conducted with such regularity as to become second nature to the ship's company. Fire was the most frequent of the drills, followed by: Man Overboard, Abandon Ship, General Quarters, etc.

Part IV

Providing a trained ship's landing party for operations ashore was one of the Marine Detachment's responsibilities. As a heavy cruiser, the Petaluma was tasked to provide an infantry company.

The Marine Detachment furnished riflemen for the 1st Platoon of the ship's landing party and trained as often as they could. Whenever he had the opportunity, the "Major" attempted to convince Captain Willis to make the bluejackets of the 2nd and 3rd Platoons available for training. The captain's cooperation and interest resulted in the USS Petaluma having the best-trained and most efficient ship's landing party in the Division. The 2nd Platoon was comprised of sailors from the deck force (affectionately known as "Deck Apes") and was trained and organized to be a rifle platoon. The 3rd Platoon was the Weapons Platoon and was made up of firemen and engineers from below ("Snipes") and a few NCO's from the Marine Detachment. The major commanded the ship's landing party.

The Marine Detachment had the usual number of NCO's and privates to include one first sergeant, the detachment gunnery sergeant, four sergeants, six corporals one field music bugler and twenty-five privates and PFC's. The detachment was additionally blessed by the presence of Platoon Sergeant Sean McBride who was an additional NCO, not officially rated but a tremendous asset to the detachment and the ship's landing party. There were six additional Marines aboard who were members of the CruDiv-7 flag allowance.

When the ship had been out to sea for a while it often became necessary to refuel or to load supplies. This was one of the dreaded events of shipboard life. Loading stores aboard was often an all-hands evolution. Every officer and man not actually on duty was required to participate in manning the long "bucket brigade" lines to pass heavy containers, boxes and assorted cargo from man to man. All hands evolutions of this type were executed with speed and caution.

It was good to be back in port and to go ashore for a bit of relaxation. Paul was walking down Georgia Street in Vallejo and turned in to the Arizona Bar. He sat down on a bar stool and was about to order when he heard laughter coming from one of the booths behind him. Then he heard a

familiar voice speaking and knew why there was laughter. It was the voice of "Mad Mike" Madigan, a sailor he had known in Shanghai. Mad Mike had been a saxophone player in the Asiatic Fleet Band and was a natural comedian. He could turn the worst situation into a hilarious experience. He would probably have done very well in civilian life but seemed to be having such a good time in the Navy, he wouldn't think of getting out.

Mad Mike stood out as a rare and unique character indeed in the old peacetime Navy where characters were commonplace. Paul, temporarily forgetting his lowly rank, turned, looked at the booth where the laughter was coming from and exclaimed, "Wow, it looks like the zoo keeper at the monkey house left the door to one of the cages open. I see one of the berserk deck apes has gotten out." Brave words uttered by a lone Marine private in a Navy bar that was sure to provoke a fight of major proportions. The laughter suddenly subsided and a roar from the booth demanded, "Get the hell out of the way so I can get to the jarhead that uttered those blasphemous words!"

Sailors scrambled and Paul slid off his barstool to confront the raging sailor and to the amazement of all present, they embraced like long lost brothers. Mike roared," Shanghai you damned seagoing bellhop, it's good to see you. Pooley asked, "What has the Navy got you doing now Mike?" He answered, "I've got my own band now. I finally got my chief's hat so they gave me the CruDiv-7 Band.

"Actually Shanghai, I guess I'd better tell you what really happened. The way I've got it figured, there was an administrative error in BuPers back in Washington. They were screening records to see who was going to be kicked out of the Navy. My record book fell off the desk and some dumb Marine passing by must have picked it up and accidentally put it in the wrong pile, those were the guys to be promoted. So now you know how I got my hat.

"Shanghai isn't the same anymore, the 4th Marines are back down to two battalions and most of the old-timers are gone. The Japs are everywhere, even in the settlement. You were right when you used to tell us that we were going to have to fight them. I'm convinced we'll soon be at war with the arrogant little bastards."

Part IV

Paul said, "CruDiv-7 is flying his flag on the Petaluma." The chief answered, "Yeah most of the flag allowance went aboard already. My band moved into their compartment this afternoon." Paul looked at the chief and said, "Welcome aboard shipmate. I'm in the Petaluma's Marine detachment."

During all-hands evolutions while the ship was underway Captain Willis took special pride in the way his crew worked together. They were efficient and they were fast. He watched as the officers and men alike heaved-to and formed lines to pass the heavy boxes, packages and small cargo of various types from man to man across the deck down into the holds. He knew his ship and crew were better than any other in the division. He made it a point to see that his crew had turned refueling and loading ship while underway into an art form.

In the Marine Detachment there was concern and a bit of a challenge. During an all-hands evolution, especially while loading stores, the Marines had to out-do the sailors. It was a matter of pride. The sailors worked so hard and were getting so good that it was barely possible for the Marines to best them. Something had to be done. The men would be worn out almost to the point of exhaustion when passing stores.

Paul was concerned for the welfare of the men including himself. After all, how were they ever going to surpass the Navy? They needed to slow down and take a break while loading supplies at sea; contrary to what the captain thought, it was a very high priority with him. They worked so hard and so fast that they were all worn out, some to the point of near exhaustion, and this could present a real danger. Paul felt that something had to be done about it.

It was important that Admiral Rampage flew his flag aboard the Petaluma because his band was one of the best in the Navy. Chief Petty Officer "Mad Mike" Madigan was the petty officer in charge. Talented as a musician, ramrod straight and giving the impression of a no-nonsense bandmaster; his looks were deceiving as the Chief was an incorrigible comedian at heart.

After many days of steaming the ship was cutting through a glassy sea on a beautiful sunny afternoon as the supply ship came alongside. Lines were heaved over the side and the ships made fast to one another. The word

was passed, "All hands on deck!" The admiral and the captain stood side-by-side looking down from the bridge. As always, the captain had an intense look on his face. He wanted things to go perfectly, especially with the admiral watching. He spoke with pride in his voice, "Admiral, notice how smoothly the crew accomplish this evolution. They seem to acquire a little better teamwork and more speed each time."

Shanghai was perspiring as were his fellow Marines and Sailors and his arms felt like they had lead-weights attached to them. It felt as though they were about to fall off and he somehow wished they would so they wouldn't hurt so much. His aching back told him it was time to stop and rest.

That crazy captain up on the bridge had to be nuts to push his men so hard. The band was playing a rousing march, as they always did when there was an all-hands evolution, it helped to keep the men moving briskly. Finally, Paul knew the time had arrived; his arms and back couldn't hold out much longer. He made eye contact with Mad Mike Madigan and nodded his head. The chief nodded back with a smile on his impish face. He raised his baton and directed the band in playing a stirring rendition of The Marines' Hymn.

Every Marine on the ship froze at a rigid attention. Sailors, realizing that the Marines had stopped moving slowly almost one at a time rose up and stood at attention as well. It was a welcome break for the exhausted crew.

The captain, his eyes bugging out, cupped his hands around his mouth and appeared to be hollering something down to the men on deck but none could hear him, the music was loud and was being played with gusto. Hundreds of sailors slowly joined their mates by coming to attention as the red faced captain seemed to be turning purple. Nearly twelve hundred men on deck in the middle of the day were standing at attention.

The captain glanced over to where the admiral was standing and his arms fell loosely to his sides as his jaw dropped open. Rear Admiral L. P. Rampage was standing at attention with just the slightest hint of a smile on his face. Willis thought he could detect the admiral's lips moving. Oh, my God! He thought, he's actually singing the Marines' Hymn.

Later, in a relaxed moment on the flying bridge, the admiral addressed the captain, "Bill, that was a fine piece of leadership you displayed this

morning. The crew was really exhausted and for you to select that means of giving them a break was brilliant." The captain stood a little taller as he answered, "Thank you admiral, we can always count on the Marines to stand when their hymn is played and so it was just natural to take that means of resting the men. I've been thinking of making it a standard practice to have the Marines' Hymn played when the crew starts to really show fatigue during every all-hands evolution." And so it was that a new tradition was born aboard the USS Petaluma.

Sergeant Adams barked, "Shanghai, the major wants to see you down in the detachment office." Paul moved on the double and was soon standing tall in front of his commanding officer. Now his commanding officer wasn't a real major, he was a captain in the Marine Corps but Captain Willis, USN, was of the opinion that there should only be one captain aboard a warship and so the Marine captain was called "Major." It was a tradition in the old Navy to refer to the Marine commander as "major" and the Marine executive officer (generally a first lieutenant in rank) as the "soldier" so as not to confuse him with the ship's First Lieutenant.

The major stated, "Pooley, I just wanted to tell you personally that I've been observing what you've been doing down on the starboard gun mount. The classes you've been holding have generated a lot of interest and motivation on the part of the men. Gunny Neal and Platoon Sergeant McBride have told me that you've been working with the crew from the port mount as well. The gun boss was really pleased with the scores after our last live firing exercises. You know Pooley, we may be on our way to getting a Navy E on one of those mounts." Paul answered, "No Sir, we're on our way to getting two Navy E's, one on each of 'em." The major replied, "I sure wish you were right about that. Well, that's all Pooley I just wanted to say keep up the good work." Paul said, "Thank you Sir" and turned to leave,

The major stopped him with, "Oh, by the way Shanghai, before you leave, let me ask you a personal question. Do you happen to know a chief petty officer, by the name of Madigan? He's a musician." Paul answered, "Yes Sir, I know him. He was a member of the Asiatic Fleet Band when I was out in Shanghai and he used to frequent the Marine Staff NCO Club. He seemed to

like Marines a lot and I know he played in a combo that, except for him, was made up of all Marines from the 4th Marines Regimental Band."

The major responded, "I was sure you were going to tell me that you knew him. You were the only Marine on the ship that would have been able to convince him to do what he did when we were loading stores. You see Shanghai, the Top and I knew he had served in China just from his ribbons and of course we are familiar with your time in China and that helped the Top and me make the connection. What you two did was pretty gutsy you know you could wind up in the brig for something like that. The good news is you may be off the hook. I've seen the captain twice this afternoon and he hasn't said a word to me about it as yet.

"Now on a personal note, and I'll deny saying this to you if it ever should come up but, I think what you guys did was pretty neat. It probably screwed up the captain's timetable and it may have made him mad as hell but it was just great for morale. I will be surprised if it isn't talked about in every Marine Detachment in the fleet before long."

Steaming in Pacific waters bound for Oahu Paul was admiring the depth of color in this part of the ocean. The blue was so vivid it almost seemed artificial. He watched as a school of flying fish leapt from the sea as though actually flying. Paul was reminded of something in a book he had in his locker below in the Marine compartment. It was the Complete Book of Rudyard Kipling. He hadn't opened it in some time but opening the book wasn't always necessary, he had much of it committed to memory. The school of flying fish reminded him of Kipling's Road to Mandalay (where the flying fishes play), which he enjoyed reciting when sufficiently lubricated and if in the right company. It also caused him to think of his former life and Lillian. He missed her but kept it in mind that "No one is really dead unless they're forgotten."

Among the myriad of duties that befall the captain of a man-o-war is one that may be a bit distasteful to some. It is the brig suggestion box. It is a steel box, not unlike a machine gun ammunition box but painted haze gray and with a slot for prisoners to drop their "suggestions" into. Each day while at sea, the captain's Marine orderly is sent below to the ship's brig to

retrieve the suggestion box and deliver it to the captain. The captain keeps the key to the box on his person, there is no other.

When there is a Marine Detachment aboard a cruiser, one of the many assignments that fall to the Marines is that of guarding the brig a generally distasteful, boring and monotonous job. The ship's brig is located well below the main deck in a secluded part of the ship's bowels where almost no one has occasion to go. Watches are for a period of four hours. The prisoners are on one side of the bars and the Marine guard on the other side. The guard, who has not committed an offense, is subject to the same environment and restrictions as the prisoner, who has. There is no sound, other than the subdued throbbing of the ship's engines. Guards should be forgiven if on occasion they succumb to boredom and resort to imaginative ways to kill the monotony of their dull tour. Such an occasion occurred one watch when Private "Gabby" Hayes decided to have his prisoner give a demonstration of his singing ability. Hayes thought the prisoner showed real promise when he enthusiastically belted out the first verse of the Marines' Hymn. So Hays requested to hear the second verse. The seaman/prisoner did not know the second verse of the hymn and took offense when "Gabby" endeavored to teach it to him. He grudgingly managed to learn it but with less enthusiasm than desired.

Cruising through a glassy sea on a sunny morning, all seemed right with the world. The bridge was businesslike as usual. The captain seemed pleased at the performance of the Underway Officer of the Day. The ship's navigator was nearby going over a chart and an alert quartermaster had the helm. The captain took a sip of his coffee then turning to his Marine orderly said, "Alright Adam, go get the damn box." Corporal Adam Baum saluted smartly as he turned about uttering the appropriate, "Aye aye, Sir!" and went below. He descended one ladder after the next as he worked his way down to the brig deep in the bowels of the ship. Upon his arrival, he caught his breath, greeted PFC Simonovitch, the current brig guard, glanced at the prisoner, then started back up the series of ladders that would take him to the bridge. His ascent was slower than his descent had been. He knew the captain did not like receiving these "secret" messages from prisoners he had

locked up. Corporal Baum remembered the last time he had orderly duty on the bridge the captain was discussing his "pen pals" with the executive officer, Commander O' Toole. He was thoroughly fed up with the nonsense they had been writing to him. Baum found that the captain had moved out to the flying bridge so he reported to him there. Captain Willis took his binoculars down from whatever he had been staring at out on the horizon and said, "Al right Baum, I guess we'd better open it. He reached into his pocket, withdrew the key and proceeded to open the box. It held one slip of paper. The captain read it, crumpled it up in his hand and with a look of complete disgust on his face he muttered something about The Marines' Hymn then threw the crumpled paper into the wind which carried it far over the side and away from the ship. Corporal Adam Baum was disappointed; he would like to have seen what was written on the paper. Next, the salty old captain did something completely out of character; he heaved the metal box from the flying bridge into the deep blue sea. It landed with a small splash and sank innumerable fathoms to the bottom. At the Navy's next ship's annual inspection, the USS Petaluma's Marine Detachment would receive a demerit for not having a suggestion box available to prisoners but they did have two Navy E's for gunnery.

Standing on deck in the afternoon after a long, trying day of classes, gun drill and the usual effort spent on spit 'n polish, Shanghai was alone thinking of better times. He felt a rough hand on his shoulder and heard a gruff voice demanding to know; "Dammit isn't there enough work aboard this ship to keep the jarheads busy? All the bluejackets seem to find things to do while we're underway but you seagoing bellhops just stand around on deck wasting time." Paul turned and exclaimed, "Hi Chief, how's it going?" The gruff answer, "Forget the Chief stuff you know my name's Mike.

"We'll be making landfall tonight so I'm glad to have caught you here. Do you have liberty tomorrow?" Paul's answer, "Yeah, I've got two four to eight watches to stand today then I'm off tomorrow and my section does rate liberty. What makes you ask?" The Chief had an incredulous look on his face as he roared, "What! What the hell do you mean, what makes me ask? There are two reasons why you'd better be ashore tomorrow you damned

ungrateful jarhead! The first one is I was going to play "Home On The Range" during the all hands evolution last Thursday but just for you I made my whole band play that distasteful Marine hiking song, the Montezuma Trot or whatever you call it. You owe me buddy and I'm not lettin' you off the hook. There's a nice quiet little neighborhood bar down on Hotel Street where I think they may be willing to serve Marines as long as they're buying and are well-behaved and have a Navy escort.

"The other reason should be very obvious to you. The damned Navy umpires were obviously hung over and couldn't keep score during the firing exercises and they awarded the ship two E's for gunnery. To our everlasting shame, they were both Marine gun crews. Of course it really doesn't mean anything because we know the judges had to have been cheating.

"I've been in this Boy's Boat Club since 1918 and it's the first time I've ever seen anything like it. Your port and starboard batteries both, damn. You sure as hell need to be ashore celebrating that! The Chief of Staff 's yeoman told me himself that he was typing up a Bravo Zulu message for the admiral to give your squirrely captain yesterday." Pooley couldn't be more pleased. He knew they had both done very well but he had needed to hear this confirmation.

Pearl Harbor was a familiar place and Paul was glad they could tie up alongside the pier. As he started walking along the pier, he heard a rough growl, looked up and there was Mad Mike with a Chief Boatswain's Mate standing on the pier looking up at their ship. Mike gestured with his best bandleader's flourish and directed Paul's attention to the forecastle. Looking up, Paul saw a sailor suspended on the outside of the starboard gun tub. He was painting and was just putting the finishing touches on the coveted Navy E. The chief boatswain's mate assured Paul that the E on the portside was already painted. After all, he should know, the sailor doing the painting worked for him.

The nice quiet little neighborhood bar on Hotel Street turned out to be a standard, large, smoke-filled Honolulu bar catering to servicemen. There were scores of sailors in whites apparently from all the ships at Pearl shouting and scrambling to get drinks from the bar.

As they worked their way through the smoky sea of white uniforms Paul was amazed that right ahead of Mad Mike was an empty table. It was the only available table in the entire place. Mike got to the table and sat down, matter of factly, as though he had known it would be there and acted as if it had been reserved just for him. A waitress miraculously appeared and took their drink order.

A heavyset man in a colorful aloha shirt pushed his way through the crowd and approached their table. Mike stood up briefly and shook hands with him then the man nodded to Boats and said hello to him and shook hands. Looking at Paul, he said, "I don't think we've met." Mike spoke up and said, "This is a friend of mine, Shanghai Pooley. Shanghai meet Shipwreck McCloon." Paul shook hands and heard a "Glad ta meetcha Shanghai" as the heavy man turned and started moving through the crowd.

Mad Mike looked up from his frothy schooner of beer, smiled and said, "Boats, I guess we've fulfilled our obligation." Then casting an eye toward Paul, he said, "No self-respecting sailor ever comes ashore in Honolulu without first stopping for a "cool one" at Shipwreck McCloon's Bar. Drink up Shanghai and Boats and I will take you someplace where you can see some real live Hawaiian Hula girls and get a cold drink that's served in such a fancy manner you'll think you've magically become a rich tourist."

Working their way back out through the almost solid mass of sailors in whites they left the din of Shipwreck McCloon's where Paul was able to take a deep breath and inhale the fresh Honolulu air which, though smoke free, wasn't really as fresh as Paul had hoped. The warm afternoon Hawaiian air was significantly humid.

Mad Mike hailed a taxi, much to Paul's chagrin, he felt compelled to split all expenses three ways and felt at some disadvantage being a Marine private in the company of two chief petty officers. Their difference in pay was considerable. When the taxi deposited them at their destination Mike reached into a pocket and pulled forth a wad of currency and paid the driver. Paul was amused that Mad Mike had started a conversation in pidgin with the driver. It wasn't the same pidgin that Paul had been used to in Shanghai; it was different in that every fourth or fifth word was in Kanaka. At the

conclusion, they shook hands vigorously and the beaming driver looked at Paul and Boats and said something to the effect; "Dis da kind haoli guy, he's kamaina, he's my bruddah." Mad Mike's talents never ceased to amaze Paul.

Mike was on cloud nine as he looked up at the neon sign over the door proclaiming, "Cocoanut Cabaret," his beaming face was reminiscent of a little boy's on Christmas morning as he approached the door and held it open for his two companions while admonishing them to step lively so the air conditioning wouldn't all be lost into the humid Hawaiian evening. As they stepped through the door they observed a clean, modern restaurant with potted palms and white tablecloths and linen. They hadn't gone more than a half-dozen steps into the place when Mad Mike was engulfed in the arms of an attractive, middle-aged Eurasian lady who shrieked, "Mona, Mona! Look who's here, Mike's back!"

Mona turned out to be another Eurasian lady, clad in a colorful mumu who also embraced the beaming chief. She exclaimed, "Mike, you didn't write, we had no idea you were coming. Why didn't you tell us so we could make a big luau for you?" Mike feigned a scowl as he stated, "I didn't write because this is supposed to be a surprise inspection, I thought I might catch you shacked up with some rich pineapple grower from Molokai and neglecting the business." Mona scolded, "Oh Mike, you know better, I . . ." But before she could utter another word he was kissing her again.

Mad Mike finally stopped to take a breath and said, "Mona, you remember Boats Shaughnessy?" She answered, "Yes sure, I wasn't ignoring you Boats, I was just so glad to see my favorite Leprechaun that I wasn't thinking of anything else. It's good to see you again. Gee, it must be seven or eight years since we last saw you." The Boats answered, "That's right Mona, Mike and I haven't been together since we were in the battleship division aboard the USS Texas; it has been nearly eight years. We're temporarily together now while Mike's boss is flying his flag on my ship. We're on the cruiser Petaluma. She's one of the new ones, a beautiful ship."

Mad Mike growled "Lani, you and Mona meet my jarhead friend Shanghai Pooley, we used to drink together once in a while in Shanghai before he got orders back to the states. He got promoted to private out in

China and became my hero. He's on our ship now too. Whenever you see him, his money's no good. He drinks on the house. I'll tell you why later.

"Now, dammit, give these guys a table and take care of them. I'm going to see if your piano has been tuned lately and whether it has or not, I'm going to drive some of your customers away." Mike stepped up to the platform that was used as a bandstand and sat down at the piano and began to play. Lani walked over to the piano and placed a large glass snifter on it in case anyone wished to leave a tip. Then she came back to the table and said to Paul and Boats, "My real name's Leilani, Lani is just for short." Paul took notice of the attractive Lani and decided that she and Mona as well must have been real beauties a few years back.

Paul listened as Mad Mike played a couple of popular tunes on the piano then, completely ignoring the microphone which he never turned on, he roared out a routine that Paul had heard before in the Marine Staff NCO Club and in some of the rooftop ballrooms in Shanghai. His masterful playing was entertaining and his style unique. Some of his routines were not unlike those of the popular comedian of the time, Jimmy Durante who used a piano as a prop but Mike could really play and in Paul's opinion he was much funnier.

The customers loved Mike and by the time Paul and Boats Shaughnessy had finished their dinner, Mike didn't bother to eat, Paul noticed Lani had emptied the overflowing snifter and returned it to the piano as Mike beamed. He finally took a break and came over to the table and sat down. Mike was thoroughly saturated with perspiration. When he did his act he went all out. He entertained from the heart and people loved him for it.

Mona, sitting beside Mike said, "Tell Lani and I about Shanghai." Mike looked at her with eyes that were no longer twinkling with mirth and the comedian's face took on a very serious look as he started to explain, "I followed Shanghai's court-martial pretty close, because I knew him and like everybody else out there I believed that he was being railroaded. Girls, this Marine was a gunnery sergeant when I knew him but he beat the hell out of a couple of the Jap's secret police and instead of giving him a medal they court-martialed him.

Part IV

"If they had been Americans or anyone else they would have just taken him before a Captain's Mast. This guy didn't deserve to be busted down to private! Let me tell you something, the Japanese you've got here on Oahu are a hell of a lot different than the ones out in China. When Shanghai first mentioned it, I didn't believe him but now I'm sure of it, we're going to go to war with Japan. You can ask any sailor in the fleet, if he's been out on the Asiatic station recently he'll tell you war with Japan is inevitable. Only our diplomats and the American public seem to be unaware of it or they choose to ignore it."

Lani spoke up with, "We've been hearing a lot about the problems with Japan but Mike surely we're not going to war." It was the Boats who spoke next, "Lani, you just don't understand them. They really hate us for opposing their takeover of China and for the embargoes. They've whipped the hell out of the Chinese and they think they can do the same to the Dutch, the British and to us." Mona changed the subject by sending Lani for a bottle of chilled champagne and cuddling up to Mike. She mentioned to Boats and Shanghai that whenever they were ready to let her know. She was having her bouncer drive them back to Pearl Harbor.

Mike went back up to the piano and started playing again. It wasn't long before he launched into another of his comedy routines and Paul noticed that every set of eyes in the restaurant was on him. He was really good and seemed to enjoy what he was doing. The overwhelming applause indicated that the audience enjoyed it too.

Back at the table, Shanghai and Boats were saying their goodbyes to the girls when Mad Mike came over to the table to say he'd see them on the ship in the morning. Paul noticed that the impish twinkle had returned to Mike's eyes and he looked like he was eager to say something. "Shanghai, before you shove off, I think we should toast those Marine gun crews on the forward AA mounts. The Navy E is always good but you guys got a pair of 'em. That's really worth toasting." He raised his glass and they all joined in toasting the Marine gun crews and their Navy E's as Lani asked, "Why do you keep calling them Navy E's when the Marines earned them? They belong to the Marines now so I think you should call them Marine Corps E's." Paul said, "Thanks Lani, here's to the Marine Corps E's."

It was at that moment that Mad Mike came up with an insane plan. "Okay Jarhead if you want to call them Marine Corps E's it's all right with me but when you look at them, they all look the same, they look like Navy E's." Boats exclaimed, "Oh no! The crazy leprechaun is about to strike again. Look out Shanghai, you're already a private this comic is about to get you into real trouble now."

Mike cut him off with, "Boats can read my mind he knows what I'm about to say. It's not to get you into any trouble, it's just a test of you're Marine Corps pride and spirit. Who controls the paint on our ship Boats? Isn't that your paint locker back on the fantail? You know the place where we have to hold reveille whenever we're looking for a missing deck ape?"

Boats responded, "Okay Mike, Shanghai and me will work it all out on the way back to the ship but we really have to shove off now. Mona's got one of her boys waiting to drive us back to Pearl." Mike stood up and gestured goodbye as he commented, "Okay shipmate but when I go ashore in San Pedro next week I expect to look up at the forecastle and see green E's painted on the gun tubs to remind me of my Marine buddies." Shanghai and Boats simultaneously bid Mike and the girls *aloha* and *mahalo nui loa*.

On the drive back to Pearl Harbor, Boats Shaughnessy and Paul formulated a plan. The ship was scheduled to weigh anchor right after morning colors on the day after tomorrow. Liberty for the crew expired at 2400 tomorrow night. Chiefs and commissioned officers could stay later but most would be on board early. There would be very little activity on the pier or around the ship after midnight tomorrow and anyone coming aboard that late wouldn't be inclined to scrutinize the gun tubs anyway. Paul said, "Boats, if I knew where to put my hands on some green paint, we could get the job done during the mid-watch tomorrow night. That way, no one aboard would even see the E's before we drop the hook in the States next week."

During the drive back to Pearl, Shaughnessy said, "Well Shanghai, you Marines are supposed to be responsible for the ship's security, let's perform a little test tomorrow night. The paint locker has to be locked. Suppose we unlock it

just to see if your Marines are alert enough to catch it. If it is still unlocked the next morning, you have obviously failed to do your jobs. If the Marine guard tries to walk into that locker he'd better proceed with caution 'cause it's dark in there and there is going to be an open can of green paint right in the middle of the deck; if he knocks that can over, there will be hell to pay." The Boats looked over at Paul grinning and said, "Shanghai, if you go through with this caper you're just as crazy as Mad Mike himself and he's got a reputation that's worldwide." Paul answered, "Well Boats, that may be so, but I think Mike's right, it would be a hell of a morale booster for our Marines."

Back at the Cocoanut Cabaret, Mad Mike was sitting at the bar and watching the staff clean up for the night. Mona and Lani were both standing behind the bar facing Mike. He was chuckling to himself as he nursed a Jameson and water. "What's so funny Darling?" Mona asked innocently. Mad Mike answered with, "Aw, you girls wouldn't understand. You're both *hapa-haoli's* and you aren't qualified to understand the workings of a true leprechaun's mind." Lani asked, "Oh come on Mike, try us." The chief finished his drink and sliding his glass across the bar toward Mona said, "Oh all right, maybe you'll understand enough to enjoy it.

"Boats is gonna make the green paint available to Shanghai and he's gonna have the Marines paint the E's green, supposedly in honor of the Marine Corps. They'll do it late tomorrow night since we put out to sea early the next morning. That means no one will see them until we pull into San Pedro next week. San Pedro is home for the Pacific Fleet so there is sure to be several ships and thousands of sailors in Pedro that morning. As the ship pulls into port, my band will be up on deck playing and do you know what I'm gonna have them play?" Mona answered, "No Mike. How would we know what you'll be playing, the Marines Hymn?" He spoke up with, "I knew it! You two just can't be expected to understand. You've led a sheltered life out here in the islands all your lives. The day we're scheduled to arrive in port I'll be playing, "The Wearin' O' The Green" it'll be March 17th, Saint Patrick's Day and those poor Marines will think everyone is cheering for them. Pretty funny don't you think?"

Mona spoke up with, "No! I thought you said Shanghai is your hero.

Why would you want to get him in trouble?" Mike retorted, "I knew it! One of the funniest capers I ever came up with and you don't see the genius in it. Normally, the Marines, especially Shanghai would be suspects but on Saint Patrick's Day, it could have been done by anyone on the ship. When the captain starts to investigate, he'll have over 1,200 suspects. Shanghai will never get nailed for this one." When he'd spoken to Shaughnessy and Shanghai at the Cocoanut Caberet Mad Mike Madigan was totally unaware of Captain J.C. Willis' personal plans.

Captain Willis had to be in Denver, Colorado on the 19th of March for a wedding rehearsal. He was giving away his only daughter and wanted everything to be perfect. His ship was scheduled to arrive in San Pedro on the 17th at which time he would turn the command over to his capable executive officer, Commander K.P. O' Toole and leave the ship immediately in order to catch his train to San Francisco where he was to transfer to another which would take him on to Denver. The timing was dangerously close but he had no choice. If he didn't have the damned flag aboard, he might have influenced the day of departure and left 24 hours sooner. As it was, the Admiral, his nemesis since Naval Academy days, had previously scheduled an important golf date in Honolulu and didn't care much about weddings anyway. The admiral was a bachelor.

The ship was steaming eastward and expected to make landfall before dawn on the 17th. The captain's bags were packed. He would leave the ship after she was made fast to the Navy pier and immediately following morning colors. The ship's executive officer would assume command while the captain was on leave.

He wouldn't deny it; Captain Joseph C. "Bill" Willis was in love with his ship. She was a beautiful cruiser and handled perfectly. His executive officer had a reputation for competence throughout the fleet. His Engineer Officer and Gun Boss were as good as any he'd served with. The Navigator was new on board but came well recommended. He was well satisfied that he could take leave for ten days and things aboard would be just the same when he returned. As he crossed the quarterdeck, the captain could see a taxi waiting for him down on the pier.

Part IV

Sailors and Marines manned the rail as the ship slipped in beside the pier. The admiral's band was on deck and played Morning Colors and the stirring National Anthem as the beautiful flag of our country rippled from its halyards. The captain arrived on the quarterdeck. Side boys were posted and the shrill notes of a boatswain's pipe pierced the air as the captain went over the side and down the officers' accommodation ladder. He was a proud man and had no qualms about leaving for a few days. Everything was shipshape, the sign of effective leadership.

Before the captain's feet touched the pier, a strange feeling of uneasiness began to descend upon him. The band up on deck had varied from their usual routine and instead of military and patriotic music; they were playing a medley of rollicking Irish ditties. He shook his head as he entered the waiting taxi and as it proceeded down the pier, he checked his wristwatch; with a little luck he could just make it to the train. He looked through the taxi's window up at the great ship. His eyes swept her from stem to stern taking in the magnificent view of this classic cruiser of which he was so proud; until his eyes spotted the Marines' forward gun tub.

The coveted Navy E had been desecrated! The bright white E's edged in black were now painted green. Damn those Marines!! Thanks to them, his ship would be the laughing stock of the fleet. The cab picked up speed as it left the pier bound for the railroad station.

Commander Kevin Patrick O'Toole had heard about the green E's so he went over the side to get a look at them. He returned aboard and was walking forward on the starboard side of the ship talking to the ship's First Lieutenant when he noticed a couple of sailors with lines and tackle and a can of white paint up at the forward gun tub. He turned to the First Lieutenant and asked, "Stu, what the hell are those men doing at Mount 2-1?" The First Lieutenant answered, "Sir, they're going to repaint the E's on Mounts 1-1 and 2-1. I had hoped you hadn't seen them yet." The commander cut in with, "Why? It's still Saint Patrick's Day, leave them alone until tomorrow." The ship's First Lieutenant broke into a smile as he responded, "Aye, aye Sir." They both hoped the captain would enjoy his time away from the ship and his daughter's wedding.

In the early afternoon the admiral was on the quarterdeck about to be piped over the side to attend a meeting somewhere ashore. Seeing Commander O'Toole standing nearby, the admiral commented to him, "Kevin, I hope Captain Willis got away without noticing the E's on those AA Mounts. I'm sure he'd have a blue fit if he ever saw a thing like that on his ship." O'Toole replied, "They'll be gone in the morning Admiral." Admiral L.P. Rampage winked as he commented, "Good for the crew's moral little things like that."

While the ship was in San Pedro, the major took advantage of every opportunity to exercise his troops ashore. They had two weeks before they were scheduled to leave for fleet maneuvers off the coast of Baja California.

The two years of sea duty went fast for Paul Pooley. He liked the people he was serving with, he liked the ship and he enjoyed being at sea.

When he was off duty and they were underway Paul enjoyed being on deck up forward near the bow as the sleek ship sliced through rolling seas. It was a great place to be alone with his thoughts. He reflected on his time as a young Marine in Nicaragua, the excellent training he'd gotten from ONI and his years in China. It had been a great life so far and there was bound to be more. He had been aboard nearly two years and was due for orders. He had no idea where the Marine Corps would send him next but he knew few assignments could be as rewarding as sea duty. Whatever was in store, he was ready for it.

The First Sergeant sent for Pooley and confronted him with what he had been expecting for some time, his orders. He was to be detached from the ship and was to proceed to the Marine Corps Base, San Diego, California, for duty with the Sixth Marines. He was granted the usual travel and proceed time and offered leave. Paul decided on 10 days leave and then wondered what he was going to do with it.

The Sixth Marines

In the early spring of 1941 the 2d Marine Brigade, now redesignated the 2nd Marine Division, passed in review at the Marine Corps Base, San Diego, California. The parade uniform consisted of the steel helmet of the

style worn in World War I, a cotton khaki shirt and field scarf, winter service green trousers wrapped tightly into tan, blanco'd leggings, and polished field shoes. Weapons and equipment were essentially the same as the Marines had in the First World War, 23 years earlier: the M1903 rifle and bayonet; the Browning automatic rifle (BAR); the .45-caliber M1911 pistol; cartridge belt; and combat pack. Web equipment was scrubbed and blanco'd to a light tan shade. Metal parts were painted dull black, and leather items spit-shined a dark brown.

Field training for the 6th Marines and the other 2d Brigade units was conducted in the scrubby hills and arroyos of Camp Elliott where large wooden, yellow-painted, Navy designed barracks housed the brigade. Some units were in nearby tent camps.

Unit training consisted of weapons schools, drills, and firing of individual and crew-served weapons. Companies ran small unit tactical exercises, and there was a considerable number of long-distance hikes. The Marines had virtually no vehicles so nearly all movement was by foot. There were very few battalion-sized exercises and night training was minimal.

In April the 6th Marines' landing teams began a series of amphibious training exercises, Ship-to-shore drills were held on San Clemente Island, west of San Diego, using the recently developed Landing Craft Personnel or "Higgins Boat." This boat had no ramp in the bow, so the Marines had to roll over the gunwales to debark.

The regiment received a warning order in May 1941 for a possible move to the East Coast to join the 1st Marine Division for contingency operations related to the war in Europe. At the time, the regiment was not yet up to peacetime strength, so the call went out to both the 2d and 8th Marines for volunteers to augment the 6th. There was no lack of volunteers.

For its move, the regiment was to be reinforced by the 2d Battalion, 10th Marines (with 12 75mm pack howitzers); Company A, 2d Tank Battalion, minus one platoon (with 12 light tanks); a parachute platoon; an antitank platoon; and the 1st Platoon, Company A, 2d Service Battalion. The regiment and its supporting units were brought up to a strength of 204 officers and 3,891 enlisted Marines and Sailors. Following the arrival of 58

officers and 577 enlisted men from the other units of the division, the word came down from division headquarters that the reinforced regiment was to take 10 units of fire for all their weapons."

Most of the Marines embarking with the 6th believed that the force would go to the Caribbean region. One credible rumor was that they were going to Martinique to guard an impounded Free French aircraft carrier against a potential German takeover. Still another rumor held the Azores as the objective.

The regiment, with attached units, departed San Diego on the 31st of May with orders to report to the Commanding General, Fleet Marine Force, Atlantic Fleet. The regiment still did not know where they were going.

Their convoy headed south, bound for sunny tropic seas. They were advised that they would be transiting the Panama Canal and when they got into the Atlantic they would head north and go up the coast of the U.S. and could look forward to liberty in Charleston, S.C. their first port of call. They arrived at Charleston on the 15th of June 1941. On the 16th of June the force was given a new name, they were re-designated The 1st Provisional Marine Brigade, under the command of Brigadier General John Marston, USMC.

When the ship was approaching Charleston, the Marines not on duty flocked up to the deck to see the sights. Sergeant Andy Anderson turned to Paul who was standing next to him at the rail and asked, 'Have you been here before Shanghai?" Paul answered, "No Andy I never have. I've heard a lot about it though, it's supposed to be a real picturesque old southern port city. I'm looking forward to going ashore and looking around. How about you?" The sergeant responded, "Sure, I'm up for going ashore if they decide to grant us liberty." Some of the Marines, those not on working parties, were granted liberty; went ashore and found Charleston to be every bit as hospitable, historical and picturesque as they had heard.

Most of the men were not unhappy to leave the hot, humid and noisy Navy yard. While in Charleston many of the Marines were kept busy loading ships with additional supplies and equipment procured ashore including such incongruous items as skis, ski-poles and winter protective clothing purchased by supply officers at a local Sears Roebuck store.

Part IV

The convoy that left Charleston harbor was an impressive force, it consisted of 25 vessels, including two battleships, the USS New York and USS Arkansas, and two light cruisers, the USS Nashville and the USS Brooklyn. After leaving Charleston, the convoy headed for the open sea and took a northern course. They were advised that their next destination was Argentina, Newfoundland.

Paul Pooley had long ago learned not to be surprised by any turn of events. Thus far, his Marine Corps career had been replete with many things he could never have anticipated and this one was no different. With very few exceptions, the other Marines of the 1st Provisional Brigade were taken completely by surprise when told that after leaving Argentia, their ultimate destination was to be Iceland.

Iceland was strategically located between the British Isles and North America, ideally situated for air and naval control of the North Atlantic "lifeline." France had already fallen and Britain alone faced Nazi Germany. Iceland could not be allowed to fall into enemy hands.

When Marines are embarked as passengers on a Navy ship, life is different than when they are a part of the ship's company. The hours at sea seem to stretch into days and then keep repeating themselves so that one soon loses track of times and dates. Lieutenant Donovan, ably assisted by Platoon Sergeant Stevens, insisted on daily formations, weapons inspections, and training on general military subjects.

The ship's captain did his best to keep the troops awake and alert by conducting General Quarters drills, Fire drills, Abandon ship drills, and life vest inspections at odd and often unexpected times. Few things were as distasteful to the Marine passengers as standing in the long; slow, chow lines aboard the transports. They were always monotonous and frustrating.

Our ships did not have the new surface radar yet, so Marines were added to the continuous submarine watches from special posts above the main deck. The periodic appearance of U.S. Navy PBY aircraft flying anti-submarine warfare patrols was reassuring.

On 5 July, life suddenly took on a more serious aspect when they were ordered to wear their life jackets at all times, the convoy had entered

the European war zone. The next night a destroyer on the starboard flank picked up a lifeboat with 14 survivors, four of them women. A German submarine had sunk their ship.

The next day the convoy went through the flotsam and jetsam of the British battleship HMS Hood that had been sunk by the Germans on the 24th of May. Items of debris and equipment from the battleship floated alongside the ship and brought the seriousness of war ever closer to the Marines leaning over the rail.

The troopships the Marines were embarked in included transports each named for former Commandants of the Marine Corps; the USS Biddle, the Fuller and the Heywood. They arrived at Argentia on the 27th of June and departed on July 2nd. The convoy arrived at Reykjavic, Iceland on 7 July 1941.

Entering the harbor Private Scooter McClosky and Field Music Windy Easton were on deck leaning on the rail and talking as the ship pulled in to the port of Reykjavic. Corporal Mayer, the "Governor" overheard their griping as Scooter grumbled, "Man, what a helluva dismal place this is, there's nothin' here except that black sand and cold rain driven by the arctic wind." The Governor spoke up with, "Lad, it's obvious to me that you are not very observant. The Marine Corps has gone to a lot of trouble to bring you here to an exotic place where only a few Americans have ever been before.

"You should count your blessings and look around you, there's plenty for you to see; Iceland has glaciers, volcanoes, fjords, geysers, mud pots, Lava fields, lava tubes, flood plains and waterfalls, and if that's not enough, it even has a respectable amount of snowfall now and then. What more can you ask? You young Marines just don't appreciate anything. It sure wasn't like this in the "Old Corps."

In Iceland, there was little local labor for offloading the ships. The Marines would have to do the job themselves. Pressure to get the ships offloaded in the shortest possible time was considerable. Fortunately at this time of year there was 24 hours of daylight; this would aid tremendously in the offloading. Only 2 ships could dock at a time in Reykjavic. The rest of

the convoy totally vulnerable to possible attack from the air or submarines was riding at anchor in the harbor.

Building their own camps and preparing for winter became top priority missions. In addition, the Marines had to build housing and facilities for the U.S. Army troops who were expected to arrive any day. The Marines got the job because there simply wasn't anyone else left to do it.

They approached this task with considerable enthusiasm since they felt the sooner camps were built for the Army, the sooner they would be relieved and could get away from Iceland. Some teams of Marines became experts at constructing the British-made Nissen huts. They set up assembly-line operations where teams of men specialized in constructing certain parts of the huts. The British wooden-fronted Nissan hut, heated by a coke and coal pot-bellied stove was the predecessor of the American Quonset hut that came later in the war.

Standing the duty here was different. Paul thought he had been cold before but that was nothing compared to what he felt now. Encumbered by multiple layers of heavy clothing, he still felt the icy wind blowing through him. The dull black volcanic terrain exacerbated by the dull sky overhead was depressing. He was reminded of the timeworn saying, ". . . 'till hell freezes over," and that is precisely what the landscape around him looked like, hell frozen over.

Paul had been certain since his tour in Shanghai that war with Japan was inevitable. As he contemplated the brigade's mission; strategically located for the air and naval control of the North Atlantic "lifeline" he knew that Iceland must be protected from falling into the hands of the Germans. He was certain that if we went to war with the Nazis it would leave us vulnerable to Japan in the Pacific and Far East. Yet, he knew that the British did not have adequate men or the means to defend Iceland and protect their own shores at home. The situation was grave.

The Icelandic landscape was black volcanic rock and soil. The terrain was mountainous and the Marines were told that it was the most volcanic region in the world. The humidity was high and the erratic rains were frequent. Steady winds often reached gale force. Private Scooter McClosky

looked at Field Music Windy Easton as he asked, "Pongyo, does this place remind you of anything?" Windy responded, "Hell no! I've never seen a place like this before in my life." Scooter said, "Neither have I but this is just what I thought hell would look like, only the wind got so bad the fires have blown out." Windy had a concerned look on his face as he answered, "Yeah, Scooter, I guess you're right, this probably is what hell looks like, I just never thought about it before."

While the brigade spent much of their time as stevedores and builders, they were also responsible for the defense of a goodly portion of the island. With borrowed British motor transport the Marine Brigade was a "mobile force" for use at any point along the winding coastal road leading from Reykjavik to the naval base at Hvalfjordur. They also provided air defense with the mission of protecting the city, the harbor and the airfield from German attack.

When the brigade had first arrived, the British major general in command of the 49th (West Riding) Division honored the Marine brigade by offering them the shoulder patches of the Division. Major General Marston accepted and for the first time since the First World War, the U.S. Marines wore shoulder patches. Each Marine was to sew his shoulder patches on his green blouse and overcoat. The Polar Bear patches were worn on both shoulders with the bear facing forward.

The Marines began to refer to one another as "Polar Bear." Polar Bear Easton, Polar Bear Fitzgerald or Polar Bear whatever their last name was. This was due to the fact that the Icelandic people had told them that there were no polar bears in Iceland. They could not understand why the British and now the Americans wanted to sew polar bears onto their uniforms. The Marines felt totally qualified to call themselves polar bears because of their frigid living conditions. "The Marines Have landed and now there are plenty of polar bears in Iceland."

The men of the 3rd Platoon were in formation prepared for inspection. They were wearing full greens with overcoats and fur arctic caps. Lieutenant Jim Donovan was inspecting with Platoon Sergeant Stevens. They were especially interested in the shoulder patches and cap emblems. The lieutenant

was not pleased with the lack of uniformity of the black plates behind the cap emblems.

The lieutenant noted that apparently each of the men had cut his own emblem plates from metal probably salvaged from tin ration cans. They were irregular, of varying sizes and generally unprofessional. The plates were to be 2" X 2" square and painted non-reflective black. They were to be worn centered on the front of the artic fur caps at an angle so as to present a diamond configuration.

At the conclusion of the inspection, the lieutenant stepped a few yards out to the left flank of the formation and conferred with Platoon Sergeant Stevens. After a few moments discussion, the platoon sergeant saluted smartly and the lieutenant strode off. Stevens walked back over to face the formation and raising his voice to be heard above the howling wind he reported to the men that Lieutenant Donovan had been disappointed with the inspection. The platoon had failed. The platoon sergeant then sneered, "I didn't know that failure was an option in the Marine Corps but you birds have managed to start something new to the Corps, you've failed.

"The lieutenant says those metal hat plates you're wearing on your "Mongolian Piss Cutters," as we used to call them in North China, look like hell. None of them are uniform! The real reason for the lieutenant's disappointment is that we wear those plates to keep the fur from obstructing the emblems so people will know we're Marines. Some of the British troops are wearing those Mongolian piss cutters and the army will soon be sending troops here to relieve us and they'll be wearing them too.

So here is what you are going to do; Fitzgerald, I want you to take one man with you and go over to the engineers' camp, procure a sheet of metal heavier than those tin cans you used before. Have them cut into 2" squares: then have holes drilled in the center of each plate. Bring 'em back here and give them to Scooter. Scooter, you will take one man and go see the quartermaster and procure some dead black paint. If they don't have any, find out who does and get all the plates painted. After they are dry, present them to me for my inspection and approval. If they are satisfactory we'll mount 'em on our fur covers and invite the lieutenant to come back and inspect again.

This time, we'll show him the platoon with the best and most uniform hat plates in the brigade.

On Saturday, the 16th of August it was a really nice day by Icelandic standards, Prime Minister Churchill visited The Iceland Base Command on his way home from a meeting with President Roosevelt at Argentia Bay in Newfoundland, where they had forged the Atlantic Charter. The British and U.S. Marine forces put on a grand review and parade, which consisted of several miles of troops with platoons in line stretched along a major road under a bright sky. Mr. Churchill, with his cane and cigar, walked the entire line.

When Churchill passed along the ranks of the 6th Marines, he stopped to speak to some of the older men wearing campaign ribbons. One senior Marine staff sergeant had groused earlier about parading for the British Prime Minister, but when Churchill stopped and asked him, "You're an old soldier aren't' you?" The Marine retorted, "No Sir, I'm an old Marine." Churchill then said, "Well an old sea soldier, is that a good term?" The sergeant replied, "Yes, sir. We like to regard ourselves as sea soldiers." Churchill asked him if he would shake hands with another old soldier. Winston Churchill won that Marine over as well as all the others he spoke to that day.

Churchill's visit was one of the highlights of the 6th Marines monotonous deployment to Iceland. The Brits and Marines got along well in Iceland with the Brits providing most of the motor transport since the Marines had little of their own. The cordial relations lasted throughout the 8 dreary months the brigade was stuck in Iceland.

The fire watch was posted, the lights extinguished and the residents of Nissan Hut #1-6-14 rolled up in the two wool blankets the Marine Corps had generously provided to each of them. They covered their blankets with their shelter halves to insure a modicum of added heat and then they shivered as they waited to drop off to sleep.

It seemed like only an hour or two until one of the cooks from the battalion messhall opened the hut's door accompanied by an icy blast of wind, made his way to "Windy" Easton's bunk and awakened him saying, "Okay Field Mouse, it's time to get up and sound reveille."

Part IV

Spending long hours on post gave men time for reflection. Paul knew that the situation was grave; the British did not have the means or the manpower to defend Iceland and protect their own shores. Iceland was important to the allies because it is strategically located between the U.S. and Great Britain. It is critical for air and naval control of the North Atlantic "lifeline."

One of the things the men were constantly reminded to be alert for was the danger of Nazi raiding parties coming ashore from submarines. Paul talked it over with Corporal Governor Mayer over a couple of brews one evening and decided that any German sailors being put ashore in this bleak, cold, desolate place would promptly get back aboard their warm, comfortable U-Boat submarine and get the hell out of here.

Private Scooter McClosky asked, "How the hell are we gonna wash our duds in this damn place? The rain and this terrific humidity will soak anything you hang out to dry and there's hardly enough room for us to turn around in here without hanging clothes up to dry inside." Sam Sloat complained, "Yeah, like Scooter says, we're livin' in a sardine can. How do they expect us to hang our clothes up to dry?"

The Governor interrupted, "You guys better stop feelin' sorry for yourselves and start thinkin' like Marines. If you don't, this is going to be one hell of a trying tour of duty. We have to use the elements to our advantage. Don't worry about dryin' your duds. This is Iceland! Use the ice to dry your clothes. Just think about it; you wash your long-johns then hang 'em out, they promptly freeze solid. What is it that really freezes? Water, that's what freezes so you just bring your things inside and chip and break the ice off 'em before it can melt and your long-johns will be free of water. Put 'em on and if they feel a little damp, so much the better, your body heat will react with the dampness and you'll feel warm faster."

The Governor had a look of satisfaction on his face as though his answer had been brilliant. He went on by asking, "Shanghai, you were in Nicaragua. Remember how bad it used to get? It was hotter than the hinges of hell, especially on the days when we had long patrols. Those big blue horse flies bit us all day and the mosquitoes tried to devour us at night. We were always sweating and that led to chafing, heat rash and sores. They

made us wear the same hot, canvass leggings we're wearing now and our felt campaign hats absorbed the heat from the blistering sun and it radiated right down though us. When we were on patrol we'd get so damned hot and sweaty we'd be weak as kittens. At night it was too hot to sleep and you were afraid to sleep anyhow 'cause if you did, some of your Guardias may sneak off and go home or some might even join the insurrectos. You guys just don't know how well off you are here in Iceland. It sure as hell wasn't like this in the "Old Corps."

During their time in Iceland, members of the 1st Provisional Marine Brigade looked forward to mail call with great enthusiasm. Shanghai Pooley got fewer letters than anyone else in his squad but when he did get mail it was generally from a Navy Chief friend; a character by the name of Mike Madigan. The letters were lengthy and they were hilarious. Paul found them well worth sharing with the other Marines in his squad and platoon. The Marines practically adopted Mad Mike and whenever mail call was sounded, they would crowd around Shanghai to see if there was a letter from Mike.

In one of his letters Mike added a PS reporting his transfer to take over another band. This time, he was back on a battleship and was delighted. He had served aboard her before and loved the ship. Aboard the new ship he would be spending much more time in Hawaii. The Navy was transferring their Pacific Fleet Headquarters from California to Pearl Harbor. He shared with Paul that the time for his retirement was rapidly approaching; this would be his last ship. On his retirement day, he and Mona were to be married; they had been engaged for eighteen years and were already partners in business. Mike explained that they should have married earlier but the Navy was a jealous mistress and Mona wasn't willing to play "second fiddle" to a ship. Mike's new temporary home was the BB-39. Paul was happy for Mike and Mona.

Scuttlebutt circulating among the Marines and even their officers was that the Army would relieve them in September; it was soon October then November. Their eventual return to the United States was well overdue. On the 7th of December the Japs bombed Pearl Harbor and Paul Pooley's prediction of war with Japan was now a reality.

Part IV

Between the 4th and 8th of March 1942 the 1st Provisional Marine Brigade finally packed up and departed Iceland bound for the United States; now at war with the Axis powers. Paul always looked forward to his letters from Mike Madigan but they had suddenly stopped in December. The USS Arizona, BB-39 was one of the first major casualties of the war.

The 6th Marines arrived in New York City on the 25th of March where the Brigade was disbanded but not before a generous liberty was granted to the troops. Thus, the 1st Provisional Marine Brigade became the first American fighting unit to return to the United States during World War II. New York welcomed them with open arms.

Lieutenant Colonel Oliver P. Smith took the 1st Battalion, 6th Marines back to San Diego to rejoin the 2nd Marine Division now stationed at Camp Elliott. Many of the old hands from the 6th were reassigned to fill out the ranks of the new division's other regiments, the 2nd and 8th Marines. Paul Pooley, now a PFC was assigned to the 8th Marines Paul found himself back in San Diego only to learn that the 8th Marines were in American Samoa, far across the Pacific and he would have to hitchhike to Samoa.

The Eighth Marines

In December 1941, the Japanese had bombed Pearl Harbor; in February 1942, the 8th Marine Regiment went to war. It was the first American ground combat unit to go overseas after the bombing of Pearl Harbor. The regiment was embarked on the liners, Matsonia, Lurline, Monterey and Mariposa. Still painted white and manned by their civilian Merchant Marine crews. The Marines were fed rations intended for passengers that had paid for luxurious accommodations on the beautiful liners. Of all the U.S. forces in World War II, they were the one regiment that went to war in style. As the war progressed, their luck would change drastically. Their first destination was Pago Pago on American Samoa.

When Paul Pooley finally arrived in Samoa he found that he was to be assigned to the regimental Weapons Company. An assignment he relished because of the company commander, Chief Marine Gunner Henry Pierson Crowe, an officer he had known and respected in Shanghai. Gunner Crowe,

known throughout the Corps as "Jim" was a legend in his own time. With Crowe in command, the company was destined for great things.

The 8th Marines spent ten months in jungle training and in building up the defenses of American Samoa. Paul was interested in an assignment to help train the 1st Samoan Marine Battalion, USMCR, but was informed that they were only looking for senior staff NCO's. He appealed to Gunner Crowe based on his experience but Crowe, even though he was familiar with Paul's past and was somewhat sympathetic, wanted to keep Shanghai Pooley now a corporal in Weapons Company.

The purpose of training a Samoan Marine Battalion was so they could take over defense of their home islands when the regular U.S. Marines left to fight elsewhere in the Pacific. After ten months in the steaming jungles of Samoa, the 8th Marines left to reinforce the 1st Marine Division, already heavily engaged in fighting the Japanese on Guadalcanal in the Solomons.

Their training on Samoa proved invaluable but nothing could adequately prepare them for the horrors of "condition black." Condition Black or Phase Nine was the warning of imminent attack from naval gunfire. Naval gunfire was accurate and it was deadly. The Marines were also vulnerable to attack from the air. Sometimes it was just "Washing Machine Charley" making his nightly run over the island to drop a couple of bombs and hope for a lucky hit, but at other times it might be a flight of Japanese fighters and bombers arriving overhead to really raise hell; until driven off by the brave fighter pilots of the "Cactus Air Force."

On the ground, the Japanese were a brave and cunning enemy but even they were not prepared to fight dual enemies, the U.S. Marines and the jungle. Many succumbed to Malaria and without adequate treatment, hundreds died. The Marines too were subject to the ravages of Malaria and other tropical diseases, but with a difference; they received adequate medical treatment.

Many were evacuated back to the United States or to New Zealand. Eventually rumors were circulated that the 8th Marines were going to New Zealand to rejoin the 2nd Marine Division, but not until the U.S. Army's Americal Division had relieved them.

Part IV

The Americal came ashore as untested green troops. They were integrated into the Marine positions and learned to fight the Japs through "on the job training" by their veteran Marine brothers. They fought like Marines and a mutual respect was established between the soldiers and Marines on Guadalcanal.

While on Guadalcanal, the Weapons Company Commander, Chief Marine Gunner Henry Pierson Crowe was promoted to Captain and would subsequently be transferred to the 2nd Battalion, 8th Marines.

Lieutenant Sam Griffith who had been one of the "Language Officers" at the U.S. Consulate in Shanghai was now a lieutenant colonel with the 1st Marine Raider Battalion and would assume command when "Red Mike" Edson Left the Raiders to command the 5th Marines as a colonel. Paul remembered him as a captain in Nicaragua. Captain Puller who Paul accompanied on the long patrol to Agua Carta when Puller commanded M Company of the Guardia back in Nicaragua now was a lieutenant colonel and had a battalion in the 7th Marines. Captain W.M. Greene, Jr. who Paul had respected so much when they were in the R-2 Office in Shanghai was a major (destined to be a future Commandant of the Marine Corps).

Paul Pooley thought long and hard about the transformation of the Marine Corps. The Corps he had joined that could boast hardly more than eighteen thousand was now growing rapidly its top strength during the height of World War II would reach almost 500,000. So many people that he had known and served with had assumed positions of greater responsibility and at much higher rank. Even the Major General Commandant of the Marine Corps had been advanced to three stars; he was a lieutenant general now and a fourth star would soon be added. Pooley was a corporal still seeking his mission in life. Remembering the words of Chang Wu, the ancient fortuneteller of Nantao, he wondered again what it could be that he was sent here to do?

When the 8th Marines arrived in New Zealand from the hell that had been Guadalcanal, the men were delighted. To many, it seemed very much like what the United States would have been like fifty years earlier. The climate was healthy and the people friendly. It was an ideal place for men to

recover from the trauma of combat and the ravages of Malaria and a number of other tropical diseases.

They were here not only to recover and to defend the New Zealanders but also to train for the next campaign. The training was intense almost brutal but necessary and went on continuously except for an occasional break for liberty in Wellington or one of the small villages or farm towns between Paekakariki and Wellington.

Shortly after arriving in New Zealand, Shanghai Pooley was transferred from the Regimental Weapons Company to the 2nd Battalion. He reported to the sergeant major who looked at him in astonishment. "Pooley, is it really you? The guy I knew out in China? You were a gunnery sergeant. What the hell happened? Did you get out of the Marine Corps and then come back in at a lower rank?"

"No John, oops sorry, no Sergeant Major! I had a little trouble with the Japs out in China and got reduced to private. That's why I'm back in the infantry, I no longer have a security clearance."

"Well, somebody must be lookin' out for you, the "Old Man" is Chief Gunner "Jim" Crowe. He's a major now and is in command of the battalion. He told me to assign you to Fox Company and to let him know when you came aboard. He wants to see you."

"Well, there's nobody I'd rather see. I'm glad they made him a major. He's really a great guy. I knew him in China when he was a Chief Gunner and on Guadalcanal he was my company commander."

The sergeant major leaned back in his chair and said, "Sit down and I'll have Dinatelli bring us a couple of cups of joe, then I'll let the old man know you're here. If he can see you now you won't have to come all the way back from Fox Company later on. Music! Bring us some coffee and then see if the old man will have time to see Corporal Pooley in about ten minutes."

The Field Music Corporal grabbed a couple of mugs from the top of a bookshelf and started for the coffee pot. "Cummin' right up Sergeant Major."

The sergeant major reached into his desk drawer and took out a pack of Lucky Strikes and held them out to Pooley who obligingly took one.

Part IV

Then the Sergeant major retrieved a half-smoked cigar from the ashtray on his desk and attempted to relight it. Finally meeting with success, he leaned back and looking at Shanghai asked, "Okay, old man, now tell me just what the hell happened to you out in China?"

"I got a General Court Martial. They tried me, convicted me, reduced me to private and sent me back to the States. Under the circumstances, I guess they gave me the lightest sentence possible. The Japs were right there in the courtroom throughout the whole trial so they had to throw the book at me. As soon as I got aboard ship, I was told that my brig time and fine were vacated but that the reduction in rank had to stand."

The door to the C.O.'s office swung open and standing in the doorway was a very impressive Marine major with a chestnut mustache, waxed points sticking straight out to the sides. Major Henry Pierson Crowe glared at Pooley. "What the hell are you doing out here? I left word that I wanted to see you. Are you too good to drink your coffee in my office?"

Pooley, now standing at attention replied, "No Sir!"

"All right then, get your butt in here. Bring the coffee and cigarette with you."

A full fifteen minutes passed before Shanghai Pooley stepped back into the sergeant major's office. The sergeant major glanced up and said, "Okay Corporal, PFC Nearny here is the runner for Fox Company, he'll take you over so you can report in to the first sergeant. Here's a set of your orders with our battalion endorsement on them. Just hand them to the top when you get there." Looking around the room at Nearny, the Music and the two clerks, the sergeant major nodded to Pooley indicating that he wanted to say something privately. He and Pooley stepped out of earshot of the others and looking at Pooley he said, "Tomorrow morning, there's a battalion formation. Be sure you are present. They'll have all persons to be decorated front and center first, then they'll ask for persons to be promoted to front and center. That will include you. I don't know if the old man told you or not, but in case he didn't, I just finished typing up your warrant. I thought you might like to know that you'll be a sergeant again by this time tomorrow."

Mare Island to Saipan

Reporting in to F Company, Corporal Paul Pooley handed his orders to the first sergeant who told him to leave his sea bag and pack in the company office and go to chow. He was to report back in an hour to complete checking in to the company. He felt a bit of uneasiness at the way the first sergeant had looked at his ribbons and three service stripes then at his corporal's chevrons but was a bit more at ease when the first sergeant asked him if he thought he could handle a rifle squad.

About to enter the messhall, Pooley was surprised to see the familiar face of an old shipmate he had served with in Nicaragua. They shook hands and then went through the chow line and sat down together.

Pooley remarked, "Boy Chief, what a small world it is. You and I sitting down together here in New Zealand after not seeing each other since Nicaragua so many years ago. We're probably the only two corporals in the Corps still wearing the Nicaraguan Medal of Valor." Chief smiled and answered, "Yeah, I guess you're right. Everyone else that got one is an officer or a senior staff NCO now; in fact Captain "Looie" Puller, who always called me Indian and refused to call me Chief, is a lieutenant colonel now. I heard that he has a battalion in the 1st Division. I guess you and me haven't done so well in the Corps amigo. Here we are each wearin' three hashmarks and we're only corporals." Pooley responded with, "You know there's a lotta guys in the Corps now who've only been in a couple of years and they're already sergeants."

Chief replied, "Hell Pooley, it's worse than you think. I'm not even a real corporal. My permanent rank is PFC. Corporal is just an organizational warrant, they can take it away from me at any time if I screw up." Shanghai Pooley looked at his old friend and smiled as he admonished, "Well I guess that's a pretty good reason for you not to screw up, isn't it?"

Chief answered, "Yeah, it is but there's a lot more to it than that. It's not about me anymore Paul. I've got to stay out of trouble so I can help these new replacements that we've been getting. They're just a bunch of kids and they need all the help we can give them." Pooley responded with, "I've noticed that most of them are right out of boot camp with no previous duty stations and not much advanced training. I guess that's all we can expect

when the Marine Corps is growing so fast? It's sure not the same outfit you and I joined back in 1930.

The Indian answered, "Yeah it is; there's just a lot more of it now."

"By the way Chief, what outfit have they got you in around here?"

"I've been in Fox Company for over a year now the 2nd Platoon. What about you Paul, where did they assign you?" Pooley answered, "Boy, talk about a small world, I'm in Fox Company too and the "Top" told me he was going to give me a squad in the 2nd Platoon if the company commander approves it." Chief was obviously pleased as he raised his mug and took a sip of coffee then asked, "Do you think they can stand having two triple hashmark corporals in the same platoon? It would probably be the only outfit in the whole Marine Corps to have a couple of mis-fits like you and me in the same platoon."

Pooley's tone was serious as he answered, "I don't intend to stay a triple hashmark corporal very long Amigo. No way." As they ate they talked of previous duty stations and mutual friends and each told the other something of where he had been and what he had done during the past several years. Chief was surprised at Pooley's schools and special training and to learn that he had once been a gunnery sergeant.

Chief mentioned the next day's formation and told Pooley he was being awarded his second Silver Star Medal. "Pretty good for a guy that can't hold his booze or his rank, don't you think?" Pooley answered, "Yeah Chief, I really am impressed. By the way, I'll be in the same formation. I'm picking up sergeant again tomorrow. I want to learn more about why you can't hold your rank but it's going to have to wait 'till next time 'cause I'm due back at company headquarters to see the top and finish checking in." Pooley left hurriedly while Chief decided to linger and have another cup of coffee and count his blessings. He wanted to reminisce about some of the things he had liked so much about Paul Pooley when they were both privates in Nicaragua.

Liberty was much sought after. The men spent most of their time in the field and it was a rare treat to have a break from training and be permitted to go ashore. Sergeant Pooley the squad leader had admonished the men to,

Mare Island to Saipan

"...be ever watchful on liberty. Relax and enjoy yourselves and have a good time but for God's sake, don't get into trouble. I want every one of you men back here by 2300, Clean and Sober, is that clear?" He was concerned for his men; they were all young and inexperienced in the ways of the Corps, they were "Wartime Warriors," in for the duration and then back to their homes and civilian life, if they survived. Paul thought about the "new Corps" and Chief's comment when he had said "it's sure not the same outfit you and I joined back in 1930." The Chief had said, "Yeah it is, there's just more of it now." Paul thought about Chief's comment and remembered that they had been green recruits themselves when they had arrived in Nicaragua and learned their craft from the professional Marines they were serving with.

The men were milling around in the hut when Chief sounded off, "All right you men, First Call! You know what that means. You've got just five more minutes before Assembly and when Assembly sounds, I want to see your butts out in the company street standin' at attention just like you wuz real Marines. Do you people understand me?

A disgruntled voice answered, "Yeah Corporal, we understand. This ain't our first formation you now.

Chief detected little enthusiasm in the voice and responded with, "Well Sonny Boy, it is your first formation with your new squad leader, Shanghai Pooley lookin' on! He's going to be out there checkin' to see what kind of Marines he's inherited. If you men know what's good for you, you'd better be the sharpest squad in this battalion because I happen to know the new squad leader and he's a professional who will demand and extract the absolute maximum effort from everyone of you."

Chief contemplated the squad as he thought to himself, "Nice kids, most of them probably from average American homes. Volunteers, eager to do their part for the war effort, but they're not Marines, not real Marines anyway. These kids were not like the men who had served with him back in the 1930's and stayed on through the great depression. They were the old timers, the professionals, or they had been driven into the Corps by the depression and had stayed on to become professionals. Chief knew that he and the other pre-war veterans had a formidable challenge. The days of the

professional private were over. He hoped he was up to the task of setting the proper example for these young men.

Chief's thoughts were shattered as the field music bugler blasted out the crisp, clear notes of Assembly and a wave of green surged from the huts. Three ranks started forming and by the time the field music had repeated the call, the battalion was in formation. That's the way it was in 2–8; Major Crowe wouldn't have it any other way.

Platoon Sergeant John Black "Blackjack" sported a magnificent imperial dragon on his left forearm, a souvenir of time spent serving in Peking, China. He had a varied career that included time as a Drill Instructor at Parris Island and he had served at the Marine Barracks in the old Philadelphia Navy Yard and he had served in two ship's detachments afloat. Paul felt fortunate working for such a well rounded, professional.

First Lieutenant David Stacey, the platoon leader was a former enlisted Marine who had been commissioned in Samoa at the temporary Officers' Candidate School affectionately known to the aspiring officers as "Tiny Fraser's Concentration Camp" after the officer in charge. The lieutenant had proved his value repeatedly in the fighting on Guadalcanal. The nine survivors, who were still in the platoon, spoke of him with admiration and respect. Blackjack and Lieutenant Stacey worked well together and Paul was glad to have joined their team as a squad leader. Shanghai Pooley had been in the 2nd platoon less than a week when Blackjack approached him during a smoking break in the field one day and asked what he was doing after evening chow. "What is there to do? I'll probably square my gear away and clean my rifle then maybe write a letter. What do you guys generally do around here at night?" Blackjack looked around cautiously to be certain none of the troops could hear then softly mentioned that, "The lieutenant and I are going to have to drive in to Paekakariki to do a little reconnaissance on a training area were hoping to use for a night problem next week. Want to come along just for the ride?" Paul answered, "Sure, it will be great to break the monotony of sitting around in the hut all night. But, you said ride. Where are you and the lieutenant going to get a vehicle around here?" Blackjack responded, "Captain Barrett, the company commander rates a

jeep and he lets the lieutenant use it occasionally when it's for official business." Paul said, "Okay then I'll see you right after evening chow." Blackjack retorted, "Be wearing Winter Service A so you can get out the gate."

Standing in front of the C.P. hut, Shanghai had waited less than five minutes when a jeep rounded the corner and stopped. Lieutenant Stacey was at the wheel with Blackjack sitting next to him. Paul hopped into the back and they were on their way.

Driving past a meadow Blackjack indicated, "That's one of the training areas the lieutenant has selected for our night, platoon in the defense, exercise next week. We've already got the farmers permission for us to use it." Paul said, "Looks good to me," as he nodded his approval although he thought to himself, any other area would have done just as well. The lieutenant turned his head and shouted to Paul, "Blackjack and I were thinking of stopping at that little pub over there and getting a glass of milk or something, do you mind?" Paul smiled and answered in the negative as the lieutenant turned in and parked.

As they entered, it was obvious that Blackjack and the lieutenant were no strangers to the landlord or the local customers as they were warmly greeted. A charming New Zealand girl approached the table where they were sitting with, "Hi Yanks, what'll you be having tonight?" Blackjack looked at her and said, Good evening Grace, Mr. Stacey and I would each like our usual glass of warm milk and you may as well bring the same for our new friend." She smiled and winked as she said, "Too right, Yank." and disappeared behind the bar. She reappeared a few moments later with the same smile and a tray containing three pints of foaming lager. It was a warm cozy pub and its occupants, all New Zealanders, were friendly.

The lieutenant looked at Paul and said, "The skipper let's us take his jeep out once in a while when he's not using it himself. No one else but our other squad leaders and the platoon guide have been here with us. I'd like to get all the men out but since that's not possible, we've limited it to squad leaders and above.

We come to this place because none of the other Marines seem to have found it yet and it's a good place for us to talk, relax and brainstorm. The

conversation promptly turned to the platoon and how to make it more effective. The lieutenant asked, "Well Shanghai, you've been with us long enough to have gotten to know a little something about each of the men in your squad. What do you think so far?" Paul's response, "Well Lieutenant, since you asked, I'd say we've got a long way to go. Most of these kids are pretty green." Blackjack interrupted with, "Yeah Shanghai, we've only got nine men left in the platoon from Guadalanal and that includes the lieutenant and myself." Paul responded, "Wow! That equates to approximately 80%, casualties you really got hit hard!" Blackjack retorted, "No, no don't let me mislead you, I don't mean we had that many killed and wounded. We lost almost as many to malaria as to the Japs."

Blackjack reminded Paul, "Shanghai, we're experiencing something that is not new to the Marine Corps, it's happened before on several occasions. The most recent was how rapidly the tiny Marine Corps had to expand in order to fight in the First World War. Their combat record was superb and yet, as you think about it, you realize; most of them too were just "Wartime Warriors." They were kids that had been recruited, trained and sent right over to France and into combat. When the war ended, most were quickly mustered out and sent back to civilian life as the Marine Corps once again was downsized drastically." The lieutenant added, "We're especially fortunate to have nine seasoned men with combat experience, many of the other outfits aren't as lucky as we are."

Blackjack took a long draught of his beer and looking up at the girl who had returned to the tableside he said, "Grace, bring us another round and if you don't mind, I'd like some steak and eggs." Shanghai agreed, "An order of steak and eggs would be just fine right now." The smiling lieutenant nodded his concurrence.

Blackjack was speaking again as he fixed Paul with a very determined look and said, "Shanghai, by now I'm sure you've figured out that Lieutenant Stacey and I are pretty close. We've been through a lot together and we think a lot alike. There's something we'd both like to share with you." The lieutenant interrupted to call Paul's attention to the fact that he was now an "old salt" and there were damned few of them around. His mission

in life was clear, "Turn these kids into Marines!" Blackjack interjected, "You know very well that there's a helluva lot more to making an individual a Marine than just teaching them military subjects. We can follow the training schedule to the letter. We can have them fire their rifles 'till they're all experts. We can teach them the functioning of the Browning Light Machine Guns; water-cooled and air-cooled until they can recite it letter for letter, but that, along with all the other training they're getting now isn't going to make them into Marines! That'll teach them combat skills; it'll teach them to kill, but they'll think and perform like soldiers."

It was the lieutenant's turn to speak and he appeared eager to share his thoughts with Paul. "Shanghai, There's more to being a Marine than what these kids are being taught in the field. It's a state of mind; it's damn near a religion. You know what I'm talking about because you've already got it; it's in your heart, it's the spirit of Semper Fidelis. The kids we've got have to be taught to embrace our history and traditions, they need to feel that special sense of belonging like you and I and Blackjack they need to know that the Corps is really a close-knit brotherhood. They have to feel the pride and understand the responsibilities of being a Marine. Once these qualities are inculcated into them and combined with their regular military training then and only then, will they really be Marines and many of those that survive this war may get out of the Corps but they will remain Marines for the rest of their lives."

Grace was back with their steak and eggs and she served them with her usual smile. Blackjack said, "It's up to us; and there's only a few of us left. You know how big the Corps was when you were in China, there were only about 18,000 of us and now we're into the hundreds of thousands and there's no telling when it might stop, it may even go as high as a half-million. For a mere 18,000 men to transfer their beliefs and standards and loyalties to hundreds of thousands means every one of us has to be in there pitching all the time. It's up to us to set the example and show the kids what being a Marine is all about."

Paul exclaimed, "I'm with you all the way Blackjack but, it's really worse than you've stated. We have already lost some of the best. The 4th Marines

from Shanghai were captured in the Philippines along with all the other Marines in the Philippines; the American Legation Guard Marines were captured in North China and the Marines on Guam and Wake Island were all captured or killed, as you well know. Over two thousand professional Marines were lost from the very start of the war. They won't be around to help the rest of the 18,000 regulars mold the new wartime Marines."

The lieutenant interjected, "What were trying to say is, we're here for one reason, to train these kids to fight in the next campaign as Marines. If we don't do it right those of us that survive will have to start all over again so we'd better do it right. There's a hell of a lot more to training a Marine than just following the training schedule. We've got to make them know that they are the best trained fighting men in the world and we've got to show them, by example, that they've got the finest officers and NCO's." He stopped talking abruptly as Grace approached their booth.

She picked up their empty plates and took their orders for another round. After bringing three more beers to the table she smiled as usual and stated, "I'm off now so if you Yanks want anything else, just tell Mr. Frank, the landlord, and he'll take care of you." Blackjack said, "Thanks Grace, we'll be seeing you next time."

The lieutenant continued, "We've got to make these kids understand about their heritage, their history and traditions. They have to know that no matter how tough things may get, there's always another Marine covering their back. That's what makes Marines different. Knowing about their Corps and understanding it's history and the dedication of one Marine to another, seems to motivate them.

The next two days were spent in the field carrying out the training schedule. Whenever they took a break, Shanghai gathered the second squad around him and talked of the Marines who had gone before them from fighting the Barbary pirates during the Tripolitan adventures of Presley N. O'Bannon to the storming of the castle at Chapultepec in 1847. He told them of the seagoing Marines that went ashore in Korea in 1871 and fought at the Salee River Forts and of Lieutenant Waller and his Marines fighting side by side with the British Marines against the Muslim fanatics in the

inferno at Alexandria, Egypt. It was working; he could tell that they were interested. They wanted to know more. Lieutenant Stacey and Blackjack were right, these young Marines were eager to know about the Marines who had gone before them and had been in harm's way down through the pages of history.

Throughout the week, whenever time permitted, he would tell them of the hardships and adventures, of Marines, including the repelling of a cavalry charge in China during the Boxer Rebellion. He told them of the fighting in Nicaragua and then went on to describe ways of surviving in the often-hostile jungle. Paul made a special point of teaching his men all he could about tracking and detecting a hidden enemy and about deceptions. They were starting to talk about such things among themselves and Paul knew he was succeeding.

The 2nd Division had settled into a routine of intense training that the men understood was not only designed to help them take their objectives, but may also keep them alive. All worked hard and unit pride soared. New Zealand was becoming like home to many and some were even convinced the division would have to stay to defend New Zealand from invasion by the Japanese.

There were always skeptics who found it difficult to accept reality. Such was the case of a few lovesick Marines who didn't want to leave New Zealand. They were taken by surprise when rumors started circulating that they would be leaving Camp MacKay for another campaign in the not too distant future; after all, that's what they had been training for.

One of the company field music buglers, FM-1/c W. Max Netherland, dispelled such rumors by explaining that they were only going on an amphibious exercise and would be gone for about four days. He claimed to have seen a draft of the orders himself. In an effort to gain credibility he secretly agreed to divulge the code name of the exercise and even the name of the location where it was to take place. The code name was to be Operation Galvanic and the location was to be the island of Efate in the New Hebrides. After all, as the "Music" explained it, they couldn't be gone more than a few days, as the division was needed for the defense of New Zealand.

Part IV

The 8th Marines were trucked to Aotea Quay in Wellington to go aboard ship on the 28th of October 1943. Land on Efate they did, but it was only a landing exercise. Operation Galvanic was something else altogether. Paul Pooley had learned long ago never to be surprised at anything that happened in the Marine Corps and so it came as no surprise to him when the word was passed for the 2nd Platoon to lay up to hatch #2 on the main deck for a briefing. Lieutenant David Stacey armed with a relief map of the island they were to assault briefed his platoon. At approximately 0800 on the 20th of November, they would assault and capture Betio Atoll, Tarawa, in the Gilbert Islands. The lieutenant gave a complete and thorough briefing and at its conclusion he assured his men that they were well trained and ready for whatever may lie ahead.

The lieutenant stated that he had complete confidence in them. The conquest of Tarawa, a small stretch of land not over 2½ miles in length and only ½ mile across, lasted for 76 hours of sheer terror and was the bloodiest and most costly landing in Marine Corps history up until that time. In taking fortress Tarawa, the 2nd Marine Division had flung open the gates to the Japanese Empire.

It was a much smaller 2nd Platoon that went aboard ship to depart what they considered hell on earth. Even the dreaded transports seemed luxurious compared to the hot sands and cloying smell of death that was Tarawa. They were told that their destination was Hawaii. Most were disappointed; New Zealand had been their destination of choice. The 2nd Marine Division never returned to New Zealand.

Once at sea, the millions of flies that had infested steaming Tarawa diminished until by the second day at sea, they were nearly all gone. The intense heat subsided as well and all hands welcomed the fresh sea breeze on deck. The Navy did its best to provide a traditional Thanksgiving dinner to the embarked troops. The turkey went mostly uneaten; the cloying smell of death remained in the nostrils and the memories of the Marines and tainted all the food they attempted to consume. It was however, a very special Thanksgiving to those who survived. Life suddenly had taken on a special meaning and had become more precious to them than ever before.

Blackjack put his hand on Shanghai's shoulder and said very frankly, "You know the system, for the time being, Sergeant Childs is our new platoon sergeant. You're older and more experienced, and I think you'd be the perfect man for the job but he is senior, so that's the way it has to be." Paul answered, "Blackjack, I shouldn't have to tell you that it doesn't mean a damned thing to me. I like Childs and I think he'll do a good job; I certainly have no hard feelings. In the meantime you've still got me in the platoon and you know you can count on me for anything you need. Frankly, I'm glad to be staying with the 2nd Squad; those men have become like sons to me and I really don't want to leave them. You know they're the only family I have. I hated like hell to leave four of them behind on that stinking island."

Landing in Hilo Harbor, the 2nd Division got aboard open trucks for the ride to their destination. They started moving up Saddle Road, Route 200, at a speed of about 35 miles per hour. With each passing mile it seemed to get colder until the myth about Hawaii being a tropical paradise was dispelled. The men learned much to their chagrin that it snows up in the volcano areas of Hawaii. Their destination was to be another "Rest Camp" located on the Parker Ranch. They named it Camp Tarawa and hoped there would be more "rest" than at their last rest camp at Paekakariki. Once the tents were in place and the messhalls operational, it was right back to training.

Blackjack and Shanghai anguished over the men returning from hospitals. They trickled slowly back to the battalion one or two at a time and were sent back to their respective companies and returned to duty. The two NCO's wondered about their lieutenant. He had been hit hard on Tarawa and it looked as though the war may be over for him but rumors began to circulate from returning Marines and Navy corpsmen friends that Lieutenant Stacy was in the Aiea Heights Naval Hospital over on Oahu and was recovering. The men of the 2nd Platoon missed their lieutenant and all hoped he would be returning to duty soon.

The training at their "rest camp" on Hawaii became even more grueling than it had been at the previous rest camp in New Zealand. Liberty for the troops was rare indeed. The only real city on the island was Hilo, 60 miles South

Southwest. There was no public transportation on the big island but there was one taxicab at nearby Kamuela, which boasted little more than a general store. Honokaa offered less. It was closer to the coast but nearly inaccessible.

It was the final day of a three-day field training exercise. The men were to have one more class and witness one more demonstration and then break for chow. The battalion mess personnel were bringing hot chow out to the men for their final meal in the field.

The 2nd Platoon of Fox Company was conducting the assault against a fortified position demonstration. After Tarawa they were now the undisputed experts. At the conclusion of the demonstration, Blackjack covered some of the salient points he wanted the men to remember and answered their questions. When finished he turned to leave and go over to where the platoon had mustered when he heard a, once familiar, voice from somewhere out in the sea of troops ask, "What are you tryin' to teach these men? Those tactics went out when the South lost the Civil War!" He retorted with, "I don't recall there ever being a civil war, all the ones I've ever fought in have been anything but civil." By the time the words were out of his mouth, he had covered the distance from where he had been speaking to the place from where the voice had emanated. Directing a quick salute in the direction of the newly promoted Lieutenant Colonel "Jim" Crowe, Blackjack embraced Lieutenant David Stacey while repeatedly slapping him on the back. Glancing at the colonel, a smiling Blackjack blurted, "I'm sorry Colonel but you don't know how we've missed this guy." Smiling, Crowe answered, "It's alright Sergeant, I'm pretty glad to see him back myself."

Colonel Crowe suggested to the lieutenant that he ride back to camp with him in the jeep, "I had Dinatelli drive it out pulling a water buffalo, you know how the men never seem to get enough drinking water in the field." Stacey answered, "Thanks Colonel but if it's all the same to you, I'd like to march back with my platoon. It's been over a month since I've seen them and it may help me catch up on any of the lyrics to their raunchy songs that I may have forgotten while I was hospitalized." An understanding Jim Crowe answered with a smile, "Have it your way Dave," then he turned and strode in the direction of Captain Barrett.

Mare Island to Saipan

The training was intense and effective. New replacements soon filled the gaps left by those killed and seriously wounded and time passed quickly. Everyone was obsessed with the next campaign. They did not know where it would be but all knew that it would be another Pacific island. Lieutenant Stacey and Blackjack were proud of their platoon's state of readiness. Shanghai Pooley was equally proud of his rifle squad. He had taught his men everything he possibly could to help them accomplish their mission and still remain alive.

The convoy of 2-1/2 ton trucks moved along the seemingly endless road at a leisurely 35 miles per hour. They passed through the lava flows between the great volcanoes Mona Loa and Mona Kea having departed the Parker Ranch and Camp Tarawa forever. The Dragon of Destiny had chosen them to participate in Operation Forager, which had no meaning whatever to the Marines being transported; it was just another code name for another campaign. The convoy slowly wound its way down through the dust along the highway until finally the city of Hilo was in sight. As they moved closer to Hilo the highway became paved and the dust created by the trucks diminished. The troops looked at Hilo as they would any other mundane sight along the way, without emotion. Many wished they had been given an opportunity to visit Hilo while on the island but only a few were so favored. Now, it was too late, they were just passing through on their way to new excitement and new adventures.

Operation Forager

Time spent aboard troopships was always boring and was much too long. The men did not look forward to another contested amphibious landing but they were looking forward to departing the steamy, cramped quarters, diminished rations and shipboard drills that were so much a part of life on the Navy's amphibious transport ships. They were briefed on Operation Forager and learned that they were to invade Saipan in the Northern Mariana Islands. None had previously heard of Saipan. Finally the moment of truth was upon them. It was the fourteenth of June 1944 and they had arrived at their destination. They could see fires burning in many places

throughout the island and some wondered whether they were to invade the burning beaches of hell or the island of Saipan. The fifteenth of June was D-Day and H-Hour came much too quickly.

Crossing the line of departure and heading, full throttle, for the beach made everyone clutch his rifle a little tighter. Several of the amtracks took direct hits and were demolished in the lagoon. Shanghai Pooley could hear and feel small arms fire and shell fragments hitting the sides of their amtrack. Private Jerry Bronson lost his head. "Dammit!" Pooley thought, "I told the men not to put their heads up when we were going in." Nearly all of the others were splattered with Bronson's sticky blood, but no one else stuck his head up.

Directing Mc Laughlin to pick up one of Bronson's dogtags and the little Star of David attached to it before leaving the amtrack, Shanghai roared at the others to follow him ashore.

At the waters edge, the amtrack had groaned to a pitiful halt. It would go no further. Shanghai Pooley had gotten past the smoke and stumbled onto the beach, his men fanned out beside him. There was no way the amtrac could have taken them on to the 0-1 line as planned. At least 20 of the amtracs had already been blown out of the water before even getting to the beach.

The white sandy beach was littered with dead Japs who were soon joined by hundreds of dead Marines. Shanghai looked around at his men. He had lost one, Jerry Bronson, before they'd even left the amtrac. He thanked God that most of them still seemed to be alive and alert. Some, following his orders, were running down the beach toward Green Beach II where the amtracs should have put them ashore. He watched as Eddy Malone was nearly vaporized when hit with what must have been an artillery round. He wished he could recover what remained of Malone's body but it was out of the question until later when the beach had been secured. The terrifying volume of deafening Japanese artillery was punctuating the nearly continuous small arms fire. The enemy was well prepared and had carefully registered their artillery and mortars on the reef and the beach areas. There was almost nothing left of Eddy Malone.

Mare Island to Saipan

Shanghai raced down the beach, dropped behind a large rock, fired a few rounds in the direction of the enemy and saw that Chief was only a few feet away. He looked at Chief and said, "You really got lucky running down this beach old buddy. When you killed that Nip with your rifle butt you saved the Knife Fighter's life; but you could easily have been killed yourself. You know that don't you?" The Chief didn't bother to answer his squad leader; he was busy returning the fire of an unseen enemy in the brush ahead.

Once on Green Beach II the survivors rapidly attempted to reorganize in preparation to taking the next objective, the Charan Kanoa airstrip. Shanghai's squad now had three dead. Some were wounded but they would go on. In the first minutes ashore, the replacements had all become combat veterans.

The Marines spent the first sleepless night on Saipan withstanding heavy artillery shelling and periodic infantry counterattacks. It seemed as though the dawn would never come, but come it did, and with it the horrors of a new day of terror. Every hour of every day presented challenges to the raggedy assed Marines of the 2nd Squad and every other squad fighting in this God-forsaken place. Hours became days and days became weeks.

One of the more distasteful tasks endured by combat Marines was being sent back to the beach or wherever the supply points happened to be to resupply their units by carrying heavy expeditionary cans of water and boxes of ammunition—anguishing over the excessive weight he had to carry Private Stahoviak lamented, "These bastards are really heavy after you've carried them awhile." Hashmark Jones replied "Don't concern yourself about how heavy they are Ski just think about how good its gonna feel after you put them down—you won't even remember how heavy they were. And think about how exhilarating its gonna be when you sight in, depress the trigger and kill a few Japs with that ammo you're carrying, that will make it all worthwhile." Stahoviak, remembering his many dead and badly maimed buddies had an immediate change of heart as he hollered to one of the men handing out bandoleers of 30-caliber ammunition, "Hey Mac, throw a couple of them bandoleers over my head will ya? I guess I can handle a few more pounds. We're gonna do some getting even for the "Choirboy" and a bunch of other guys that aint around anymore."

Part IV

Slowly with time seeming to stand still and after severe casualties had been sustained on both sides the ferocity of the Japanese artillery fire began to diminish.

Lieutenant General Yoshitsugo Saito was in overall command of the Imperial Japanese Forces on Saipan. He was wounded on July 4th. By the 6th, his aviation assets and tanks were gone and his artillery was in a pitifull shambles; there was little chance of receiving reinforcements from the Imperial Navy. His troop strength now numbering hardly more than 5,000 effective fighting men and with his ability to defeat the enemy on Saipan severely in doubt he had arrived at the point of decision. Saito decreed that on the double seven (the seventh of July) there would be a *Gyokusai.*

The *Gyokusai*, a fight to the death, was intended to reduce the American forces by seven dead Americans for each Japanese life lost. The Marines referred to a Gyokusai as a "Banzai" attack. General Saito took his own life ceremoniously, in the manner expected of a great Samurai general. He promised his spirit would greet his men when their spirits arrived over the Yasakuni Shrine in Tokyo. The great Gyokusai resulted in over 4,200 Japanese dead on the battlefield. On the 9th of July, the island of Saipan was officially declared secure.

The statement that an island is secure or that a campaign has ended does not normally come from the PFC's or corporals who are doing the actual fighting; but rather from a general or an admiral. The infantry action on the ground, though somewhat diminished, continued for weeks with many casualties on both sides. The Marines combed the island looking for guerrillas or Japanese holdouts in the jungle. The patrols varied by size and length. On some days the full company would be on a combat patrol together. At other times it may be a series of platoon or squad-sized patrols.

PFC Yancey was glad to be back with the platoon and to be on patrol. He had been away for several days on a bizarre but exciting adventure with the Japanese in the jungle; culminating in his escape first from the Japs then from an Army field hospital. Shanghai kept him close at hand, wanting to make certain that he was recovered enough to resume his full duties. He decided to have Yancey share his foxhole the first few nights he was back, to keep an eye on him.

Mare Island to Saipan

The time for the coming assault on Tinian Island was drawing closer. Back in the company area, the men's nerves were on edge. No one was looking forward to hitting another beach but none could refrain from discussing it. They all wondered how many more of their buddies would be killed or seriously wounded?

On one hot July morning, the company had been broken down into squad-sized patrols. The area assigned to the 2nd squad held a particular interest for Shanghai; he had been through the area a week before. That morning, as the men were finishing their C-Rations, Shanghai directed that all empty ration cans, cigarette butts, papers and trash be put into two empty sandbags. They were taking them along on patrol. He cleverly distributed the trash to indicate that Americans were occupying a former Japanese command post and supply point. Instead of patrolling further, he employed his squad in "setting the stage" to include even hanging an American flag over a cave opening and igniting a cooking fire just inside the cave's mouth. Shanghai claimed he was setting up a deception. Talking among themselves, the men wondered about Shanghai's sanity. All were significantly impressed two days later when Shanghai's trap had been sprung resulting in eight dead Japanese soldiers with no Marine casualties.

On one particularly dark and quiet night, sitting in their fighting hole, Shanghai looked at Yancey and quietly said, "You've wanted to know about my interest in the Japanese for a long time. Now that you've told me all about your adventures with them in the jungle, I guess the only way I'm going to keep you from asking so damned many questions is to go ahead and tell you my story. You may not like what you are about to hear and it may surprise you to hear it but you asked for it. If you ever tell this to anyone else I'll kick your ass right up between your shoulder blades and I'll never forgive you. I want you to know that I have not discussed this with anyone since my court-martial. I didn't think I would ever be able to talk about it again, but it's eating me up inside and you seem to be interested. I just can't forget what happened.

I was given a bum rap; I was reduced in rank, lost my security clearance and was transferred out of China, yet I did nothing that any other Marine would not do under similar circumstances. This sure as hell isn't going to be what you had expected to hear kid, but I believe you really want to know so here it is.

He talked all through his watch and through Yancey's watch. It took the whole night, but the sergeant related his moving story just as it had happened years ago out in China. Yancey was thankful it was a dark night, too dark to look Shanghai in the eyes. He knew the salty old sergeant was deeply moved and from the sound of his voice, there had to be a tear coursing down his cheek from time to time when he spoke of his Lillian. Though Shanghai may never have told anyone the story before the young Marine could sense that he was haunted and tortured by his memories. He had to have re-lived it a thousand times. The salty sergeant and the young PFC sat in their foxhole and watched the darkness gradually drift off to the west as it was replaced by the beauty of a tropical sunrise.

This night would not be spoken of again yet neither of them would ever forget it. Shanghai had spoken of his great love that knew no bounds and how it had filled his heart and brought him great happiness. Paradoxically, it was that same love which caused the tragic consequences over which he had no control. He spoke of his lost love as one who knew he would never love again. The young Marine tried to understand but had some difficulty doing so as he had never been in love. He knew he could not reveal Shanghai's story yet he would never forget it. Few men are privileged to share the innermost secrets of another. Yancey was beginning to realize just how tragic and unfair life could be. In the Corps, there's a time worn verse that seemed to be appropriate in Shanghai Paul Pooley's case,

"And when he dies and goes to heaven,
To Saint Peter he will tell
Another Marine reporting Sir,
I've served my time in hell."

Shanghai Pooley was jungle-wise he could read the signs and sounds. More importantly as a professional he seemed to have an intuition about some things. If they had to be on a patrol in hostile territory in the jungle, he was a good man to be with.

The Duel

An effort was underway to rid Saipan of all effective Japanese fighting men before the 2nd and 4th Marine Divisions left for the next campaign, Tinian. This was being accomplished in several ways including daily platoon and squad-sized patrols.

Shanghai was leading his squad on another routine morning patrol. The men were carrying their rifles at sling arms. The squad rarely moved through the jungle at sling arms, but this time it was different. There may have been a bit of over-confidence. Enemy activity had been minimal the past few days and after all, the island had been officially secured for some time. The dreaded Saipan—Island of the Dead—was beginning to feel like home now that the Marines knew they would be leaving for Tinian soon. Shanghai was always teaching. He had read the tracks and shown them to the two point men.

"Alright men, listen up. You had better learn to read the obvious signs if you expect to stay alive and accomplish anything when you are on patrol. If you've got any questions that I can't answer, ask Chief, he taught me most of what I know when we were back in the jungles of Nicaragua while most of you were still wearing diapers."

The Chief chuckled quietly to himself as he thought of Shanghai's way of always trying to give credit to others. He hadn't taught Pooley a damned thing about reading tracks. They had both been green recruits newly arrived in Nicaragua when they learned tracking in order to stay alive. Native experts, Mosquito Indians who were members of the Nicaraguan Guardia Nacional, had taught them. Chief knew that Shanghai thought he would have credibility with the troops because he was an Indian. He also knew that Shanghai was aware that in spite of his heritage, he didn't know the first thing about being an Indian. He had left the reservation at an early age and had never returned. Most of what little Indian lore he knew he had gleaned from books and movies.

Shanghai was speaking, "There are signs that someone has been moving around here. There aren't many tracks just a few. Look at the footprints. Footprints are not always a nice clean outline of someone's shoe or foot on the ground. Be realistic look for something sensible. Do you see those little broken twigs? They're fresh do you see that? Someone has stepped on them and crushed or broken them under his feet. The broken twigs are on the trail right? You don't see any broken twigs off the trail or under the bush. Now, look at the dirt and the rotting vegetation on the ground. Do you see how it has been disturbed here and there? About the same distance between the turbulence on the ground as a short man's stride would be right? Okay, now, look at the trees and bushes. Look up and see if anything is disturbed, fragile things like small branches and twigs. They may indicate to you that it was a man. Do you see that little broken branch? Now see here? There's a couple more broken in the same way. That gives you a pretty good clue that it was a man or something just as tall as a man and if you'll look closely, you can see the direction he was moving in. Now if there had been a lot of foot traffic around here, the rotting vegetation and dirt on the trail would be churned up much more than it is. This indicates that there has only been one or two. Someone has used this trail in the last couple of hours. They're probably hiding out around here, close by. Get those rifles off your shoulders insert a clip of ammo and stay alert."

Deadly Dave and Epstein were the point men. They had entered the clearing first then stepped aside and waited for the others. Shanghai Pooley stepped into the clearing and automatically sensed someone's presence. His attention was riveted to the little lean-to shack at the far end of the clearing; it was recently put together; of green limbs. He didn't know it yet, but he was now finally about to learn his karma; he had re-entered the domain of the Dragon of Destiny.

As the men filed into the little clearing, they fanned out to the sides. They all looked at Shanghai who had stopped at the top end of the clearing and was standing with his feet apart and was facing down toward the little lean-to his eyes were fixed on it. It seemed as though the whole thing had been rehearsed. The men thought it was almost like a dream, they felt that it just couldn't really be happening. There were two rows of Marines, facing each other. The men looked at their sergeant and then glanced down in the direction of the lean-to.

Ross was closest to it. He was a tough wiry little character from Illinois, who had proven to be a good boxer in the ring and a good combat Marine in the field. He was the shortest man in the squad but one of the most effective. His buddy, Muldoon was standing next to him, the two were inseparable. Shanghai hollered something in Japanese and then waited. He yelled something else then waited again.

Ross spotted him first and sprang into action. He whipped his rifle around and went into a crouching position with his muzzle pointed right at the lean-to shack not more than twenty feet from him. Pooley's voice rang out loud and clear, "Hold your fire! He's mine, I've got him!"

There, at the lower end of the clearing was a Japanese officer climbing out of the lean-to in uniform. How he managed to look so neat and clean in the steamy hot jungle was a mystery. This was apparently the moment he had been waiting for. He was about to die for his Emperor and he wanted to do it in style.

He stood looking at Shanghai as a cunning and slippery suggestion of a smile crossed his face. His narrowed eyes had a glint in them that was ugly to behold. It was a look of pure hatred and Paul Pooley realized that this was Morio Takahashi, his longtime nemesis.

Paul remembered the words of Chang Wu the old fortuneteller in Nantao just as clearly as though Wu was right here beside him. "My dear Master Poo-Lee, always remember, we don't come here to stay, we come here to go. Missy Lillian has gone; you are here. Do what it is that you were sent here to do, fulfill your karma. Then perhaps someday, somewhere, you will rejoin her. There are few gifts more precious than pleasant memories of a loved one,"

Takahashi stood up in front of his little lean-to fearlessly facing the Marine sergeant as though the rest of the squad wasn't even there. He didn't glance to the left or right, just stared at Shanghai. None of the Marines could have guessed what was going on in the Japanese officer's mind at that moment or in Shanghai's. Morio Takahashi was totally surprised and shocked. It was simply beyond belief that there before him, among all the other American barbarians on the island was the hated Pooley.

Pooley whom he hadn't seen since 1938 when he had personally observed as the American Marine was taken under guard, placed aboard ship and departed for the United States. He himself had submitted a report of the incident to his superiors in the kempeitai. Now here on Saipan-shima in the vast Pacific Ocean the hated Pooley was standing right before him with a gun in his hand

Paul Pooley realized that he had reached the most important moment of his life. He knew that finally this was his karma. The Dragon of Destiny had brought him to this place in the jungle on a tiny island in the Pacific to confront the hated Takahashi who he seriously regretted not having killed six years before in Shanghai.

It was Pooley's voice, "All right you guys, steady now, don't any of you move. This one's gonna be mine!" Paul thought of the thousands of Japanese fighting men and US Marines on Saipan Island and couldn't believe that fate would bring he and Takahashi together face to face. They were looking directly at one another as he remembered the meanness and hatred in the ugly little bastard's eyes.

Again, Shanghai spoke in Japanese; "It is my most pleasant duty to send your disgraced spirit to your ancestors for their final condemnation." Almost softly Takahashi responded with a sneer and a grunt as he remembered his deep and abiding hatred for this Yankee Devil retorting in Japanese, "No, you die now." He then reached up with his left hand and loosened the flap on his holster. Slowly and methodically he reached across his body with his right hand and drew his pistol from the holster on his left hip; watching Pooley's every move. He stood there for a moment pistol in hand pointing down. Finally, he had his chance to kill the hated Pooley. Shanghai was moving at about the same speed as Takahashi as he loosened his holster flap with his right hand, then dropped his hand to his side.

They stood there looking very much like a couple of characters from an old western movie. None of the men observing could believe that their sergeant was apparently going to engage this Japanese officer in a duel. Then it happened! Shanghai Pooley had given his adversary the advantage, Takahashi's pistol was in his hand, and Pooley's .45 was still in its holster.

The Jap raised his pistol, taking aim just as though he was on a firing range. Shanghai drew his pistol and in what appeared to be one smooth movement, raised his arm, aimed and fired just as Commissioner William Fairbairn and Bill Sykes had taught in their classes on snap shooting in the Shanghai Municipal Police "shoot house" years before. Takahashi had gotten his wish. He died instantly as his body crashed backward from the force of the .45 caliber bullet then dropped. Shanghai Pooley of the Second Squad was still teaching as he said,

"Men, remember what I've told you before, don't ever under-estimate your enemy."

A stream of blood was coursing down the front of Shanghai's dungaree shirt as he stated, "The little sonofabitch shot me." Before any of the awe-stricken Marines could react he placed his pack between his knees clutching it tightly and laid back.

"Corpsman! Corpsman! Get up here Doc!" It was Chief's voice. He had been the closest to Shanghai and the first to realize his old friend had really been shot. This was the first time anyone in the squad had seen Chief show any visible sign of emotion when someone had gotten hit. Which, until recently, had been fairly often. Few of the younger Marines knew that this was nearly the last of Chief's old shipmates. Some had been with the old Fourth Marines and were captured in the Philippines when the Army surrendered Corregidor (Many of these had been starved or beaten to death by the Japs). The others had been killed on the 'Canal' or at Tarawa. Now here was Pooley, shot in the belly in a duel with a damned Jap when the island had been secured for days. It just didn't seem fair.

Chief wondered who was going to hold the Corps together when this damned war was over? These kids didn't understand about the real Marine Corps, they were just part-time help. They were in for the duration of the war and then would go back to civilian life. So many of the real Marines, the old timers, had been lost.

Poncho did an immediate inspection of the Japanese officer and disappointment showed on his face that indicated to the others that the Jap had no gold teeth. Lucky Lane and Stash Stahoviak checked the lean-to in hopes of finding a Samurai sword but found nothing but the Japanese officer's dirty field uniform and some small personal effects. As Chick Yancey looked at the body he noticed that the one medal the Japanese officer was wearing was the China Incident War Medal. The only Japanese award he could identify. Shanghai had told him what it was. Chick also noted a little metal chrysanthemum pin; he wondered about it and would later learn that it designated the officer as a member of the dreaded kempeitai. To the young Marine a flower blossom such as this seemed out of place on a military uniform.

Shanghai lifted his head and asked that someone get the Jap's pistol for him. Epstein already had it. He took it out of his pack and sheepishly put it on the stretcher beside his squad leader who made some remark about what a great training aid it would be when he related the sea story of his duel with a Jap officer, especially this particular officer.

Corporal Jerden asked about the camera he knew was in Shanghai's pack, The sergeant answered, "I'll take good care of it 'Cobber' don't you worry. If you want copies of any of the pictures, you guys will have to come and see me." Then speaking softly, he said, "I'm beginning to think this wound is gonna be good enough to get me all the way back to the States. It's starting to hurt like hell. Hey Doc! Are you gonna give me a *Syrette* of that morphine or not?"

The remorse started to set in immediately. Ten well-armed Marines and a Navy corpsman, any one of who could have easily blown that Jap away—and none of them did a thing. Sergeant Shanghai Pooley would be sorely missed, not only by his squad, but also by the whole company. He was a very special Marine. They all hoped he would recover soon enough to rejoin them for the next campaign. The squad would not be the same until Shanghai came back.

Chief placed his big hand on Corporal Jerden's shoulder and looked him squarely in the eyes. "You're senior, so you are in charge. Now listen to me carefully and get it straight. I'm taking the point. Follow me. I want everyone ready and alert. There'll be a round in every chamber. Don't screw up. You know I don't talk much. Watch my arm and hand signals and do

just as I indicate. We are going Nip hunting and we are not securing from this patrol until we get at least three Japs for Pooley. Not even if we have to stay out here all night. Any questions?"

Jerden responded, "Hell no Chief, I'm with you." Then he looked over his squad and said, "All right you men, listen up! Chief is going to be on the point. Little Ski, I want you behind Chief. Watch him and relay his signals back to me. Poncho! You and Stahoviak will go next. The rest of you guys follow me and be damned sure to watch for my signals. All right, lock and load. I want a round in every chamber. We are going to kill us some Nips for old Shanghai. Okay Chief, move out!"

. . . Until he's forgotten

Time has a way of passing too quickly when things are going well. When they are not going well, it seems to do just the opposite. For the 8th Marines time stood still for three long bitter months. The Island of Tinian had been secured since the 1st of August but the 8th Marines couldn't be removed from their blocking position on the southeast portion of Tinian where all the effective Japanese forces were believed to be buttoned up from Marpo Point almost to Lalo Point. It was a cat and mouse game that seemed destined to go on forever. Finally on the 25th of October, two battalions of the 8th Marines were removed from the cliffs and plateaus and returned to the 2nd Marine Division on Saipan. The 1st Battalion was destined to remain on "Hell's Half Acre" until January of 1945. Back on Saipan the 8th Marines were again privileged to sleep in tents and were provided three meals per day. The food was barely adequate in quantity and it was of poor quality but it was vastly superior to what they had been accustomed to in the field. The remnants of the 2nd squad with a few buddies from other squads who had shared the same experiences and been in the platoon for multiple campaigns banded together, calling themselves the raggedy assed Marines. It was a name that fit. Sunday was the only day of the week when no training or patrolling was scheduled and only an occasional working party. The raggedy assed Marines in groups of not more than four or five usually managed to go exploring on the far side of the island where the civilized troops lived.

Part IV

They were the Seabees, the Army Engineers, the Navy and the Army Air Force personnel. All were engaged in turning the islands into the busiest airfields in the world. They were fed rations far superior to the 8th Marines. The raggedy assed Marines had one common desire. It was to scour the island for food. They were eager to swap Japanese war souvenirs for food. They didn't care what service it came from anything was better than what they were accustomed to. They had met with some success on several Sundays but were often their own worst enemies and found themselves occasionally banned from some of the ships in the harbor and some messes ashore.

They found themselves walking on a road with freshly crushed coral they had come ashore with full stomachs. Having had a rewarding afternoon aboard their favorite ship, the submarine tender USS Orion, AS-18, she was a good feeder with a great crew. They were on the west side of the island walking down a road paved with freshly crushed white coral. They had hopes of spotting a vehicle bearing the tactical marks of the 8th Marines so they could bum a ride back to their camp on the far side of the island before the inevitable rains started. The threatening sky had darkened and was becoming gloomy. It was overcast with an occasional shaft of bright sunlight penetrating the dark clouds and sending its gleaming golden-white pillars of light earthward. A small side road appeared on their left. It had also been freshly paved with crushed white coral. Over the little road a wooden arch had been erected. The letters on the arch silently proclaiming "2nd Marine Division Cemetery" It drew them like a magnet and without speaking a word they automatically turned in to the cemetery and slowly strolled through its neat rows of countless white wooden crosses.

The raggedy assed Marines started seeing familiar names on the crosses and were overtaken by a deep sense of reverence for this hallowed place where so many of their buddies and friends were buried. It was an unusual cemetery in that there were no old people buried here, just young Marines and sailors. Dave Donahoe knelt down in front of one of the graves and made the sign of the cross. The others looked at the name stenciled in black on the white wooden cross and froze where they stood. They found it hard to believe what they were seeing but it was clearly spelled out—Pooley, Paul

(NMI), Sergeant USMC. "So that's why Shanghai never wrote to anyone," Lucky Lane said in a somber voice. "He's dead. How in the hell can he be dead? We all talked to him after he killed that Jap officer. He was hit but he seemed like he was going to be all right. The Navy even sent him out to one of the hospital ships to be treated."

Warm tears softly coursed down the cheeks of Chic Yancey as he silently prayed for the soul of the man who had taught him so much about how to stay alive and how to be a good Marine. A gentle rain started to fall and the raggedy assed Marines were glad of it; it gave them a reason to leave the cemetery. Their feelings of sorrow and depression were a heavy burden.

Back in camp, they waited until the following morning to ask the first sergeant why he hadn't put out the word on what happened to Sergeant Pooley. The first sergeant looked up and asked, "Who the hell's Sergeant Pooley"? The Top was a replacement who had joined the company on Tinian and had never met Shanghai Pooley. Yancey kept hearing a voice from within saying, "No one is really dead until he's forgotten." Lucky Lane raised his voice as he proclaimed, "The best damned Marine that ever served in this outfit, that's who Shanghai Pooley is." The captain had heard the exchange and before the first sergeant could explode, interjected; "Yes Lane, he may well be the best damned Marine who ever served in this outfit. Now, tell me what this is all about?" They related to the company commander that they had seen Shanghai's cross along with many others from the company. The others had not been a surprise, the men knew they were dead, but Shanghai was different. They had all been waiting for him to return.

Captain Barrett stood up grabbed his cover and glancing at the new first sergeant, he said, "I'm going up to battalion Top, not sure when I'll be back." He looked at his raggedy assed Marines; who by now were like members of his own family and stated, "Men, I'm going up to battalion and to regiment if battalion doesn't have the answers. When I come back, I'll have some information for you." He stepped out of the tent and bellowed, "Music! Get the jeep, we're going for a ride."

The first sergeant scratched his head as he wondered, who the hell was running this company, the captain or these raggedy assed privates? He had

no way of comprehending the deep emotional bond that existed between the company commander and his men after repeated campaigns together. The first sergeant was a seasoned Marine but he was new to the infantry. If the war lasted long enough, he was sure to learn.

In their tent after Taps that night they were discussing Shanghai's death from pneumonia, which the captain told them, had apparently been contracted during surgery aboard the hospital ship. How odd that the Dragon of Destiny would have chosen this way for Shanghai to fulfill his karma.

Chic felt it was important to remind the others of the words Shanghai had so often repeated, "No one is really dead until he's forgotten." This book is evidence that Shanghai Paul Pooley has not been forgotten.

Semper Fidelis

The Flag Circle and Court of Honor in the American Memorial Park on Saipan.